Theology of Nature

Books by George S. Hendry
Published by The Westminster Press

Theology of Nature

The Gospel of the Incarnation

The Holy Spirit in Christian Theology
(Revised and Enlarged)

Theology of Nature

George S. Hendry

The Westminster Press
Philadelphia

First edition

Published by The Westminster Press®
Philadelphia, Pennsylvania

PRINTED IN THE UNITED STATES OF AMERICA
9 8 7 6 5 4 3 2 1

Library of Congress Cataloging in Publication Data

Hendry, George Stuart, 1904–
Theology of nature.

(The Warfield lectures ; 1978)
Includes bibliographical references and index.
1. Nature (Theology) 2. Religion and science—1946– 3. Creation 4. Holy Spirit I. Title.
II. Series: Annie Kinkead Warfield lectures ; 1978.
BT695.5.H46 231.7 79-27375
ISBN 0-664-24305-3

Contents

Preface

This book contains the Warfield Lectures that were given at Princeton Theological Seminary in the early months of 1978. The first five lectures are presented substantially as they were delivered, with only minor revisions. The sixth lecture has been greatly expanded in order to develop some aspects of the doctrine of creation that are essential to the theme but could only be mentioned in the time available: these are treated in Chapters 6 to 9. The final part of the book is an attempt to answer the question: What difference does it make? I have not taken up the ethical questions, not because I am blind to their importance, but because I believe that the fundamental question is one of perception. If the priest and the Levite failed to act neighborly toward the man who fell among thieves on the Jericho road, it is because they failed to perceive him as their neighbor. In Chapters 9 to 12 I have attempted to answer the question concerning what it means to perceive the world of nature as God's creation.

I have to thank the Faculty of Princeton Theological Seminary for the honor they did me in appointing me to the Warfield Lectureship. Coming as it did from former colleagues, this honor was particularly gratifying. I am also grateful to the audience who came out to listen to the lectures on six nights of an exceptionally snowy winter.

I owe a special debt of gratitude to my wife for her patience and perseverance in the preparation of the typescript.

G.S.H.

Princeton, N.J.

Introduction

Chapter 1

The Problem of Nature in Theology

During the last few decades we have all been made acutely aware of our dependence as human beings on our natural environment, as we have learned that deterioration in the quality of the air we breathe, the water we drink, and the soil in which we grow our food seriously threatens our continued life and well-being on this earth. The crisis has brought into current speech the name of a science previously known only to a few—ecology. The science of ecology, which studies the relationships of living creatures to their natural habitats, used to be concerned with the bees, the birds, the bears, etc., but now it has been found to have an application to human life, which is not merely of scientific interest but is crucial for its survival. The immediate and practical response to the ecological crisis is the search for measures to protect the environment against the abuses that have caused its deterioration. But at the same time it is clear that some of the abuses spring from human attitudes toward the world of nature, and that these in turn have their roots in more or less conscious assumptions of a theological and philosophical character.

The question for theology may be tentatively formulated in these terms: What is the place, meaning, and purpose of the world of nature in the overall plan of God in creation and redemption? The question has been taken up by a number of theologians, and already some significant work has been done. But the enterprise is hampered by the fact that the question has been virtually ignored for the past two hundred years; nature has been dropped from the agenda of theology, which has been preoccupied with other themes, and, in consequence, has failed to develop resources to deal with it. The knowledge of nature has advanced by leaps and bounds during these two hundred years, while theology has been in the main concerned with other problems. There is thus a twofold leeway to be made up, if theology is to address itself to the problem of nature—one in the understanding of the new shape of the problem, and the other in the development of theological resources for dealing with it.

It is a formidable task, and I want to say at the outset that what I aim to present will consist, in large part, of a reexamination of the problem, and in particular one that will attempt to re-pose the problem in a more comprehensive manner than has been customary in the past, in the hope that this may uncover some possibility of a more adequate approach to it.

It will be best to begin by considering why the world of nature was dropped from the agenda of theology. We have to find an answer that is itself theological, but before we come to that, we may take note of a number of nontheological factors that have contributed. One is that the church, which theology has to serve, has been affected by the general movement of the population from the country to the city, which began with the industrial revolution and has been proceeding at a quickening pace ever since. At the birth of this nation two centuries ago, less than 7 percent of the population lived in cities; today the number is more than 70 percent and it is increasing steadily. The consequence is that most people are removed from immediate contact with the world of nature and are unfamiliar with its ways. Thus many of the parables of Jesus have become unpreachable; the ways of nature, to which he referred, have become no less mysterious to the average city dweller than the mysteries of the kingdom they were intended to illustrate.[1]

But the effects of the shift from a rural to an urban environment go deeper; they not merely affect people's familiarity with nature, they affect their real relationship to nature in radical ways, of which three may be mentioned. (1) In the agrarian, preindustrial society the family was the unit of labor as well as of life together; family relations and labor relations coincided. But when labor was moved from the field to the factory, labor relations became separated from family relations and were organized on an artificial basis. Thus the family was deprived of a large part of its former significance and tended to be reduced to the level of a dormitory or a cafeteria. (2) In the agrarian society the division and pace of work are determined by the seasonal rhythm of nature. Nature sets the hours and the conditions of labor, and they are not negotiable. In the industrial society nature is dethroned and degraded to the rank of a reservoir of materials and resources to be exploited at man's behest for his own advantage by scientific technology. The conditions, divisions, and hours of work have now to be organized, and as the industrial order becomes ever more vast and complex, these matters fall more and more under the control of a bureaucracy. (3) The strangest thing is the contradiction in economics. Although our basic dependence on nature remains, since it is by the products of nature, however processed and packaged, that our life is sustained, natural production holds a low place in the economic system. Thus we have the paradoxical situation that the production of food is discouraged in a world where millions go hungry, and when it happens that the earth produces extra-bountiful harvests, as it did in the United States in 1977, the economic effect on those most directly involved in the process of production—the farmers—is near-ruin.

If we now ask what happened in theology itself that made it turn its attention away from the world of nature, there can be little doubt that the proximate cause was the destructive criticism of natural theology at the hands of Hume and Kant, especially the latter. It is beside my purpose to rehearse the arguments with which Kant disproved the proofs of the existence of God, or to discuss their validity. That has been done often enough already. I want to suggest that the demise of natural theology is the inevitable consequence, if not, in fact, the obverse, of the demise of a theology of nature. For if it is not possible to establish a knowledge of nature in the light of God (and this may be taken as a rough definition of a theology of nature), it is hardly to be expected that it will be possible to establish a knowledge of God in the light of nature. One evidence of this is the curious fact, which has rarely been noted, that the proofs of the existence of God were perfected at a time when the existence of God was barely questioned. The little coda with which Aquinas concludes each of his five ways shows that the problem in his time was not really to persuade people to believe in God, but to help them to relate their belief in God to the nature and condition of the world and to see that their belief in God and their understanding of the world mutually illumine each other. Natural theology is like moonlight. Moonlight is reflected sunlight. Shut off the sunlight, and the moon becomes dark. This was the situation in Kant's time. Nature had been annexed by science, and it had proved much more responsive to scientific investigation than to theological interpretation; the heavens no longer declared the glory of God, but the laws of Newton, and even the light, which had been ascribed to the first act of creation, had had to wait for him, as Pope suggested in his famous couplet:

> Nature and Nature's laws lay hid in night;
> God said, Let Newton be! and all was light.

If the world receives no direct illumination from God, then it cannot reflect his light. It was not Kant's intention to disprove the existence of God or to deny that there is any place for him in relation to the world of nature. God was allowed to retain the role of honorary chairman, so to speak, but the day-to-day operations of the world reveal no trace of him. Thus if our thought takes its start from the world as we experience it—and in Kant's view it can do no other—there is no way in which it can reason from the world to God, either as the author of its existence or as the architect of its order. For whether the world had a beginning in time or not is a question which it is impossible for us to answer, when our thought observes its proper limitations, as Kant showed in the First Antinomy, and it is only when the human intelligence imposes order on sensory experience that the world is knowable by us at all. But if there is no way of moving in thought from nature to God, there is another area, or kind, of human experience which does open a way, viz., moral experience. If we want to find God, Kant taught, we must look, not to "the starry heavens above" (though they may inspire awe), but to "the moral law within." We must listen to the voice that commands us to do our duty, the categorical imperative he called it, because it is absolutely unconditioned by anything other than itself. It is not even to be identified with the voice of God, though if anyone wished to call it that, Kant raised no serious objection. He held that if we listen to it and follow it and reflect on its implications, we shall be led to the place where God is to be found, or where, at all events, it becomes necessary to think the thought of God.[2]

When Kant gave priority to the ethical over the natural as the gateway to God, he provided a city of refuge to which harassed theologians fled from their philosophical and scientific pursuers in increasing numbers in the nineteenth century. There were some who followed Kant directly in attaching theology to the ethical area of human experience, notably Ritschl and his disciples, who also took their cue from Kant in their campaign for the expulsion of metaphysics from theology. Kant's influence was also felt in Victorian England, which was the scene of a remarkable, perhaps unprecedented intensification of the moral consciousness (which does not, of course, imply a corresponding elevation of moral conduct): the project for a translation of theological dogma from a metaphysical to an ethical key appealed to a number of leading theologians. It was, of course, in Victorian England that the impact of Darwin was immediately and most powerfully felt, and it was around ethics that the most decisive battles between theology and Darwinism were fought.

There were other theologians in the nineteenth century who followed Kant's direction to the ethical, not in the strict sense he gave to the term, but in the broader sense in which Schleiermacher used it in the introduction to his *Glaubenslehre* to designate the whole area of subjectivity, or self-awareness. Schleiermacher's direction has also been followed, with variations, by several theologians both in the nineteenth century and, perhaps more significantly, in the twentieth. The existentialist theologies of Bultmann and Tillich, for all their differences, have this in common, that they relate the thought of God, not to the world of nature, but to certain aspects of the experience of the self.

This concentration of the theme of theology, however, is not an invention of modern times. It is simply a modern version of a motif that has been present in theology (better, Western theology) since the time of Augustine, who in a famous passage described the object of his reflections as "God and the soul, nothing more, nothing at all."[3] Augustine was not quite fair to himself here, for he was by no means indifferent to nature or to history, as theological themes. He laid the groundwork for a theology of history in *The City of God,* and he was endlessly fascinated with the creation stories in Genesis. But his great discovery was the inner world of the self—he was the first Christian to write his autobiography—and he marked this as the place where God is to be found. He defined the theme that was to remain central in Western theology.

Medieval theology strove to broaden the horizon and to compass the world of nature as well as the soul. But in order to do this it was obliged to draw on resources from outside the Biblical and dogmatic tradition (as I shall hope to show in a later chapter). The consequence was that theology of nature never became the concern of more than a few, who were viewed with suspicion by the majority, and it was remote from the central theme of popular piety. The dominant trend was toward concentration on the inner life, and this was intensified in several of the movements that sprang up in the period immediately preceding the Reformation.

The climax was reached with Luther. The concern that led to his eruption lay right in the heart of the Augustinian theme, God-and-the-soul. It had nothing to do with God-and-the-world. Luther showed no interest in natural theology; for it is not in nature but in the soul that God proves himself as God, and more specifically as the God of grace. When Luther turned catechist and found himself obliged to teach the doctrine of creation, he brought it all under the same *pro me,* which he had found in the gospel of grace, and he reduced the whole world of nature to a repository of goods for the service of man. His exposition of the first article of the Creed in his Small Catechism of 1529 runs:

> *"I believe in God, the Father almighty, maker of heaven and earth."*
>
> What does this mean?
>
> Answer: I believe that God has created me and all that exists; that he has given me and still sustains my body and soul, all my limbs and senses, my reason and all the faculties of my mind, together with food and clothing, house and home, family and property; that he provides me daily and abundantly with all the necessities of life, protects me from all danger, and preserves me from all evil. All this he does out of his pure, fatherly, and divine goodness and mercy, without any merit or worthiness on my part. For all of this I am bound to thank, praise, serve and obey him. This is most certainly true.[4]

The simple piety of this statement conceals a presumptuous impiety, for it makes it appear that the entire furniture of creation has been put there for my sake. Creation is merged with providence, and virtually disappears behind it. When the Bible says that God looked on his creation at various stages in its progress and saw that it was good, this is said without reference to man. It was good for God; but Luther's statement makes it sound as if it were all good for man. And this is illustrated in an even more striking manner in a classical document of the Reformed faith, the Heidelberg Catechism. It contains two separate questions, one on creation, and one on providence (Questions 26 and 27), but it answers both in terms of providence. There is no suggestion that the world of nature might have any theological significance apart from its providential service to man.

But does not the concentration of theology on the theme of God and the soul, or God and man, faithfully reflect the central emphasis of the Bible? It is true that it is primarily the human sphere with which the dealings of God are related —and so intimately related that it was suggested by none other than Karl Barth that the name of theology should really be theo-anthropology. Only, the human sphere is seen in the Bible, not as the sphere of subjectivity, or the soul, but as history. It is history that forms the dominant coordinate in the framework of human life. History is the field in which God interacts with man, and in which the meaning and destiny of human life are to be worked out. It may well be that the first creation narrative, with its elaborate sequence of six days, culminating in the sabbath rest of God, is intended, not as a sketch of the structure of the world of nature, but as a preview of the course of history as the field in which God's purpose proceeds by orderly stages toward its consummation. This does not mean that the world of nature had no place in the faith of Israel. Since history takes place in the world of nature and is largely affected by it, God could not be Lord of history if he were not also Lord of nature. But in Israel's faith history is always the primary field of the action of God, and his action in nature is secondary and instrumental to it. It is only in the context of God's redemptive action in history that Israel's faith in God as creator of the world came to expression, and, as von Rad puts it, "it performs only an ancillary function."[5] God was known by his mighty acts in the history of his people. He announced himself to them in the promulgation of the covenant: "I am Yahweh your God, who brought you out of the land of Egypt" (Ex. 20:2), not, "I am God the Father almighty who created the heavens and the earth."

Nevertheless, the God who was known primarily as the liberator of his people from Egyptian bondage came also to be recognized as the "Almighty," i.e., *Pantokrator,* the ruler over all, who created the heavens and the earth. The extension of the sphere of God from the people to the universe was implicit in the faith of Israel from the beginning, and it appears in some of the oldest traditions, but it did not become articulate until the time of the exile. In Second Isaiah, where God is first proclaimed as "the Creator of the ends of the earth" (Is. 40:28), this was done, as von Rad has shown, in order to support and reinforce the message of redemption; there was no independent interest in the creation of the world, and no attempt to develop it. It first appears as an independent theme in the creation story in Genesis 1. But it should be observed that this story reflects an interest that is unique in the Old Testament; it has no parallel until we reach some of the later Wisdom writings. The location of the creation story at the beginning of the canonical Scriptures gives a misleading impression of Biblical faith; for this is not where Biblical faith begins. Biblical faith begins with the God of the people, not with the God who created the heavens and the earth.

At the same time, the introduction of God as the creator of the heavens and the earth on the first page of the Bible indicates how firmly this understanding of God eventually established itself in the faith of Judaism. No doubt this reflects the effect of contact with understandings of God that were current beyond the bounds of Israel, primarily to the east and also to the west. It is the latter, I think, that played the more decisive role. The extended treatment of creation which is to be found in some of the writings that originated in the Judaism of the Diaspora, notably the Wisdom of Solomon, and Sirach, clearly show how easy, or "natural," it was for Jewish thinking to assimilate the characteristics of Greek thinking about God. Greek thinking about God had developed in relation to the cosmos. And it was, inevitably, in the area of cosmological theology that dialogue had to take place. It is here too that it continued in the early centuries of the Christian era, when the Western expansion of the church brought it into contact with the cosmic theology of the Greeks.

There is an age-old controversy over the question of whether the contact between Biblical faith and Greek thought about God brought a blessing or a curse. There are several questions involved in this controversy, but I want to point up just one of them, which is probably the crucial question, as it relates to our theme. It is the question of the pattern of the action of God. Where is that pattern to be looked for? Is it to be looked for in the work of God in creation, or is it to be looked for in the history of his covenant with his people? Luther's problem with the theology of his time was that the pattern of the work of God had been construed in terms that had their roots in the cosmological theology of the Greeks, and that kind of theology had no place for the gospel of forgiving grace. To recover the gospel of free grace, therefore, it was necessary to reject the cosmological framework and reinstate the history of the covenant as the model of the action of God.

Then, in turn, the work of God in creation was reinterpreted in the light of this model, and, as we have seen, creation was overshadowed by providence as an act of grace.

The point of this issue may be clarified if we consider the manner in which it presented itself in the Old Testament. Is history, or nature, the field in which the authentic pattern of the divine action is disclosed? The rulers of Israel were resolutely opposed to the cults of the indigenous Canaanites, because they looked to the world of nature as the field of the divine and found the pattern of divine action in the processes of nature; Baal, Moloch, and Ashtoreth were deities of natural fertility and plenty, and they were worshiped at local shrines with appropriate rites. God, the teachers of Israel maintained, is the Lord of nature, because he is the Lord of history; and his action in history is the model and pattern of his action in nature as well. As God said to Abram, "Go from your country" and Abram went, "as the LORD had told him" (Gen. 12:1–4), so he said, " 'Let there be light'; and there was light" (Gen. 1:3). In both realms he acts by word, and in both his word is obeyed.

> For to the snow he says, "Fall on the earth";
> And to the shower and the rain, "Be strong."
> (Job 37:6)[6]

Nature, which, like man, is God's creature, is credited with a sensibility, or responsibility, to its creator no different from that of man.

The superiority of Greek thought about God, which gave it a powerful attraction for people from the world of Biblical faith, lay in two things: (1) it offered a more sophisticated conceptuality for expressing the unity and the universality of God; and (2) it was free of anthropomorphism and offered an account of the action of God in nature which was much more compatible with the nature of nature. For evidence of this it is not necessary to go to Plato or Aristotle; it is sufficient to recall Paul's speech at the Areopagus in Athens, which is reported in Acts 17. The speech opens with a reference to God as universal creator and an argument that anthropomorphism is totally inappropriate in such a cosmic theology. We may wonder why Paul should have thought, or should have been thought, to bring this message to Athens, for there was no place that needed it less. It might have been better addressed to the people back home in Jerusalem. At all events it evoked no reaction. But when Paul switched from the ways of God in creation to his action in history, it was then that the audience grew restive, and the meeting broke up. There were few converts, but it is not explicitly stated what they were converted to. Since the speech ended with the message of judgment through Christ, and it was delivered at the court of justice, it would be reasonable to conclude that it was this part of the message that won over Dionysius and Damaris and the rest. But it may not be without significance that when an unknown author, centuries later, adopted the pseudonym of Dionysius the Areopagite in order to invest his writings with an aura of apostolic authority, his spiritual home was unmistakably the academy, not the Areopagus.

Let me now try to present the thesis of this chapter in a more formal and systematic way. The meaning of God can be understood in three different contexts: the world as a whole, the history of salvation, and the inner life. If we can speak of these as three parameters of theology, they can be described, respectively, as the cosmological, or universal; the political (I prefer this term to historical, because the reference is to the organized community in history, and political is the best way to characterize the theology that works within this parameter); and, third, the psychological. These three parameters correspond in a way to the three articles of the Apostles' Creed, the first of which refers to God as the universal creator, the second to his work in history for the salvation of mankind, and the third to the appropriation of that work in the experience of believers. Origen, who was one of the first to grapple with the problem of the Trinity, once suggested, in answer to the question why there are three persons to be distinguished and how they are to be distinguished, that they have distinct spheres of operation: God the Father, as he put it, "embraces all things . . . the Son touches only things endowed with reason . . . the Holy Spirit pertains only to the saints."[7] This distinction was not acceptable to the church, especially since Origen coupled with this idea of a successive reduction in their spheres the doctrine that the Son is inferior to the Father and the Holy Spirit still lower in degree. The church insisted that it is one and the same God, Father, Son, and Holy Spirit, who is present and active in each of these spheres, and this became the orthodox doctrine. Nevertheless, the spheres remain distinct, and it remains extremely difficult to understand how the same God is present and active in each of them.

Thirty years ago Prof. H. Richard Niebuhr of Yale published an article on the doctrine of the Trinity, in which he pointed out that while the churches continue to profess the orthodoxy of one God in three persons—Father, Son, and Holy Spirit—they tend in practice to fall into one or another of three unitarianisms, as he called them: a unitarianism of the Father, which focuses on God as the sovereign ruler, the supreme arbiter and ultimate disposer of all things; a unitarianism of the Son, which focuses on Christ as savior from sin; and a unitarianism of the Spirit, which focuses on the experience of the reality of faith in the inner life. There is no intention in any of these unitarianisms of excluding the others, but in each of them the others are overshadowed or pushed into the background. And the reason for this is not far to seek—it is the inordinate difficulty of holding them together in a real and intelligible unity.[8]

In the light of this analysis we can perceive the course of modern theology as a process of moving from one parameter to another. Schleiermacher consolidated the systematic shift to a theology of the inner life, or of religious experience. In his first publication he announced his new program in unitarian terms, declaring that the kind of religious experience he was extolling could dispense with the traditional conception of God as a transcendent being. Later, in his major work, *The Christian Faith,* he retreated from this position somewhat; he allowed that a doctrine of God as creator could have a place in theology, but only a secondary place, i.e., only insofar as it was involved in a theology of the religious emotions—and even on this he seems to have been doubtful. In the book there is a curious passage in which Schleiermacher reveals how he was torn between respect for the tradition and his own innovative approach. I refer to this because it points up the problem in a concrete way. In §30 he discusses the question, What is the subject matter of theology? or, as he puts it, What kinds of propositions does the system of Christian doctrine have to establish? His answer is that propositions describing the religious self-consciousness are the fundamental form, and propositions about God and the world are secondary and derivative. He then turns to an imaginary questioner, who sounds like his own earlier self and who asks why these propositions about God and the world cannot be dropped altogether. I give the answer in his own words, because it is hard to believe he is not being a little disingenuous:

> But if anyone were to attempt at the present time to treat Christian Dogmatics in this way, his work would be left isolated without any historical support. . . . [It] would have no link with the past.[9]

In a word, it would involve too radical a break with the tradition. In addition, it would fail to fulfill one of the functions of dogmatics, which is to keep a critical eye on the hymns we sing. It is worth giving this also in Schleiermacher's own words:

> For since dogmatic language only came to be formed gradually out of the language which was current in the public communication of religion, the rhetorical and hymnic elements in this latter must have been especially favorable to the formation of conceptions of divine attributes, and indeed these became necessary in order that those expressions should be kept within due proportions.[10]

The obvious response to this would be to ask whether the hymns describe the religious self-consciousness, and if they do not, why not discard them? But if we think of some of these grand old German hymns which celebrate the attributes of God manifested in his works of creation—such as Neander's "Praise Ye the Lord, the Almighty, the King of Creation"—we can understand Schleiermacher's problem. To suggest that hymns like this should be scrapped would be just too much; people would not stand for it. Doubtless the same applies to some of our English hymns that have the same theme: Robert Grant's "O Worship the King All Glorious Above," or Henry van Dyke's "Joyful, Joyful, We Adore Thee," which is a great favorite in these parts, and, set to Beethoven's music from the Choral Symphony, a grand hymn to sing. But I sometimes wonder how the God who is praised in these hymns—the God "whose robe is the light, whose canopy space. / His chariots of wrath the deep thunderclouds form, / And dark is his path on the wings of the storm"—the God whom "Field and forest, vale and mountain, / Flowery meadow, flashing sea, / Chanting bird and flowing fountain, / Call us to rejoice in thee"—I sometimes wonder how this God is related to the God who is preached in the sermon, and whether the sentiments expressed in these hymns have any real place in the piety of those who sing them.

The theological revolution that was led by Karl Barth may be simply described as a shift of focus from the psychological to the political parameter of theology, or from the third to the second article of the Creed. Barth vigorously repudiated Schleiermacher and his type of theology; he had an aversion to all theology of experience which was almost pathological, and which he did not overcome until his last years, when he grudgingly conceded that there might be a place for experience in theology after all. Barth's Christocentrism, or Christological constriction, came as near as any to being a unitarianism of the second article, an attempt to confine theology within the political parameter, excluding not only the psychological but also the cosmic. His volume on the doctrine of creation is certainly one of the weakest in the *Church Dogmatics.* He confesses in the Preface that he felt ill at ease with this topic and wished it could have been taken over by someone else; he says also that he thought at one point it would involve him in a dialogue with science, but he decided he could dispense with this, and he devoted the kernel of the book to an extended exposition of the creation narratives in Genesis, which provided the opportunity for a dazzling display of exegetical pyrotechnics, but did nothing to answer the question of a scientifically informed person who wants to know what light, if any, theology has to shed on the world of nature.

It is a similar position, in a more extreme form, which we have in Bonhoeffer. When Bonhoeffer asked what Christ can mean in a religionless world, he was, in effect, asking for a unitarianism of the second article. By a religionless world he meant a world that has shed the presuppositions of "metaphysics" and "inwardness," a world that no longer needs God to fill the gaps in the understanding of itself, either in the cosmic dimension, where science has taken over, or in the area of the inner life, which has "become the hunting ground of modern psychotherapists."[11] The modern world come of age has lost the sense of insufficiency in either direction and is perfectly capable of understanding itself without the need of God as a "working hypothesis."

If we read this as a sociological observation, there can be no question of its truth. But the puzzling thing is that Bonhoeffer takes it for granted that the only way the relationship between God and the world can be formulated is in terms of metaphysics, which means, in effect, natural theology. There is no hint of an alternative construction in terms of a theology of creation, which is not so much as glanced at. Bonhoeffer's remarks about the conquest of the world by modern science and the consequent demotion of the "God of the gaps" have a curious nineteenth-century air about them.

There is a well-known passage in one of his letters in which Bonhoeffer charges Barth with a "positivistic doctrine of revelation which says in effect, 'Take it or leave it!' Virgin Birth, Trinity, or anything else."[12] He did not mention creation as one of the doctrines we are asked to swallow whole, but he might well have done so, for this is how he himself had treated it some years earlier. Creation, we were told then, is an act of the divine freedom, which "no question can penetrate behind"[13] and which as such contributes nothing to our knowledge and understanding of the world. Creation has to do with the beginning, and the beginning is the point at which thinking "collapses" and "crumbles into dust."[14] The only way to escape this conclusion and derive some significance from the doctrine of creation would be, he suggests, to follow Hegel in "arbitrarily enthroning Reason in place of God." If we want an example of a positivism of revelation that says

"Take it or leave it," we have an excellent one here. In 1933 Bonhoeffer took it, in 1944 he left it.

This conclusion seems to be inevitable if the question of cosmic theology is posed in terms of natural theology, i.e., the question of establishing a knowledge of God in the light of nature. But this question, as I suggested earlier, is the obverse, or correlate, of a prior question, the question of establishing a knowledge of nature in the light of God. This is the question to which we must address ourselves first.

If we do this, there is one important difference that follows. When the question of theology and the world of nature is posed in terms of natural theology, it inevitably turns into a debate between science and theology. I wish to dispute the assumption that science and theology represent the only two viable perspectives on nature and that the question of nature is a matter of debate between them alone. I wish to demonstrate that there are other perspectives, and that if they are not so clearly defined or institutionalized as those of theology and science, nevertheless they may bring into view important aspects of the subject, which tend to be lost sight of when it is assumed that nature discloses itself only to science and/or theology.

Modern science arose out of a revolt against the implicit or explicit imperialism of the theological perspective on nature, or, less violently expressed, by the discovery that there is another way of looking at nature than that of theology. The enormous success of the scientific method in forcing nature to disclose its secrets, however, generated at length a counter imperialism, when it came to be believed that this success establishes the sole right of science to "put nature to the question." I have used the vivid phrase that Bacon used to describe the new experimental approach. It sounds innocent enough, but the phrase referred to the practice of torture, as Bacon's first readers would have immediately recognized, and it raises the other question, which Bacon no doubt did not intend, whether the information that nature yields to scientific investigation is the unalloyed truth, or answers forced from a tortured victim to please his interrogator. Be that as it may, the success of the new scientific method in forcing nature to speak so overawed all other interrogators that they were either reduced to silence or led to claim some kind of scientific status in order to gain a hearing.

Now that science has largely shed its imperialist pretensions to be the only qualified interrogator of nature, it is important that these other interrogators should be given a hearing, even if some of them have not been heard from for a long time. I propose to introduce three of them and give them a place in the dialogue.

The one with the most recognizable title is, of course, philosophy. It is the question of nature that gave rise to philosophy in the first instance, and nature continued to be a main theme of philosophical reflection throughout the greater part of its history. Contemporary philosophy has for the most part succumbed to the prevailing belief that nature is the exclusive province of science, and it has resigned itself to the ancillary role of clarifying the tools and methods with which science conducts its investigation into nature, but it does not itself directly participate in the investigation. I shall raise the question of whether there is still a place for a direct, or distinctive, philosophical perspective on nature, in spite of the severe strictures that have been placed on such a project by both science and philosophy in recent times and that have led to its almost total suppression.

But before raising the question of the philosophy of nature, it will be important to examine certain experiences of nature, or attitudes toward nature, which are as old as philosophy, which have played a much larger part in human experience than philosophy, and which may in fact form the roots from which certain types of philosophical reflection arose. There is an experience of nature that has led to (or sprung from) a sense of community between man and nature, which is not primarily conceptual, but which has sometimes found expression in conceptual form (among others). It could be called communion with nature, and that would suggest an analogy with what is called communion in the Christian church. But I prefer to speak of it as the mystery of nature, because this term, which is also used of the communion in some parts of the Christian church, better indicates that we have here something that is preconceptual, or supraconceptual, and thus cannot be adequately expressed in conceptual form. This is true also of the communion, though this has all too often been forgotten by the theologians in their debates about it. I have chosen the term "mystery," because I intend to deal primarily with forms of the experience that are to be found outside of, or on the fringes of, Christendom.

I propose next to review some of the ways in which the world of nature has been incorporated into religion. The Religion of Nature may not be the best title for this, but I could not think of a better one to delineate a perspective on nature, which is more distinctly religious than the one I describe under the heading of mystery, but less than theological—in the sense of theologically articulate and theologically responsible. I shall confine the review to the period beginning with the rise of modern science and to religious views of nature that have been presented by some people, including some very great people, who were aware of what was being done in science. It is a kind of historical excursus, but the history exhibits a sequence of phases which I think it will be instructive to trace.

There is one other perspective which I would have liked to bring into the picture, but which I must be content only to mention because of my lack of qualifications—that is the art of nature, the treatment of nature in the visual arts and perhaps also in music. The point of interest is that in the history of art, or, more specifically, in the history of the relationship between art and nature, a movement has taken place which is analogous to that which has taken place in the relationship between theology and nature—a movement toward the centrality of the artistic self. The view that art is an imitation of nature has been abandoned; it is not nature that illumines art, but art that illumines nature. Unlike the scientist, whom Bacon counseled to "obey nature," the artist constructs—or reconstructs—nature according to his own inner vision of it. Whether nature is gained or lost in the process is a question that cannot be answered here. It may be noted, however, that it is to art more than to any other human activity that the term "creative" is applied, as if to suggest that art provides the nearest analogy to creation, as it is understood in the Bible and theology. This suggestion will be examined in a later chapter.

The three perspectives that I intend to delineate—the mystery of nature, the religion of nature, and the philosophy of nature—will bring to our attention aspects, or dimensions, of human experience with nature, which will enable us to see the problem of nature in a broader context than is customary when the debate is confined to science and theology, and at the same time it may clarify some of the issues that have engrossed that debate.

PART I

APPROACHES TO NATURE

Chapter 2

The Mystery of Nature

The word "mystery" in the title of this chapter is used, not in the sense it bears in ordinary speech, that is, to denote a particularly difficult problem, one that obstinately defies solution. Gabriel Marcel drew a distinction between a problem and a mystery which has been widely regarded as illuminating. A problem is the kind of question that ordinarily arises in the course of our traffic with the world around us, the answer to which may be found by the application of scientific method, whether in a simple and unconscious way or through a sophisticated and complex technique. To be amenable to the scientific method of investigation a problem must be posed objectively and approached dispassionately. This does not mean that a problem may not be a matter of urgent, personal concern to the investigator. A medical problem, for example, may deeply concern a physician who is attending a patient; but in order to investigate the problem scientifically he must discount his personal engagement and approach it in an attitude of detachment. A mystery, on the other hand, is essentially something in which the subject is involved and which cannot be posed and approached in a purely objective manner. The question of whether there is life on Mars is a a problem that can be apprehended objectively and that can be solved, in principle, by scientific investigation of the available data; but the question of whether there is life after death is a mystery, not because the data available are insufficient to provide an answer, but because it is one in which every one of us is subjectively engaged. No one is likely to lose a night's sleep over the question of whether there is life on Mars; but the question of what is to become of me after my life is ended —when that question has seized me, I cannot escape from its grasp.

The distinction, however, goes deeper. Some suggestion of the problematic, which is inherent in the modern connotation of mystery, still clings to the term, in the sense Marcel gives it, however different it may be from a problem; and perhaps this is indispensable, if the concept is to play a role in a philosophical investigation as Marcel intended—and the human mind cannot be stopped from asking questions at any point. But the real depth of mystery is not reached until the element of the questionable is, if not eliminated altogether, at least relegated to the background. Marcel provides an important clue when he speaks of mystery as an experience of presence. Presence, for Marcel, has ontological dimensions, but we need not follow him into that; it may be sufficient to note how presence, in the full sense of presence, precludes questioning. The human experience of two persons in love has been cited as the prototype of it. Can the lover, in the presence of the beloved, ask the question, Does she love me? The question can be posed only in her absence, and even there, it may be, if it arises at all, it is already answered.

> Where the apple reddens
> Never pry—
> Lest we lose our Edens,
> Eve and I.

To reach the real depth of mystery, we have to go back to the mystery religions of ancient Greece. Indeed, it is from these that the word itself is derived.

There is, appropriately enough, something of a mystery (in the popular sense) about the connotation of the Greek word *mystērion.* There are two Greek verbs that sound very much alike: *myeō,* "to initiate," and *myō,* "to close" (the eyes or the mouth), and both of them are present in the background. Since the ceremonies of initiation were surrounded with mystery, and the initiates were sworn to secrecy—a secrecy so well maintained over centuries that much of what went on in the mysteries was never divulged—this aspect has received prominence, and the mystery religions have been looked on as secret societies. But secret societies tend to be highly restrictive in their membership, and this the mystery religions were not. To the contrary, they were remarkably wide open, admitting men, women, children, and even slaves. The core of the mystery was an open secret, but a sacred one, and the mode of initiation into it had to be kept secret to prevent its profanation.

The mystery religions were elaborate procedures designed to bring the initiate into sympathetic rapport with the generative and regenerative powers of nature and to enable the person to participate in them. In the Eleusinian mysteries, which were the most important in ancient Greece, these powers were personified in deities, Demeter and Kore, whose legendary history dramatized the process of decay and rebirth in nature. In the ritual this drama was reenacted in the presence of the initiates, probably in some oblique manner, involving the exhibition of sacred objects, and in this way the power it represented was communicated to them. The ceremony may also have included a sermon with an exposition of the mystery, but this was only preliminary to the action with the sacred objects, which formed the real heart of the matter and the real channel of communication with those present. Aristotle says "the initiates (*mystai*) learned nothing but underwent an experience."[1] It was a nonconceptual, or supraconceptual, experience, and therefore any attempt to express it conceptually must needs distort or profane it.

The secret imparted in the mysteries was the secret of life out of death, and the medium was the process of nature in which this secret is reenacted annually. The mystery religions could be described as nature religions, but they differed from most nature religions in that their object was not to influence the process of nature, but to be influenced by it. The worship of Baal, for example, was designed to promote the fertility of which Baal was the ruling power, and the means employed by the worshipers was the performance of certain fertility rites. But in the mystery religions the traffic moved in the opposite direction; the aim was to draw some of the life-giving power of nature into human life, and the assumption was that this traffic moves on lines which differ radically from those which bear our ordinary traffic with nature.

The mystery religions are long gone, but the experience they were intended to induce has not lost its importance or its appeal. Its general disappearance from modern life has left a void which aches from time to time, and never more than during the last two centuries. The desire to fill the aching void, to recapture the lost experience, is the central motif of the Romantic movement which arose in the closing decades of the eighteenth century.

The Romantic movement was a "reaction," as Whitehead correctly describes it in the chapter he devotes to it in *Science and the Modern World;* but it was not reactionary in the common, pejorative sense of the term. It was a reaction, or perhaps better a protest, against a serious deprivation which human life had sustained through the scientific and philosophical developments of the previous two centuries; for, though these developments had brought enormous gain to humanity, they had also brought serious loss, and the sense of loss became acute in the final decades of the eighteenth century. It was, to take a term that became current in the following century, a sense of alienation, or estrangement, which was felt as a threat to the integrity of man's being.

The first intimation of this malaise occurred when the Copernican revolution evicted man from his cosy, cosmic home and left him standing like a stranger in a vast and indifferent universe. Pascal is the most eloquent witness to this shock. The alienation was intensified when Descartes destroyed man's confidence in the world around him and drove him back to confidence in his own existence: *cogito ergo sum.* From this exiguous base he undertook to reconstruct our confidence in the external world—but only with the help of a God whose existence has also to be proved by the knowing self and who guarantees our knowledge of the world—an enormous burden to impose on the self-conscious self. The critical philosophy of Kant carried the development to its extreme limit and at the same time disclosed its inner problematic; the self was more and more isolated from the world, and ultimately from itself. (1) Kant could not find the real self behind the empirical self; he knew it was there, but he could not lay his hands on it. (2) Unlike Descartes, he could not prove God, and thus he had no guarantee that our knowledge of the world is veracious. (3) He knew that he knew something other than himself; for knowledge is an affair between a subject and an object; but he had no means of knowing that the object is the real world and not just the world as it appears to us and conforms to the conditions of our subjective knowing equipment. Thus critical reason, in Kant's hands, proved too powerful a solvent: it set people free from dogmatic prejudices, but it drove them back into Plato's cave, where they could see only flickering shadows and reflections of the true reality.

Kant thought to retrieve the situation and restore man's contact with reality by switching from the notion of man as a self-conscious subject of knowledge to the notion of man as a self-legislating moral agent. But he was able to do this only by ascribing to man a moral will, ethereal in its purity, and by setting up a radical opposition between this will and man's natural impulses and inclinations. The result of the critical philosophy is thus a double dichotomy: man as knowing subject is separated from the world of nature, and man as moral agent is separated from his own nature, which includes feeling, instinct, intuition, desire, as well as cognition and volition.

The Kantian dichotomies epitomized the disruptive effect of the rationalism of the Enlightenment, and it is this which aroused the Romantic reaction. The Romantics were animated by a desire for unity and wholeness, unity with nature, and unity in man's own being. Science and the critical philosophy had reduced nature to a set of objectified facts and contingent correlations, and set man over against it as a subject who knows it and opposes his will to it. The Romantics craved a more intimate relationship with nature, one that enabled them to participate in its life. And by the same token, they sought a new understanding of man as a living being, something more than a knowing and willing subject. This was the point of their appeal to feeling. To the Romantics, feeling was not an inner haven of subjective emotion, to which they fled for refuge from the real world. Quite the contrary, it was in feeling, they felt; they made contact with the real world, contact deeper and more continuous than any that could be attempted or achieved by knowing and willing. Feeling overcomes—or perhaps the word should be "undercuts"—the subject-object split which is involved in the activities of knowing and willing; it brings the subject into an immediate relationship with the object and establishes a two-way traffic between them. The subject no longer confronts the world as an object to be ordered by the forms of his understanding and subdued by the power of his will; he lives in it, and he feels the current of its life flow through him. It is an experience of union with the whole, and at the same time an experience of wholeness, in which the dichotomy of reason and sense is overcome. There is a famous passage in his *Speeches on Religion* in which Schleiermacher describes it in lyrical terms; he compares it to a bridal embrace:

> It is the first contact of the universal life with an individual. . . . It is the holy wedlock of the universe with the incarnated reason. . . . It is immediate, raised above error and misunderstanding. You lie directly on the bosom of the infinite world. In that moment you are its soul. . . . In that moment it is your body. . . . In this way every living, original movement in your life is first received.[2]

As the last word of the passage quoted indicates, the Romantics stressed receptivity in our attitude toward the world, rather than activity and domination. It is as receivers we come to the world and participate in the life which flows through it—not merely in respect to our bodies, which belong to the world of nature and are organically related to it, but also as rational and spiritual beings who are able to experience it in our distinctive manner.

The claim of the Romantics to an experience of nature radically different from that achieved by discursive reason is one that seems to stand in need of philosophical justification, and some of them attempted to furnish this. We shall examine these in another chapter. But not all the Romantics felt that the only way to oppose the disruptive rationalism of the Enlightenment was by an alternative philosophy. The majority of them found their medium in poetry; and insofar as they based their intuitive apprehension of reality on feeling, poetry may be the more appropriate medium for the expression of it. The use of poetry widened the appeal of Romanticism, but at the same time it tended to inhibit the argument with philosophy, which uses prose and which regards poetry, if not, with Plato, as subversive, at least as something to be taken less seriously than prose. Truth, for Keats, had to be "proved upon our pulses,"[3] and what Wordsworth prized were "sensations sweet, / Felt in the blood, and felt along the heart."[4] Such statements seem to preclude argument—and how can you argue with feelings? Nevertheless, it is possible to discern in the poetical presentation of the Romantic claim the elements of a rationale, and I wish to comment on some of them.

The first is one that enjoyed great popularity among the Romantics, and also the Transcendentalists, and enjoys it still in some quarters. It can be briefly stated: it is that the sense of reality celebrated by the Romantic poets is that which belongs to childhood, but which for most of us is lost as we advance in age. Wordsworth is the most eloquent exponent of this view. His "Ode on Intimations of Immortality,"[5] which some consider his best poem, is an elaboration of the theme in terms of Plato's philosophy. According to Plato, it will be remembered, the soul, prior to its incarceration in the body, was granted an immediate vision of the forms of beauty, truth, goodness, etc., and brings with it into this world some recollection of that beatific vision. In Wordsworth's view this recollection is strongest in early childhood, but in most of us it fades in the course of our traffic with the world. Only a few are able to retain it, and they only on rare occasions, or "spots of time." Such are preeminently the poets; it is their gift to recapture that unspoiled vision of reality, which is the prerogative of early childhood, so that everything is transfigured with "the glory and the freshness of a dream." But it is not only for the poets; according to Beaudelaire, "genius is nothing but childhood recovered at will."[6]

Two features of the child's vision of reality were held in particular esteem, one is the element of wonder. To the child the world is all a novelty, and the novelty excites wonder, before familiarity has bred contempt. But there is another thing. It is not only familiarity that kills wonder; there is something more lethal: it is the habit of analysis, which we acquire—and which, indeed, we must acquire—if we are to come to terms with our environment. Analysis is an activity of the intelligence, which seeks to know things by breaking them up into their component parts, whereas wonder is a passive attitude of sensitivity, or receptivity, in which things disclose themselves to us without our seeking. This was a favorite theme with Wordsworth, and I want to refer to two of his poems. The first is "Expostulation and Reply." In it the poet recalls how he was reproached by a friend for sitting half a day on a stone by Esthwaite Lake, apparently dreaming his time away instead of improving his mind by working at his books, where he might

> drink the spirit breathed
> From dead men to their kind.

To this the poet replied:

The eye—it cannot choose but see;
We cannot bid the ear be still;
Our bodies feel, wher'er they be,
Against or with our will.

Nor less I deem that there are Powers
Which of themselves our minds impress;
That we can feed this mind of ours
In a wise passiveness.

Think you, 'mid all this mighty sum
Of things for ever speaking,
That nothing of itself will come,
But we must still be seeking?

The other poem is called "The Tables Turned," and in this it is the poet who expostulates with his friend and bids him

Up! up! my Friend, and quit your books.

"Books!" he exclaims, "'tis a dull and endless strife," and he calls his friend to

Come forth into the light of things,
Let Nature be your Teacher. . . .

Sweet is the lore which Nature brings;
Our meddling intellect
Mis-shapes the beauteous forms of things:—
We murder to dissect.

Enough of Science and of Art;
Close up those barren leaves;
Come forth, and bring with you a heart
That watches and receives.

We hear the sentiment of this latter poem in Wordsworth's very different contemporary, Carlyle, who saw a threat to wonder in the progress of science with its "Mensuration and Numeration."[7] We hear it also in John Stuart Mill, who noted in his *Autobiography* "that the habit of analysis has a tendency to wear away the feelings," and who came to believe that "the passive susceptibilities needed to be cultivated as well as the active capacities."[8] This last sentiment was echoed by Darwin, who, though he spent his life exploring "the wonders of nature" (as we might say), came to feel, paradoxically, that he had lost his sense of wonder in the process. In the autobiography he wrote for his children he lamented the fact that his long dedication to scientific pursuits had caused part of his brain to atrophy, and he had lost his youthful taste for music, poetry, and the fine arts. "If I had to live my life again," Darwin wrote, "I would have made a rule to read some poetry and listen to some music at least once a week."[9]

It was also a main objective of the New England Transcendentalists to recapture the child's wondering vision of the world, "to look on Nature with the same eye, as when in the Eden of primitive innocence and joy."[10] The fall takes place, so to speak, in the life of every child when he or she eats of the tree of knowledge—not the knowledge of good and evil, but simply knowledge; for the principal activity of knowledge is analysis, taking things apart, and this is inimical to wonder, which consists in the capacity to see things whole. Wordsworth believed this to be the peculiar property of the child's mind, which

> Is prompt and watchful, eager to combine
> In one appearance all the elements
> And parts of the same object, else detach'd
> And loth to coalesce.[11]

The plea for wonder was, as we noted, a protest against the growing domination of science with its analytical procedures. It was not against science as such, at least not in every case; the fear was that increasing preoccupation with science would lead to the atrophy of something that is essential to a full life, as Darwin confessed it had done for him. The hope of thoughtful people in the nineteenth century was that the continuing advance of science would be accompanied by a corresponding growth in the countervailing capacity, however you choose to call it. Tennyson expressed it in the lines:

Let knowledge grow from more to more,
But more of reverence in us dwell;
That mind and soul, according well,
May make one music as before.[12]

But this hope of a harmonious accord between knowledge and reverence was not shared by everybody. There were some notable dissenters, the most notable being Goethe. Goethe believed that the capacity for wonder and the sense of the whole was radically threatened by science and could be saved only by an invasion of the enemy's territory; he disputed the claim that science with its analytical methods could give us real knowledge of nature. It was in particular the science of Newton that provoked him, and he waged a determined and desperate war against it for many years. The issues were varied and complex, but they may be brought to a focus in one which we may all understand. Everyone knows that one of Newton's principal achievements was the analysis of light by means of the prism into a series of colored bands on the spectrum. But Goethe would have none of it. Not only did he think Newton was mistaken in what he thought he saw in the experiment of the prism, he refused to believe that we could really see light by breaking it up in this way. It is like dissecting a dead body—and it is only dead bodies we dissect. ("We murder to dissect," as Wordsworth said.) To see light truly we must see it whole:

Friends, avoid the darkened prisons
Where they pinch and tweak the light
And in pitiful decisions
Bow to rays distorted quite,
Worshippers most superstitious
Thronged in plenty down the year.
Leave in hands of teachers vicious
Spectres, madness, cheats and leers.[13]

Newton's law of gravity was the target of Schiller, Goethe's friend, in his poem "The Gods of Greece." In it Schiller lamented how science had robbed nature of its enchantment and its joy:

> Unconscious of the joys she dispenses,
> Never enraptured by her own magnificence,
> Never aware of the spirit which guides her,
> Never more blessed through my blessedness,
> Insensible of her maker's glory,
> Like the dead stroke of the pendulum,
> She slavishly obeys the law of gravity,
> A nature shorn of the divine.[14]

It is outside my purpose to enter into the merits of this controversy. The general view in the English-speaking world appears to be that in taking on so redoubtable a figure as Newton, Goethe affords us "the painful spectacle of . . . a great man making a fool of himself."[15] In Germany there is some disinclination to believe that so great a man as Goethe was capable of making a fool of himself, even though there he found few, if any, to support him in his lifetime.[16] I cite Goethe as an instance—an extreme instance, it may be—of the belief that the world of nature can be known in another mode than the mode of inquiry which has its paradigm in scientific investigation.

I should interject here that the romantic experience of nature was not limited to poetic expression.

Goethe's preoccupation with light suggests that this may be the appropriate place to remark that the romantic vision of nature was not the exclusive prerogative of poets; it also found expression in painting. We are reminded of this in the famous couplet in which Wordsworth spoke of

> The light that never was, on sea or land;
> The consecration and the Poet's dream.

For the poem, of which these are the concluding lines, was written in response to a painting (*Peele Castle, in a Storm*): the light was not only the poet's dream, it was the painter's creation. The romantic vision of nature found expression in

English landscape painting which reached its high point with the work of Turner and Constable in the first half of the nineteenth century. It has been said that "Constable is an exact visual counterpart of Wordsworth."[17]

According to the same authority, landscape painting went into a decline in the twentieth century. Plenty of it has been done, but it is no longer at the spearhead of the creative process. If we think of the great names of recent and contemporary painting, there is not one who offers us a vision of nature suffused with "the light that never was, on sea or land."

If we ask what is the content of this experience of nature, it is hard to find a precise answer. The experience itself has been described as mystical, and mystical experience, if not ineffable altogether, is exceedingly hard to describe. The describable is the specific, and the mystical experience is of a kind that transcends specifics.

Nevertheless, there are certain terms, or concepts, that recur in accounts of the experience which are given by those who have enjoyed it, and these may shed some light on what it is and what it signifies.

One of these is the concept of presence. To Marcel a sense of presence was one of the things that distinguish a mystery from a problem, and it was also an important feature in Wordsworth's experience of nature; he uses it in his best-known statement of the experience, the "Lines Composed a Few Miles Above Tintern Abbey":

> I have felt
> A presence that disturbs me with the joy
> Of elevated thoughts; a sense sublime
> Of something far more deeply interfused,
> Whose dwelling is the light of setting suns,
> And the round ocean and the living air,
> And the blue sky, and in the mind of man.

The thought recurs elsewhere, though the word may be absent. It is clearly present, for example, in his account of some of his boyhood experiences in the first book of "The Prelude."

There has been some discussion on whether the presence that Wordsworth found, or "felt," was a presence that coincided with nature, or one that stood behind nature, and to which nature was transparent. Whitehead, in his sympathetic account of Wordsworth, favors the former alternative, and he is probably right. He writes:

> It is the brooding presence of the hills which haunts him. His theme is nature *in solido,* that is to say, he dwells on that mysterious presence of surrounding things, which imposes itself on any separate element that we set up as an individual for its own sake. He always grasps the whole of nature in the tonality of the particular instance.[18]

It must be stressed, though it might scarcely seem necessary, that this experience of presence is not offered as an alternative or superior route to the knowledge of nature. When philosophers insist on treating the mystery as a problem, subjecting it to epistemological analysis and asking what its cognitive yield is, they are usually disappointed with the result, if not downright contemptuous. Typical is the response of Kant when he encountered the romantic approach to the mystery of nature in F. H. Jacobi: he dismissed it sarcastically as a philosophy of feeling which would appeal to lazy people who wanted a shortcut to knowledge without the laborious process of inference from the data of experience.[19] But the experience of presence is of a different kind from that on which Kant built his theory of knowledge. It is not a stimulus to knowledge, but an invitation to contemplation. It is more akin to that wonder and awe to which Kant himself confessed when he contemplated the starry heaven above and the moral law within.

Perhaps it is open to a different kind of question. While there is no reason to doubt the authenticity of Wordsworth's experience of presence in nature, the question has been raised whether there is not something parochial and eclectic about his vision of nature. Aldous Huxley suggested that if Wordsworth had lived in the jungles of the Amazon instead of in "the cosy sublimities of Westmoreland," nature might have affected him differently. And, without extraditing him to Brazil, we may ask whether Wordsworth was not rather selective with regard to the nature he knew. Everyone who has been to England knows that one of its most abundant natural resources is rain, and the Lake District, where Wordsworth lived, is as well endowed in this respect as any. But I do not recall a single mention of rain in any of Wordsworth's poetic celebrations of the mystery of nature, and I have sometimes wondered how they might have been affected by it. Take the lines from "Tintern Abbey":

> I have felt
> A presence that disturbs me with the joy
> Of elevated thoughts; a sense sublime . . .

Could one have such an experience, cowering under an umbrella in a chilling rain?

A second term that plays a large part in the romantic expression of the mystery of nature is "life." The romantic seeks not merely to know nature, but to feel in himself the current of that life which flows through the whole. Here he appears to be on a much stronger ground in comparison with the philosopher, who is bent on knowledge; for knowledge is a function of life, and life is manifestly something broader and richer than knowledge.

What is meant by life here? The thought is of more than life in the biological sense, though that too comes into it, as we shall see. It is, rather, of life as a pervasive dynamism which is the spring of creative action. The experience of presence, of which Wordsworth wrote, is of a contemplative sort. It is enjoyed, as the poet has portrayed himself, seated on a rock beside the lake, or wandering lonely as a cloud. But life is a force or energy, and it is experienced in activity.

We have here the seed of a whole philosophy, and it was developed by Schopenhauer, who propounded the doctrine that the ultimate reality of the world is will, which he interpreted as a blind, primordial drive pervading all things. It was from Schopenhauer's doctrine of the will that Nietzsche, who was captivated by him in his youth, later developed his own doctrine of the will to power. I mention this only in passing and only for the purpose of showing how this is related to an experience of nature, very different from that of Wordsworth. I quote from a letter of Nietzsche's, written in 1866, when he was twenty-two:

> Three things are my recreations—rare ones however—my Schopenhauer, Schumann's music, and, lastly, solitary walks. Yesterday there was a glorious thunderstorm, and I hastened to a hill in the neighborhood. On the summit I found a hut, and a man who was killing two kids; his boy was with him. The thunderstorm discharged itself with great violence, accompanied by hail and tempest. I felt an incomparable elevation of spirit, and I saw how true it is that we only then understand Nature properly when we are forced to flee to her from our cares and harassments. What was man to me and his restless will? What did I care for the eternal "Thou shalt" and "Thou shalt not"? How different the lightning, the tempest, the hail—free non-ethical forces! How happy, how strong they are, pure will, untroubled by the intellect.[20]

We have, however, a more moderate and congenial expression of the driving force of life in nature in Walt Whitman (1819–1892). The mystery of nature was a major theme with the Transcendentalists of New England, and especially their high priest, Emerson, who had developed it into a religion, or a religious philosophy (which is why it belongs in the next chapter and not in this one). Suffice it to say here that Emerson's treatment was similar in kind to that of Wordsworth, but articulated with philosophical elements derived from Coleridge and other sources. Whitman was not a member of the Transcendentalist group, but it was the Transcendentalist message, blended with the dynamic spirit of nineteenth-century America, that found expression in his exuberant poetic imagination. Emerson recognized it immediately, and the two men associated briefly, though two more different types than the proper Bostonian and the "rough" from Brooklyn it would be difficult to imagine.

The mystery of nature is a major theme in Whitman, and it is developed with power, but with a twist that is characteristic of the author. It is not the great sublimities of nature—the mountains, the forests, the cataracts—with which he communes (although the ocean does figure prominently in his poems), nor is it the elemental forces of the tempest and the thunder, but something much lowlier, and, one must say, "democratic"—the grass. He called his book "Leaves of Grass," and this is how he introduces the theme:

> A child said, What is the grass? fetching it to me with full hands.
> How could I answer the child? I do not know what it is any more
> than he.
> I guess it must be the flag of my disposition, out of hopeful green
> stuff woven.

He continues on a more traditional note:

> I guess it is the handkerchief of the Lord,
> A scented gift and remembrancer designedly dropt,
> Bearing the owner's name, someway in the corners, that we may
> see and remark and say *Whose?*

It is odd to find such a relic of natural theology in Whitman, and it probably owes more to his Quaker heritage than to his own thought. At all events, it is immediately followed by another suggestion, which is more indigenous, and to which I shall return:

> Or I guess the grass is itself a child, the produced babe of the
> vegetation.

He proceeds to recount other aspects of the grass, one being its democratic universality: it grows, as he notes:

> among black folks as among whites.

And how did he come to feel this way about the grass? Not by contemplating it as something under his feet, but by lying on it:

Now I see it is true, what I guessed at,
What I guessed at when I loafed on the grass.

The distinctive thing about Whitman, however, is that his sense of oneness with nature was accompanied by an equal, or greater, sense of oneness with humankind. He did not escape to Grasmere or Walden. The place of his mystical experience was Manhattan with its bustling streets; there the burgeoning life of nature had its counterpart in the restless energies of men. His eye delighted in the spectacle of men actively shaping the world, and he celebrated it in those catalogs of human occupations, sometimes almost encyclopedic in their range, which recur in his poems.[21]

What is the energy that drives all these activities? It is the energy of fecundity, the drive for the continuation and increase of life, which pervades the world of nature, and which finds its elemental expression in sex:

Urge and urge and urge,
Always the procreant urge of the world.
Out of the dimness opposite equals advance, always substance
  and increase, always sex.
Always a kind of identity, always distinction, always a breed of
  life.
To elaborate is no avail, learn'd and unlearn'd feel that it is so."
("Song of Myself," sec. 3)

But elaborate Whitman sometimes did, and in more concrete terms than in that passage. "The procreant urge of the world" involves the body as well as the soul, and Whitman could not shut out one side of it:

I have said that the soul is not more than the body,
And I have said that the body is not more than the soul.

He took delight in the body, the naked body, the male body, the female body, and in their coming together. Of course, it was all mild in comparison with what we are used to nowadays. There were no four-letter words, no play-by-play descriptions of close encounters of that kind. But everybody knew what was meant, learned and unlearned alike. Many of the first readers were shocked; there were cries of obscenity; the book was banned in some places; and the author was fired from his government job in Washington. But it was not pornography Whitman was writing; he was writing of sex as the sacrament of communion with "the procreant urge of the world," or, if you prefer, the creative principle of reality. And, of course, it was nothing new; it is a motif of great antiquity in the history of humankind and its relation to nature. But it sounded new and shocking in the ears of genteel society in the nineteenth century—and again in the twentieth, when it was presented by D. H. Lawrence, and aroused the same scandal. But for both Whitman and Lawrence, it was not physical sex they were concerned with (though both of them knew there is no sex that is not physical—and on this Lawrence is much more explicit than Whitman), nor was it psychological sex (i.e., sex as a factor in mental health, according to the Freudian formula); it was mystical sex—sex as the key that opens the door to the innermost secret of being.

It is obvious that these experiences of nature, or attitudes toward nature, shade into religions and philosophies, and some notable expressions of them have been cast in these forms. It is also in their more religious and philosophical expressions that they have been subjected to criticism by the representatives of the established religions and philosophies. Whether this procedure is justifiable, or whether it exemplifies an imperialism, possibly an unconscious imperialism, is a question I leave aside for the present. What I have attempted to do in this chapter is, by means of the category of mystery, to sketch a relation to nature that is unique of its kind and that is not reducible to religion or philosophy. And that is why I have drawn mainly on the poets, because it is in them that the romantic experience of the mystery of nature has found its purest expression.

I want to conclude with some lines from Emerson. Emerson was the most eloquent spokesman for nature in this country. To him it was primarily a religion and a philosophy, and he discoursed of it as such in graceful prose. But he knew it is also a mystery, for which the proper medium is poetry. Here is one of his poems, in which his sense of the mystery is sharpened by his rage at its desecraters. It is called "Blight," and it is peculiarly apposite to our present situation:

> Give me truths,
> For I am weary of the surfaces,
> And die of inanition. If I knew
> Only the herbs and simples of the wood,
> Rue, cinquefoil, gill, vervain and agrimony,
> Blue-vetch and trillium, hawkweed, sassafras,
> Milkweeds and murky brakes, quaint pipes and sundew,
> And rare and virtuous roots, which in these woods
> Draw untold juices from the common earth,
> Untold, unknown, and I could surely spell
> Their fragrance, and their chemistry apply
> By sweet affinities to human flesh,
> Driving the foe and stablishing the friend,—
> O, that were much, and I could be a part
> Of the round day, related to the sun
> And planted world, and full executor
> Of their imperfect functions.
> But these young scholars, who invade our hills,
> Bold as the engineer who fells the wood,
> And travelling often in the cut he makes,
> Love not the flower they pluck, and know it not,
> And all their botany is Latin names.
> The old men studied magic in the flowers,
> And human fortunes in astronomy,
> And an omnipotence in chemistry,
> Preferring things to names, for these were men,
> Were unitarians of the united world,
> And, wheresoever their clear eye-beams fell,
> They caught the footsteps of the SAME. Our eyes
> Are armed, but we are strangers to the stars,
> And strangers to the mystic beast and bird,
> And strangers to the plant and to the mine.

The injured elements say, "Not in us";
And night and day, ocean and continent,
Fire, plant and mineral say, "Not in us";
And haughtily return us stare for stare..
For we invade them impiously for gain;
We devastate them unreligiously,
And coldly ask their pottage, not their love.
Therefore they shove us from them, yield to us
Only what to our griping toil is due;
But the sweet affluence of love and song,
The rich results of the divine consents
Of man and earth, of world beloved and lover,
The nectar and ambrosia are withheld;
And in the midst of spoils and slaves, we thieves
And pirates of the universe, shut out
Daily to a more thin and outward rind,
Turn pale and starve. Therefore, to our sick eyes,
The stunted trees look sick, the summer short,
Clouds shade the sun, which will not tan our hay,
And nothing thrives to reach its natural term;
And life, shorn of its venerable length,
Even at its greatest space is a defeat,
And dies in anger that it was a dupe;
And, in its highest noon and wantonness,
Is early frugal, like a beggar's child;
Even in the hot pursuit of the best aims
And prizes of ambition, checks its hand,
Like Alpine cataracts frozen as they leaped,
Chilled with a miserly comparison
Of the toy's purchase with the length of life.

Chapter 3

The Religion of Nature

The title of this chapter suggests a large theme in the science of religion, but my theme is more restricted in its scope. I wish to survey the part that nature has played in the religious thought of Western Christendom since the rise of modern science in the sixteenth and seventeenth centuries. An alternative title, which I considered, is "The Light of Nature," but this phrase is too closely associated with one phase of the story; "The Religion of Nature," though somewhat imprecise, seemed broad enough to cover all the phases. But "The Light of Nature" might also serve, provided we may play variations on the theme of light—and one of the variations is darkness.

The story exhibits four distinct phases, and the first is one in which nature plays a negative role, or one in which its light is darkness.

1. One of the enigmas of intellectual history is the lateness with which natural science arose in Europe, in the light of the brilliant beginnings that had been made in much earlier times by the Greeks and others. Several reasons can be given, but one of them is certainly the persistence in popular piety of a dread of nature as a realm of sinister and malignant forces, which it was dangerous to inquire into. The Fall, it was believed, had affected the world of nature as well as that of man, and its effects in nature were in some respects more frightening; for man could—or believed he could—identify the corruption of his human nature, but the fall of the world had turned it into a realm of darkness as well as malice. The

corruption of nature is expressed in Milton's "Ode on the Nativity." At the coming of the heaven-born Child, he writes:

> Nature in awe to Him
> Had doffed her gaudy trim . . .
> She woos the gentle air
> To hide her guilty front with innocent snow;
> And on her naked shame,
> Pollute with sinful blame,
> The saintly veil of maiden white to throw;
> Confounded that her Maker's eyes
> Should look so near upon her foul deformities.

The world had fallen under the sway of Satanic powers, who kept its secrets to themselves, and knowledge of nature could only be purchased at the price of a pact with the powers that ruled it, "the prince of the power of the air" (Eph. 2:2), who is "the god of this world" (2 Cor. 4:4). The quest for the knowledge of nature was not only a distraction from the main purpose of life, which was the salvation of the soul through the knowledge and grace of God; it was a dangerous threat to man's salvation, since it involved him in an ominous traffic with the enemies of God. This is the theme of the Faust legend, which originated in the sixteenth century and has fascinated a succession of writers from Marlowe, through Goethe, to Thomas Mann and Paul Valéry in this century. The question of whether the story ends in the damnation or salvation of Faust points up the issue: Is the pursuit of the scientific knowledge of nature contributory to human weal or woe? Goethe, by ending his drama with the salvation of Faust, gave his blessing to science, and in this he reflected the spirit of his age; but now, a century and a half later, perhaps we are not so sure.

Be that as it may, an important requirement for the rise of modern science was "the rehabilitation of nature," and this, according to Willey, was a main achievement of Francis Bacon.[1] Bacon offered a theological reinterpretation of the

Fall which limited its effect to the moral order. The tree, of which our first parents were forbidden to eat, was the tree of the knowledge of good and evil; and this had nothing to do with the knowledge of nature, which (despite the curse pronounced on it, which Bacon ignores) is cleared of the charge of being under the domination of Satan, and reinstated in its pristine condition as God's creation, in which his handiwork is displayed. It is in Bacon that we first find clearly enunciated the view that the world of nature is a medium of revelation parallel to the word, a second scripture comparable to the first, a living book from which knowledge of God is to be obtained as from the written book. Sir Thomas Browne expressed it eloquently in the following century: "There are two books from whence I collect my Divinity, beside that written one of God, another of His servant Nature, that universal and public manuscript, that lies expans'd unto the Eyes of all; those that never saw Him in the one, have discovered Him in the other."[2]

The most significant difference in this view of nature from that found in the piety of the Middle Ages, in which it was seen as a realm of dark and sinister forces with which it was dangerous to meddle, is that nature has been exempted from the effects of the Fall and reinstated in that pristine perfection in which it issued from the Creator's hand at the beginning. It is noteworthy that Calvin, despite his drastic view of the effects of the Fall on human nature, saw none in the world of nature, which he regarded as a theater in which the glory of God is abundantly displayed.[3]

If the Renaissance initiated the recovery of nature from the ill repute into which it had fallen, the scientific discoveries of the following centuries, particularly those which disclosed the marvelous order and regularity in the behavior of natural objects, completed the rehabilitation. If man had fallen into his evil state through breaking the law of God, the science of Newton demonstrated that the world of nature everywhere displayed a punctilious observance of that law and therefore provided a more suitable occasion for praise to the Creator:

Praise the Lord, for he hath spoken;
  Worlds his mighty voice obeyed;
Laws which never shall be broken
  For their guidance hath he made.

The sentiment expressed in that hymn, which dates from the beginning of the nineteenth century, is echoed in many later hymns.

It should be said that there were some dissentients from this widespread adulation of nature. Basil Willey reports on one, Thomas Burnet, an eminent cleric of his time (1631–1715), who wrote a book called *The Sacred Theory of the Earth.* Burnet admitted, in principle, as we might say, that the earth shows evidence of its Creator and his design, but he maintained that, like man, it is a damaged creature, a ruin, a travesty of what it was. Willey describes Burnet as an eccentric—and he must certainly have appeared eccentric in the eyes of his contemporaries—but he represents a protest against the tendency, which became increasingly prevalent, to idealize nature by disregarding its less agreeable aspects. I give just one quotation—which may have become more topical than when it was written:

> Though it [the earth] be handsome and regular enough to the eye in certain parts of it, single tracts and single Regions; yet if we consider the whole surface of it, or the whole Exteriour Region, 'tis as a broken and confus'd heap of bodies, plac'd in no order to one another, nor with any correspondency or regularity of parts: And such a body as the Moon appears to us, when 'tis looked upon with a good glass, rude and ragged. . . . They are both in my judgment the image of a world lying in its rubbish.[4]

Burnet was in a minority. But he was not alone; he was followed by two others, whose names are much better known than his. One of these was Bishop Joseph Butler, whose *The Analogy of Religion* was published in 1736. The argument of this famous book is rich and many-sided, but for our present purpose it will be sufficient to note the way in which he opposes the contention of the prevailing Deism of the age, that the existence and attributes of God are so clearly and unambiguously revealed in his handiwork in nature as to render any further revelation superfluous, particularly one so obscure and contradictory as the Biblical revelation. If the Bible conveys the supreme revelation of God, as the church claims, why does it need such an endless stream of commentaries to make its meaning plain? (The question may have occurred to some readers as they have wandered through the stacks in a library.) The book of nature, by contrast, has no need of such an exegetical apparatus; its revelation is plain for all to see, so plain that he who runs may read: "The heavens are telling the glory of God; and the firmament proclaims his handiwork." Butler contested the Deist assumption of the perspicuity of nature, and sought to show that nature is just as full of obscurities and difficulties and problems as Scripture. He defended the orthodox belief in the Scriptural revelation with the argument that if there are difficulties in Scripture, there are difficulties in nature too, and in fact the difficulties are analogous, which goes to prove that both nature and Scripture are the work of the same Author. As an apologetic device, Butler's argument seems perilously weak, if not in fact absurd—it appears to plead the case for one nonrevelatory revelation by appealing to another. Its significance lies in its protest against the optimistic, and one-sided, view of nature which was so prevalent in the eighteenth century. Butler was singularly out of tune with the spirit of his age, a realist in an age of romantics. While his contemporaries tended to view the world through rose-colored spectacles, he saw things as they are. Indeed, he was something of a pessimist. Anticipating the objection to his argument, which I just mentioned, that (as he puts it in the mouth of an imaginary objector) "it is a poor thing to solve difficulties in revelation by saying that there are the same in natural religion," he replied, "Indeed the epithet *poor* may be applied, I fear as properly, to a great part or the whole of human life."[5]

The other great dissentient from the rose-colored view of

nature was Voltaire, whose *Candide* was published in 1759, four years after the Lisbon earthquake. The merciless satire which he applied to the view that this is "the best of all possible worlds" is too well known to need recounting here. I pass on to the second phase of the story.

2. The view of nature as a second source of revelation in addition to Scripture, a revelation of God in his works as well as in his words, enjoyed a great vogue in the seventeenth and eighteenth centuries, and it received much support from the insights into the order and regularity of nature which had been gained by the new scientific method. The leaders of the new science—Kepler, Boyle, Newton—were themselves devout believers, and their scientific discoveries enhanced their admiration for the wisdom and power of God displayed in his creation. The revelation of God in nature became a staple theme in popular piety, which was nourished on a stream of books that developed the theme in variety and detail. Not only the stars in their courses but the behavior of all kinds of natural objects—fire, water, birds (How do migrating birds find their direction?), and insects—were cited as evidences of divine providence and design. Some writers, in their zeal to trace the wisdom of God in his creation (to cite the title of one of the most popular books of the century) were carried to extreme and ridiculous lengths, but some laid their fingers on phenomena that are genuinely impressive. One natural phenomenon, which was hailed as a particular testimony to divine providence, is the birth ratio, i.e., the fact that the ratio of male to female births remains constant at close to equality; as one English scientist wrote, "By this means it is provided that the species may never fail nor perish, since every Male may have its Female, and of a proportionable age." A Dutch scientist of the period devoted an extensive treatise to it—and it is a rather remarkable fact, in view of the disparities found in individual families.[6]

The problem for theologians in this period was to develop a conception of the action of God in nature which was compatible with the insights of science. The naive anthropomorphism of the Bible could still be entertained as indigenous to faith at the time of the Reformation, though it was already becoming difficult, as any reader of Calvin's tortuous chapter on providence can gather.[7] It became impossible with the increased knowledge of the built-in regularities of the natural order that became general with the rapid rise of modern science in the following centuries. God could no longer be thought of as acting immediately and directly at every turn—though he might still do so on special occasions —and it became necessary to devise a conception of the action of God in a manner that did not set aside the action of the forces which had been found by scientific observation to regulate the processes of nature. The divine, providential action and the action of the immanent natural forces were correlated as first and second causes, which were conceived as operating at different levels in the production of any event. The conception has abundant analogies in ordinary experience, where human agency, as first cause, causes mechanical agency to operate as second cause—as in driving a car. In an earlier, less mechanical age, a favorite example was found in writing. Here one could see not only two, but three modes of causality operating at different levels; for what causes the writing—is it the pen, or the hand, or the writer? Clearly all three are at work. On this analogy God was understood as the first cause, who is at work unseen behind the second causes, which can be observed.

At the same time, the remaining gaps in scientific knowledge of the immanent regularities of the natural order were sufficiently large to leave God a foothold in the realm of secondary causes. The most famous example from the history of science is the hypothesis of Sir Isaac Newton, that, since the laws of motion, so far as he had been able to define them, were not sufficient to account for the regular movement of the planets, God intervened from time to time to adjust them. I may add that it was perhaps this hypothesis to which Laplace was referring when he made his famous reply to Napoleon—in which case he may not have been the type of godless scientist such as he has been so often portrayed, but the methodical scientist who saw the impropriety of introducing God to fill the gaps in scientific knowledge.

At a less exalted level, the idea of direct divine intervention in the realm of secondary causes still survives in popular piety in regard to that natural process which appears most recalcitrant to any rule of law that science can discover—the weather. Prayers for rain, or for the cessation of rain, are still held in some places on occasion; and it was widely believed in Britain that the spell of remarkably (and unusually) fine weather that made possible the evacuation of a large part of the British army from the beaches at Dunkirk in June 1940 was a special act of divine providence. God's control of the weather is celebrated in many popular hymns, for example, Isaac Watts's "I Sing the Mighty Power of God," which contains the lines:

> And clouds arise, and tempests blow,
> By order from Thy throne.

The belief that there is a place for the action of God, whether at the level of primary or secondary causality, was particularly strong—and, indeed, still is for many people, in regard to the organic field, where vital processes and not merely mechanical forces are involved. Paul expressed a sentiment that is widely shared, when he wrote: "I planted, Apollos watered, but God gave the increase" (1 Cor. 3:6). And if the vital processes are those of human life, the impulse to see the action of God in the mystery of generation is deeply rooted in many people, and deep feelings are roused when it is challenged. The controversies that are going on today, especially among Catholics, over contraception, abortion, and the like, reflect a deep fear that the desacralization of generation would exclude God from a critical place in human life and reduce life to the level of a chemical process.

No theologian devoted himself with a more sustained intensity and in a more original manner to the theme of God's work in nature than Jonathan Edwards. According to a statement in an unpublished manuscript, Edwards early in life conceived the idea of writing a "Rational Account of the Main Doctrines of the Christian Religion," in which he proposed to show how "all the arts and sciences, the more they are perfected, the more they issue in divinity, and coincide with it, and appear to be as parts of it."[8] It was to be a *Summa,* in which theology would be restored to her throne as the queen of the sciences, and all the sciences, especially the science of nature, which had been developed so magnificently by Newton, would bring their tribute to her feet. Edwards did not accomplish this project, but he left a number of manuscripts in which he had accumulated several series of notes in preparation for it. One of these was published under the title *Images or Shadows of Divine Things,* with an introduction by Perry Miller, in 1948. It contains 212 entries, some quite short, others developed at greater length. Internal evidence shows that Edwards had made these entries, off and on, throughout his life.

At a first reading the book may appear to be nothing more than a compilation of illustrations for sermons drawn from the world of nature. The use of illustrations from nature was a prominent feature of the preaching of the New England Puritans, and some of them exhibited a luxuriant fancy in doing it. But Edwards was suspicious of illustration as a rhetorical device, informed only by the imagination of the preacher. It might hold the attention of the hearers, but it ran the risk, as many preachers have found, of diverting attention from the truth it was intended to illustrate. Edwards' concern was with something deeper than the rhetorical embellishment of preaching. He wanted to demonstrate that the world of nature not merely happens to contain phenomena which, to an imaginative observer, resemble spiritual realities, as a shape in a cloud may resemble a human face, but that there is an ontological continuity, or congruity between the worlds of nature and of spirit, and that the resemblances between them are not accidental, or fanciful, but perceptions of a deep underlying affinity.

It is in this way, according to C. H. Dodd, that the parables of Jesus are to be read. The realism of the parables, by which he means their use of the realities of common, everyday, human experience in this world, is not the product of a particularly observant eye in Jesus. "It arises from a conviction that there is no mere analogy, but an inward affinity, between the natural order and the spiritual order; or as we might put it in the language of the parables themselves, the kingdom of God is intrinsically *like* the processes of nature and the daily life of men. Jesus therefore did not feel the need of making up artificial illustrations for the truths he wanted to teach. He found them ready-made by the Maker of man and nature. That human life, including the religious life, is a part of nature is distinctly stated in the well-known passage beginning 'Consider the fowls of the air . . .' (Matt. 6:26–30; Luke 12:24–28). Since nature and supernature are one order, you can take any part of that order and find in it illumination for other parts. Thus the falling of rain is a religious thing, for it is God who makes the rain to fall on the just and the unjust . . . and the love of God is present in the natural affection of a father for his scapegrace son. This sense of the divineness of the natural order is the major premiss of all the parables."[9] To Edwards what was perceived in natural phenomena was not something epiphenomenal; it was the appearance of the truth. One simple illustration: Edwards was a dedicated student of the science of his time, and the science of Newton in particular. He knew that Newton's discovery of the law of gravitation was limited to the measure of its force—in the famous formula of the product of the masses and the inverse square of the distance between them. Newton was not able to answer the question, What is gravitation? and neither, for that matter, is anyone else. Here is what Edwards says about it:

> The whole material universe is preserved by gravity or attraction, or the mutual tendency of all bodies to each other. One part of the universe is hereby made beneficial to another; the beauty,

> harmony, and order, regular progress, life and motion, and in short all the well-being of the whole frame depends on it. This is a type of love or charity in the spiritual world.[10]

Edwards also argues that there are natural phenomena which are unintelligible except as types of spiritual things—they make no natural sense. This sounds like a novel form of the "God of the gaps" argument—except that Edwards' world of nature presented not only types of the ways of God but as many, if not more, of the ways of the devil. Consider, for example, the way of a cat with a mouse. There are several puzzling things about this. How does the cat learn this game plan? No one has ever observed a kitten being instructed in the game plan by its mother, and there is no school where they go to be taught it. Yet take any cat, take one that has been raised in a house without ever seeing a mouse—just let it see a mouse, and it puts the game plan into operation immediately; it pounces on the mouse, then lets it go, then catches it again, and so on, until it finally devours it. And what is the point of it all? Does it make the meat more savory, more tender? It is hardly likely. And, after all, the mouse has on occasion, gotten away. Edwards' answer is that it "is a lively emblem of the way of the devil with many wicked men."

> So many wicked men, especially false professors of religion and sinners under Gospel light, are led captive by Satan at his will, are under the power and dominion of their lusts, and though they have many struggles of conscience about their sins, yet never wholly escape them. When they seem to escape, they fall into them again, and so again and again, till at length they are totally and utterly devoured by Satan.[11]

We can scarcely restrain a smile as we read this, and there are other entries in the book which are just as quaint. But we should remember that these notes were not intended for publication; they are only the author's musings with himself, and we do not know how they would have been transformed in a theology of nature in the *Summa* he had hoped to write.

As they stand, they seem to me to fall into the category of the religion of nature, as it took shape in the mind of an intensely religious man, one who, I sometimes think, deserves even more than its original recipient the appellation of a "God-drunk man." As I said, Edwards did not complete the project. The short treatise on creation that he wrote in the closing months of his life presents only a bare skeleton; whether he intended later to clothe it with flesh, or whether he felt this was the farthest he could go, it is hard to say. Perry Miller says that the whole project bespeaks a combination of arrogance and humility in the author, which is at once sublime and pathetic—humility in the recognition that the ultimate truth of all things is in God, arrogance in the assumption that a man could articulate it. It is interesting to note that the same charge, in only slightly different terms, "presumptuous humility," was leveled at Hegel, who conceived a very similar project, and executed it, after a fashion, with what success we shall have the opportunity to consider in a later context. I am not sure how apposite the charge of arrogance may be in such a case—all intellectual endeavor is arrogant. The main question is whether the task he undertook is necessary—and of this Edwards was profoundly convinced. If he failed to accomplish it, that cannot be laid to arrogance. What is unique about Edwards is his vision—his heavenly vision—of the unity of all things in God, and the single-minded devotion with which he obeyed it throughout his life.

3. The preference for nature over Scripture as the revelation of God, which was the chief tenet of Deism, reduced the role of God to that of Creator at the beginning, and by so doing, it clearly threatened to abolish him altogether. The God of Deism had performed his creative function in so superb a manner that he had in effect rendered himself superfluous. The third phase of the story is marked by the gradual disappearance of God behind nature, which ceases to be merely a source of religion, or a medium of revelation, and becomes an object of religion. The Deist conception of a

revelation in nature gave place to a religion of nature. The change took place quietly, imperceptibly, and perhaps even without the consciousness of those who contributed to it. There was a continuing effort to hold nature and God together, when, in fact, they had fallen apart. Several examples may be cited. One is the Declaration of Independence. When it speaks of "the laws of Nature and of Nature's God," the operative word is "Nature," and the reference to "Nature's God" sounds suspiciously like a conciliatory gesture toward traditional belief.

Another example is Wordsworth. Wordsworth's celebration of the mystery of nature, to which reference was made in the previous chapter, has obviously religious overtones; but the question is: What religion? Wordsworth was a devout member of the Church of England, and increasingly so in his later years; yet nowhere in his verse is there any indication that what he found in nature—or should I say, what nature gave him?—was revelatory of the God who is worshiped in the church of which he was a member. He speaks of a presence and of a spirit, but it is not the presence or the spirit of the God and Father of our Lord Jesus Christ; rather, it seems to be something that is peculiar to nature and discloses itself only in communion with nature. It is significant that on the one occasion on which Wordsworth set forth his vision of nature within a philosophical framework, in what many regard as his greatest poem, it is the philosophy of Plato he chose; and here nature does not declare the glory of God, it recalls "the glory and the freshness of a dream"—the dream of a vision which we enjoyed before our birth, and which we dimly recollect as we enter this world.

The third example is Schleiermacher, the Schleiermacher of the *Speeches,* and especially the second Speech. The religion which Schleiermacher wants to commend to the cultured among its despisers consists in a feeling of unity with all that is: "True religion is sense and taste for the Infinite." The Infinite is one of several terms that Schleiermacher uses as equivalent to the "Nature" of Spinoza, to whom he pays homage; others are the world, the universe, the whole. His treatment of outward nature is somewhat cool and unromantic; he does not appear to have shared that enthusiasm for the world of forest, field, and stream, which we find in Wordsworth. The religious significance of nature is to be found, not in the aesthetic delight it affords, nor in its material immensity, but in that regularity and uniformity which "cannot escape even common perception," and which attests to the fact that it is a work of Spirit. This is, of course, the cosmological argument; and if we ask how so sophisticated a piece of philosophical reflection can have a place in a religion that consists fundamentally in feeling, Schleiermacher's answer is, "Through the gradual operation of the fellowship between knowledge and feeling they [i.e., the most ancient sages "to whom the World-Spirit showed itself"] have arrived at the immediate feeling that there is nothing even in their own nature that is not a work of this Spirit."[12] The notion of an immediate feeling brought about by a cooperation of knowledge and feeling seems hardly to conform to Schleiermacher's own principles; but the sentence quoted leads him to his main point, which is that man's sense of unity with the world originates in his own spirit. And, more importantly, it originates primarily in his communion with his fellowmen. It is through his sense of unity with all humanity that man comes to a sense of unity with the whole universe of being, including the world of nature.

The crucial question is whether the experience of unity with the whole, which forms the heart of religion, according to this account, involves God. I do not propose to go into this question, because if Schleiermacher in the *Speeches* was commending a religion of nature for which the idea of God was expendable, or optional, the position to which he moved in his mature work, *The Christian Faith,* was closer to orthodoxy. I turn instead to Emerson, whose spiritual pilgrimage took him in the opposite direction.

The religion of nature was a main element in the Transcendentalism of New England, and especially in the thought of Emerson, its leading spokesman. Emerson's own career epitomized the change I have attempted to describe, from a religion of nature, which is compatible with or an adjunct of the religion of God, to one that is not, although some vestiges of the old religion still cling to the new. When Emerson left the ministry, it was because he could no longer rest content with a historical revelation received from the past; he sought an immediate experience. He refused to celebrate the communion of the Lord's Supper because it commemorated a past event; he found a substitute in communion with nature, which could be enjoyed directly and without mediation or tradition.

Like Schleiermacher, Emerson used a variety of terms to denote the object of his religion: he spoke of the Universe, and of God; but the proximate object of his devotion was nature, and it was under this title that he propounded his creed in his first publication. By nature he meant specifically what I have been calling the world of nature, the world of forest, field, and stream (and, perhaps, I should add snow, to which he appears to have been particularly sensitive) and many of his allusions are quite concrete. But it was nature set within a certain philosophical and theological framework.

The philosophical underpinning which Emerson gave to the religion of nature consists of elements drawn from various sources, but chiefly from German idealism as modified by Coleridge and the post-Kantian idealists. Emerson did not work out his philosophical position in a systematic way, and transcendentalism sounds too pretentious a name for what he offered, which, as professional philosophers have often pointed out, consists of a patchwork of bits and pieces thrown rather than sewn together. But it is doubtful if it could be done in any other way, because Emerson's doctrine is not the conclusion of a philosophical argument, but an "intuition" of a primordial unity between man and the reality which encompasses him. It is prior to discursive thought with its distinction of subject and object, for which nature is a comprehensive term for the NOT ME.[13] The delight we have in nature rather conveys the suggestion of "an occult relation between man and the vegetable," an organic relation, such that each comes to itself in and through the other. Of the person who has grasped or intuited this primordial oneness —and Emerson, like Wordsworth, believed this is the person "who has retained the spirit of infancy even into the era of manhood"[14]—he writes: "He shall see that nature is the opposite [i.e., the counterpart, or complement] of the soul, answering to it part for part. One is seal, and one is print. Its beauty is the beauty of his own mind."[15] Emerson grounds this view of the relationship between man and nature on a monism, strongly reminiscent of Neoplatonism, "the sublime creed," he calls it, "that the world is not the product of manifold power, but of one will, of one mind; and that one mind is everywhere active."[16] It is active both in nature and in man, so that man comes to himself, not by setting himself over against nature, as a being opposed to nature, but by the realization that he is organically related to nature as the leaf to the tree. The experience Emerson describes this way:

> Standing on the bare ground,—my head bathed by the blithe air, and uplifted into infinite space,—all mean egotism vanishes. I become a transparent eyeball. I am nothing; I see all; the currents of the universal Being circulate through me; I am part or particle of God.[17]

The religion of nature was not, for Emerson, a romantic indulgence but a message of salvation to be preached. It was an effort to rescue man from dangers that threatened to deform him at that time. He had already been rescued from the shackles of a rigid Calvinistic orthodoxy by the more liberal creed of Unitarianism, but the coming of the industrial era exposed him to a new kind of threat. The Transcendentalists sensed what Marx called "the alienation of man"; we hear in them "the first outcry of the heart against the materialistic pressures of a business civilisation."[18] The religion of nature was proclaimed as a means to the recovery of wholeness, and in his original manifesto Emerson spelled out the benefits to be expected from it in some detail: Nature supplies man's needs, it opens his eyes to beauty, it provides him with the raw material of language, it teaches him morals by imposing a discipline on him, and, above all, it leads him to spirit, for one cannot live with nature, as Emerson recommended, without coming to see it as manifestation of spirit.[19] "It is the organ through which the universal spirit speaks to the individual, and strives to lead the individual back to it."[20]

The doctrine that nature and man are expressions of one and the same spirit can be made to appear theologically orthodox, or at least innocuous, if the spirit is called the Creator or "the Supreme Being."[21] But there is an important difference between them. While nature and man are alike creations of God, nature is a better revelation, or vehicle, of God, inasmuch as it has no will of its own to oppose to God. Does Emerson then preach the renunciation of the will, in a Buddhist sense? Not precisely, so far as I know. But since nature, which is will-less and impersonal, is a better revelation of God than persons possessing wills of their own, something of the sort appears to be implied. It was one of his complaints against the Christianity of the churches that they place an exaggerated emphasis on the personal—and on the person of Christ in particular. In this way, he thought, they lend support to a dualistic view of man as a being separate from and over against God, while they ought to be preaching what he calls "soul." "The soul knows no persons. It invites every man to expand to the full circle of the Universe."[22]

The question arises whether, then, the religion of nature entails withdrawal from the society of men. This has sometimes been a reproach against Romanticism, and Byron, for one, felt constrained to defend himself against it:

> There is a pleasure in the pathless woods,
> There is a rapture on the lonely shore,
> There is society, where none intrudes,
> By the deep sea, and music in its roar:
> I love not man the less, but Nature more.[23]

Emerson nowhere addresses himself to the question of how love of nature comports with love of man; but he was by his own account of a "chilly" disposition, and one of his reasons for quitting the ministry was his failure in the more intimate personal relationships of the pastoral ministry.

The religion of nature, in its Transcendentalist trappings, has few, if any, followers today, but a secularized, etiolated version of it has come to be widely accepted. It is held by many people that some degree of communion with nature—or should I use a more prosaic word, association with nature?—is essential to human health and happiness, and this is what multitudes of city dwellers seek on their vacations. If this is something we have learned from the Transcendentalists, the lesson was unintentional; for, oddly enough, they did not themselves draw this consequence from their doctrine. Thoreau was the lone exception, and he was regarded as a freak when he went off to live at Walden; even Emerson had reservations about it. But now practically everybody wants to go camping or hiking or exploring the great out-of-doors, often renouncing the amenities of modern civilized living and reverting to primitive conditions of dependence on nature. And they do it not only for the good of their physical health, they look also for a lift to the spirit.

4. The fourth and final phase in the story of the religion of nature may be briefly told. It is characterized by the total emancipation of nature from religion, and its secularization. It is the industrial revolution that was mainly responsible: it effected the conversion of nature into material of scientific technology under the exploitation of capitalism. Both the Romantic movement in Europe and the transcendentalism of New England were, in part, attempts to arrest this process, which had already begun, and which, as they saw, was fraught with grave consequences for human life. But they were rearguard actions, powerless to stem the advancing tide. The idea of nature as an inexhaustible reservoir of materials and forces which could be harnessed and put to work for the improvement of the human condition exercised a far more

powerful attraction than the sense of nature as a presence that inspires with thoughts sublime of something far more deeply interfused. The steady advances of science and technology in the nineteenth century gave to the romantic vision of nature more and more the quality of a childhood dream, although some of the poets who were sensitive to the changes that were taking place attempted to invest the new and more utilitarian vision with a romantic light. One feature of the new era that appealed to some of them was train travel, surely one of the strangest sources of poetic inspiration, especially if we recall that the first railroads were built for the conveyance of coal from the mines to the factories, not for the conveyance of passengers (and perhaps the last railroads will revert to the purpose of the first).

The alienation of nature from religion was accompanied, and intensified, by the alienation of religion from nature. I am referring to the religion of the churches, which became unconcerned with nature. Two things contributed to this change. The first is the great migration of the population from the country to the city, to which I referred earlier. What relevance did the theme of nature have to people who worked twelve hours or more in noisy factories and lived in crowded hovels in smoke-grimed streets? The second factor was the new aggressiveness of science which developed in the second half of the nineteenth century. But the long neglect of theological consideration of nature and withdrawal into the supposedly impregnable fortress of the inner life left theology with no recourse but to fall back on the nature lore of the Bible; and the attempt to make a stand here before the advancing tide of scientific knowledge in the latter decades of the nineteenth century led to debacle: theology was ignominiously driven from the field of nature, which was annexed by science and technology.

Theology was forced into an apologetic posture, and I would like to refer to a book that acquired an enormous popularity in the 1880's. In a period when Religion was being called to justify itself at the bar of Science, the Free Church of Scotland took the innovative step of appointing a Lecturer in Natural Science in its theological colleges at Edinburgh and Glasgow. The Lecturer at Glasgow was Henry Drummond, a remarkably gifted man, a trained geologist, who had conducted geological expeditions in various parts of the world. He was also a devout evangelical Christian, who worked with Moody in both of his revivalist campaigns in Britain, being particularly helpful in the counseling sessions (as they would now be called) which followed the big rallies. He was a man of great personal charm, and an accomplished public speaker, who influenced the lives of many students. His book *Natural Law in the Spiritual World,* which was published in 1883, was an immediate best seller.[24] The thesis of the book is, in the author's words, that "the laws of the Spiritual World, hitherto regarded as occupying an entirely separate province, are simply the Laws of the Natural World.[25] It is developed with an abundance of fascinating illustrations culled from the author's wide knowledge of science. I cite only one. A bodily organ, which is unused, will tend to atrophy. Thus burrowing animals, like moles, which spend their lives beneath the ground, have no occasion to use their eyes. "And Nature has taken her revenge upon them in a thoroughly natural way—she has closed up their eyes."[26] It is so also in the spiritual world; if we do not exercise the talents God has given us, they will wither and die.

It became evident, however, as we read, that the spiritual world of the title is a world only in a metaphorical sense; it is the world of the inner life, the spiritual experience of believers; it has nothing to do with the spiritual constitution of the world. The constitution of the world is determined by the laws of nature, and this is not affected by the fact that there is another world, the spiritual world, where the same or similar laws obtain. The tracing of these analogies, therefore, becomes what Edwards would have regarded as an exercise of the imagination, or a rhetorical affair. It bypasses the real problem, which is not natural law in the spiritual world, but spiritual law in the natural world. That problem remains.

Chapter 4
The Philosophy of Nature

"The Philosophy of Nature" is the title of this chapter, and "The Science of Nature" that of the chapter that follows, but I must hasten to say that it is not possible to draw a clear line of demarcation between them. For a long time the discipline we now call science was conducted under the name of natural philosophy, and indeed this name has been preserved in the four older Scottish universities, in each of which physics is taught by a professor of natural philosophy. It is only in comparatively recent time, with the rise of modern science, which we associate with the names of Copernicus, Galileo, Kepler, Newton, etc., that a distinction began to be drawn (though the full title of Newton's great work, published in 1687, was *Mathematical Principles of Natural Philosophy*); and in the centuries since then the study of nature has come to be regarded more and more as the domain of science, and philosophy has been all but driven from the field. Contemporary philosophy (as it is taught in the schools) has for the most part accepted the situation; it has conceded the realm of nature to science and limits its own role to critical scrutiny of the methods and procedures of science. If philosophy was once called the handmaid of theology, it has now become the handmaid of science.

The complete disjunction between philosophy and science as intellectual disciplines is reflected in the organization of academic studies, in which they are assigned to separate departments. The question persists, however, and now perhaps becomes more urgent, whether the scientific account of nature is exhaustive, and whether philosophy may not have something of importance to say. The question arises from the side of science as well as from the side of philosophy, and it must be examined from both sides. It will be examined in this chapter from the side of philosophy.

When people first began to ask the kind of question that was to develop into philosophy—this took place in the coastal cities of Ionia in the sixth century B.C.—we are told by both Plato and Aristotle that they were prompted by wonder. Wonder at what? It was wonder at the world of nature. The questions they asked were about this world.

There has been much discussion about what kinds of questions they were. Were they scientific, or metaphysical, or theological? The prevailing view among English-speaking historians is that these early questioners were the founders of science, because, as one authority has put it, they rejected "mythological solutions to problems concerning the origin and nature of the universe and the processes that go on within it . . . [and] substituted the faith that was and remains the basis of scientific thought . . . that the visible world conceals a rational and intelligible order, that the causes of the natural world are to be sought within its boundaries, and that autonomous human reason is our sole and sufficient instrument for the search."[1] The opposing view, which is more often taken by German scholars, is that the Ionians were doing ontology, or even theology.[2] They argue that if the Greeks had the foundation of science laid for them so early in their history, it is strange that they did so little to build on it, and they point to the fact that science did not get off the ground until it learned to ask a different kind of question than those asked by the Ionians.

It is not necessary to take sides in this debate. For one thing, science, philosophy, and theology were not formally distinguished until long after the time of the Ionian sages, and it is anachronistic to apply the distinction to them. For another, there is truth on both sides. Greek thought (to use a neutral term) originated in questions about the world of nature which have a scientific appearance, but in its search for answers to these questions it went beyond the limits of legitimate scientific inquiry as it is recognized today. The early thinkers, however, did not all transgress in the same way; they moved in a number of different directions, which it will be useful to consider, since it is these same directions that have been pursued in most subsequent philosophies of nature.

The attempts of the earliest thinkers in Ionia and the Greek colonies in southern Italy to find the basic material of which the world is composed bear the closest resemblance to modern science (physics and chemistry). And the resemblance becomes most striking when the initial theories, which consisted in choices among the four elements, individually or in combination, were succeeded by the atomic theory, first propounded by Leucippus, and developed by his more famous disciple, Democritus, who blew it up into a full-fledged mechanistic materialism, and established a precedent, which has often been followed by scientists of modern times.

The answers given by these men to the question of a primal element or elements were not pure guesswork or speculation; they were based on empirical observation of the properties of the element or elements chosen. Thus, if the world with all its varied contents can be traced back to one element, then water, which is liquid, but can be solidified into ice and vaporized into steam, seems as likely as any. Of course, the answers given far exceed the warrant of the evidence. But the significance of men such as Thales lies, as has been pointed out, not in the answers they gave, but in the direction in which they looked for them: they asked questions about the world of nature and they sought the answers in nature itself. If science consists in "putting nature to the question," as Bacon phrased it, these men were doing science.

This remains true, even if it is plain that they did not observe the rules of responsible method that are accepted today. To jump to such grandiose conclusions from such meager evidence seems quite unscientific. Nevertheless, it exemplifies the fact that scientific investigation tends to press beyond the limits of responsible scientific method, which requires that all facts be empirically verifiable, and to frame hypotheses, which are unverified or, perhaps, unverifiable. Thus, to take an example from contemporary science, the study of observable facts has led some astronomers to the theory that the universe had a beginning, but any such theory is both in fact and in principle unverifiable. Such theories are sometimes described as metaphysical, but since they do not involve a transition from a scientific to another mode of discourse but an extension of scientific investigation beyond regular limits, they could more properly be described as metascience.[3]

This term is also applicable to the thought of those who introduced an important change in the direction of the inquiry into the world of nature. The most original and creative of these was Heraclitus. He appeared to follow the path of his predecessors when he opted for fire as the primal element, but in fact he shifted the direction of the quest from an element to a principle, or law. His predecessors had noted the pervasive presence of change in the world, and had sought for an element, or elements, that would account for it. Heraclitus was interested in the process of change itself, and he sought to discover the law or principle that governs it. He found it in the conflict of opposites, which, despite their opposition, interact harmoniously, according to the regulation of a principle, which he called the Logos and invested with divine attributes.

Heraclitus certainly appears to have been doing something other than science, and the style of his few surviving utterances shows that he cast himself in a kind of prophetic role. But in fact he pointed a new and important direction for scientific inquiry by focusing on the form rather than the substance of what goes on in the world of nature. A somewhat more sober, or less unscientific, version of this new direction appears in Empedocles, who ascribed the changeful process of the world to the operation of two opposing forces which he called Love and Strife. He is sometimes said to have anticipated modern theories of attraction and repulsion.[4]

A more important step in this new direction was taken by the Pythagoreans, who anticipated in the most remarkable way the role that mathematics was to play in modern science. The Pythagoreans were led to their distinctive view of mathematics by the observation that musical intervals correspond to the arithmetical ratios of lengths of strings on a musical instrument. In this way they discovered the possibility of establishing a connection between disparate spheres, one qualitative and one quantitative, by means of numbers. This was a momentous discovery, and it is not surprising that they were so entranced by it, they jumped to the conclusion that all things are numbers. In saying this, they sounded like the earlier sages who had said that all things are water, or another of the four elements; but in reality they were pointing to something quite different, viz., that the unity of the world is to be sought, not in some substance from which it is derived, but in a conception to which it conforms.

The Pythagorean theory of numbers appears to have been validated in modern science which has found the world to be more amenable to mathematical comprehension than to any other. It is a question, however, whether such comprehension is scientific or philosophical. If we may isolate the Pythagorean theory of numbers from the philosophical and religious features of the Pythagorean community, we may say that, though they exceeded the bounds of science, the excess was metascientific rather than metaphysical. It has become vastly more difficult to ask whether the role of mathematics in modern science oversteps the dividing line.

Anaxagoras presented a variation on the thought of Heraclitus, with which he may or may not have been acquainted. Like Heraclitus, he was deeply impressed with the orderliness of the world as a *kosmos* and he ascribed it to *nous,* Intelligence, which he endowed with properties peculiar to conscious beings. This seems to be a clear violation of the principle of seeking explanation of the natural world within that world itself, but this was not the intention of Anaxagoras, who described Nous as one of the elements, finer than all the others, and who was evidently seeking an explanation of the world in terms of a factor immanent in itself, and not of a transcendent, intelligent being. Anaxagoras' conception is not the prototype of the teleological argument. But whether immanent or transcendent, his Nous contains an ambiguity which appears in the comment that Plato puts in the mouth of Socrates. In an autobiographical passage in the *Phaedo,*[5] Socrates relates that he was greatly attracted to the philosophy of nature in his youth and was specially delighted when he heard of Anaxagoras' idea of Mind as the principle of all things, but he was disappointed to find that, when it came to the actual study of things, Anaxagoras fell back on air and water and the other elements, as his predecessors had done. Had Anaxagoras been in a position to reply, he might have said that the presence of order in the world points to the existence of an ordering mind or intelligence, but that the specifics of the order are to be discovered only by direct inspection of the things of the world. This is the position taken by modern defenders of the teleological argument, which reasons from observed instances of order in the world to the existence of an intelligent divine being as the author of that order, but does not pretend to ascertain the order of the world by direct inspection of the divine intelligence. (See below, p. 110.) Socrates, however, took the view that, if the order of the world is derived from a designing intelligence, it should also be deducible from that intelligence. And in this he spoke for Plato.

Plato's account of the world, which he offers in the *Timaeus,* is unmistakably metaphysical, despite the inclusion of a great deal of ostensibly scientific material. Two notes are dominant. One is aesthetic. The dialogue is a celebration of the beauty of the cosmos, and in this Plato discerns a divine quality, since it is derived and deduced from the divine perfection of the forms, which serve as a blueprint for the unnamed Craftsman, who thereby produces a world which is "a perceptible god, supreme in greatness and excellence, in beauty and perfection."[6] The beauty of the world lies for Plato in its mathematical structure, and by applying this to the four elements he is able to incorporate them into his system. The world is thus the perfect-imperfect reproduction in a bodily medium of forms which have an ideal being in a supramundane intelligence. The other note is axiological. In Plato's theory of forms the highest is that of the good, and the good plays an important part in his account of the world. Plato was the first to ask why God (or whoever) created the world, and the answer he gave has been repeated by Christian theologians throughout the ages and has virtually acquired the status of dogma. It is that God is good, and the good is ever generous, desirous of imparting itself to others; so God did not wish to be God by himself alone, he wished to share his goodness with another than himself, and so he created the other.[7] Plato, however, does not dwell on this thought. Since God is only a marginal, if not dispensable, figure in the "story" (as Plato calls it), he has no interest in extolling the moral virtues of the creator.[8] His interest lies in the goodness of the product of the divine creativity, and it is to the demonstration of this that the main body of the dialogue is devoted. The doxology, which comes at the end, is offered, not to God, but to the world which he created and which is hailed as a visible reflection or expression of the divine. And in this respect Plato is closer to the Genesis narrative, which ends with God's attestation of the goodness of his creation, than the theologians who have shifted the emphasis to the goodness of God.

The concept of value, which has come to prominence in recent philosophy, is an attempt to express the Platonic emphasis on the objective rather than the subjective aspect of goodness. Though it may not be possible to strip from it all subjective reference, it is intended to direct attention primarily to the objectivity of value as a quality that is intrinsic to things or actions, and is not derived from their relationship to appreciative or active subjects. The endeavor of philosophical cosmology has been to demonstrate the values resident in the world itself, whether or not these are traced to a divine creator. Leibniz argues that this world, being the work of a perfect God, is the best of all possible worlds, despite its manifest imperfections, which Leibniz, like Plato, ascribed to the fact that the divine perfection cannot be perfectly reproduced in a medium that is not divine. And for Kant it might almost be said that the world creates God as much as God creates the world, since his conception of the supreme good as the junction of virtue and happiness in the creatures entails the postulate of God.

The pioneering approaches of Greek thought to the world of nature exemplify the philosophic method that Whitehead described as "the utilization of specific notions, applying to a restricted group of facts, for the divination of the generic notions which apply to all facts."[9] Thus the earliest sages and the atomists thought to find in matter and its movements the clue to the explanation of the world as a whole. But the second generation discovered that there are certain aspects of the world which are not amenable to explanation in terms of matter and motion—such as complex regularities of order—and this led them to seek more comprehensive explanatory principles in terms derived from the observed and experienced behavior of intelligent beings.

To describe these philosophical generalizations as "speculative" and "imaginative," as Whitehead does, is not to suggest that they were irresponsible flights of fancy. To the ancients they were a matter of profound practical importance, inasmuch as they formed the framework for the understanding of human experience in the world, and they were judged by the measure of their adequacy to the full range of that experience.

This is partly concealed during the classical period of Attic philosophy, but is plain to see in some of the pre-Socratics, and even plainer in the great systems of the later, Hellenistic period.

Socrates diverted the attention of philosophy from the

world of nature to human life. In seeking an answer to the question of the good life, however, he had first to find the context or framework in which it is to be sought. He found it in the *polis,* or city, and his great disciple, Plato, followed in his steps. The question of the good life was resolved into the question what it means to be a good citizen. Plato's most famous treatise is *The Republic.* And Aristotle took the same approach; the *Ethics,* which is one of his best-known works, was intended as an introduction to the *Politics.*

But with the collapse of the Greek city-states after the Macedonian conquest, the polis could no longer serve this function, and people were forced to look elsewhere; they looked to the world of nature.

This turn had been prepared not only by the early philosophers of nature but also by Plato and Aristotle, both of whom accorded the world of nature a high place as an object of philosophical contemplation, though neither of them connected it with the question of the good life. In the *Timaeus,* Plato praised the world of nature as a superior manifestation of the divine than man, who, according to this account, does not come directly from the Creator's hand, but through the mediation of inferior gods. Plato, in contrast to Genesis, saw the image of God in the world rather than in man. Aristotle was explicit about it: "There are other things much more divine in their nature than man, e.g., most conspicuously, the bodies of which the heavens are made."[10] And he argued that supreme philosophical wisdom is knowledge of the things that are highest by nature, and it is superior to practical wisdom, which is concerned with human good.[11]

The turn from the polis to the cosmos as the context in which the question of the good life must be asked was completed by the Stoics. The integration of man with nature and the quest for a corresponding life-style was the outstanding feature of Stoicism, and it helps to account for its wide popularity; for the Stoic was cosmopolitan; he took the cosmos for his polis. And the laws he honored and obeyed were not the laws of any political state, but the laws of nature itself. The concept of natural law is one of the most enduring elements in the heritage of Stoicism; it made an impact on the Western world, which is discernible to this day.

With the coming of Christianity the need for a philosophy of nature as the normative context of human life was greatly reduced, as the concept of nature was replaced by that of creation, but it was not entirely abolished. The concept of natural law was retained; it was equated with the law of God delivered to Moses at Sinai and, putatively, to Adam in paradise. But the concept has been controversial, especially in Protestantism, with its voluntaristic tendency to stress the law as the expression of the divine will; the idea of a law, inherent in the order of nature (even if it be called creation), has been felt to be injurious to the sovereignty of God and to have its roots in a philosophy of nature which is incompatible with Christian faith. Such a philosophy has become increasingly suspect with the growing belief that science alone is competent to answer questions about nature, and that philosophy, if it intrudes, can only build castles in the air.

This attitude was greatly encouraged by Kant, who, as we observed earlier, had great influence in pointing the direction for modern theology. Kant was deeply impressed by the success of the scientific method, but, unlike others who were led to believe in its omnicompetence, he realized that the success of the method depends on its strict confinement to the specific area in which it was achieved, viz., the observable. Kant was well aware that there are other areas of human experience that are not amenable to the scientific method, and his problem was to find some way of accounting for them. His solution was to assign those areas to something other than knowledge, something which he called faith, which operates with ideas, postulates, principles, and the like. Thus moral experience, to which Kant gave the greatest importance, is grounded exclusively in the good will, which not only is unrelated to any objective standard of good in nature but is fundamentally opposed to nature. If the Stoic ethic said, "Live according to nature," the Kantian ethic said, "Live contrary to nature." Kant dreamed of a resolution of this contrariety beyond the limits of this present life, but for the present our experience remains fragmented and disjointed.

It is not surprising to find that some people had difficulty accepting Kant's conclusions. However deeply they may have been impressed by his analysis of human cognitive experience, they felt unable to acquiesce in a situation that gave theoretical primacy to this mode of experience and set other modes of experience aside from it, if not in opposition to it. They craved a "unified field theory" by which to bring these different modes of experience into unity here and now, without having to wait for a resolution of the discord in a shadowy hereafter.

The question was again one of the adequacy of a philosophy to the range of human experience, and it may be illustrated by the contrast between Kant and Coleridge. Both men were giants, but in different directions, one in depth of intensity and the other in range of extensity; and this difference is reflected in their philosophies.

It would be unfair to say of Kant what Mill said of Bentham, that his was "the empiricism of one who has had little experience." Kant was a man of wide-ranging sensibilities, but when he attempted to offer an account of moral, aesthetic, and religious experience, he found it difficult to break through the empirical barriers he had erected in his account of cognitive experience. In that account itself, however, there are elements which fail to satisfy the empirical test and to which Kant assigned an inferior cognitive status. According to Kant, knowledge is the product of the unifying action of the understanding on the "manifold" of sense impressions, but our knowledge would be fragmentary and uncertain unless the rules by which the understanding performs its unifying function could be assumed to belong to larger, comprehensive unities—and these are the "ideas of reason." These ideas are necessities of thought, but they do not refer to realities that we can know; in Kant's language, they are regulative, not constitutive. Real knowledge is possible only when the rules of the understanding are applied to the data of sense; but the ideas of reason are not applied to the data of sense, they are applied to the understanding in order to bring its procedures into systematic unity.[12] In Kant's words, "Reason never applies itself directly to experience or to any object, but to understanding, in order to give to the manifold knowledge of the latter an *a priori* unity by means of concepts, a unity which may be called the unity of reason and which is quite different in kind from any unity that can be accomplished by the understanding."[13]

Samuel Taylor Coleridge (1772–1834) was not an academic philosopher, and he received little or no formal schooling in philosophy during his irregular and checkered academic career. He is known primarily as one of the towering figures in English literature, both as a poet of genius and as a critic. But Coleridge was one of those people for whom philosophy is an absolutely vital necessity; he could no more do without it than he could do without the opium of which he was an incurable addict. He was a voracious reader of philosophy, and he is said to have acquired a more extensive knowledge of the history of philosophy than anyone outside of Germany.[14] The decisive philosophical event in Coleridge's life was his encounter with Kant. He became acquainted with Kant's writings during a semester at Göttingen in 1799.[15] It was a Damascus-road experience for him: Kant, as he put it, "took possession" of him "with a giant's hand." He became a diligent student of Kant, but he did not swallow him uncritically; quite early he dissented from him on a central issue. If Kant gave a superior rating to understanding than to reason as an instrument of knowledge, Coleridge reversed this judgment. He held, with Plato and the classical tradition, that reason is able to rise above the experience and judgments based on the senses and to know a reality that transcends them. He was encouraged to contest the authority of Kant, which he did not underestimate, by the belief that Kant himself in his *Inaugural Dissertation* (1770) had ascribed to reason a real as well as a logical function in the matter of knowledge; perhaps we may say that he opposed the author of the first *Critique* to the author of the *Inaugural Dissertation* as Kant phenomenon to Kant noumenon. Coleridge was of the opinion that the whole movement of modern philosophy, which aimed at the restriction of knowledge, was a kind of psychological malady, resulting from a narrowing of outlook, or something like what is now called specialization. His difference with Kant was based not on technical criticism of Kant's argument, but on the premise that Kant's "metaphysic of experience" was incommensurate with experience as Coleridge knew it; for Coleridge was a richly endowed and many-sided genius. His passionate interest in philosophy was combined with a wide range of other interests; he was a literary artist with a brilliant, creative, and critical mind; he was a close student of the science of his time and he had a profound respect for the autonomy of science; he was a deeply religious man, firmly convinced that the tradition of Biblical religion, as well as that of classical philosophy, entails a unity that embraces all areas of experience. He refused to let Kant tell him that he could have no knowledge of truths which are superior to sense and understanding; he was sure that he did. It was impossible for him to rest content with the critical philosophy, which had the primary effect of taking things apart, and postponed their unification to a visionary realm beyond present experience. To him the root and ground of philosophy was a unifying vision of the whole, and he ascribed this vision to imagination.

Imagination is a key concept in the thought of Coleridge. It plays a major role in his literary criticism, where its meaning has been the subject of much discussion, and in his philosophy, where it comes close to Kant's reason, but with this difference, that it is not an ideal to which we aspire, but an idea of unity which we grasp intuitively. In one place Coleridge quotes some lines from *Paradise Lost* in which the archangel Raphael explains to Adam and Eve the difference between divine and human knowledge:

> The soul
> Reason receives, and Reason is her being,
> Discursive or intuitive: discourse
> Is oftest yours, the latter most is ours,
> Differing but in degree, of kind the same.
> (V, 486–490)

Imagination is that which differs least in degree from the intuitive knowledge of divine and angelic beings. It is, he says, "the living Power and prime agent of all human perception, and as a repetition in the finite mind of the eternal act of creation in the infinite I AM."

A good example of the exercise of the imagination in this sense may be seen in Coleridge's best-known poem, "The Rime of the Ancient Mariner." The poem is a classic portrayal of the condition of alienation, and it is done with sufficient psychological insight. The mariner, after his guilty act, is progressively alienated from his comrades, from wind and rain, from reality, even from God:

> So lonely 'twas, that God himself
> Scarce seemed there to be.

Then came the moment of healing—not after protracted (and expensive) sessions on the psychiatrist's couch, but when he looked over the side of the ship and watched the water snakes as they coiled and swam and flashed their brilliant colors in the light. It was at that moment that his heart was strangely warmed, and the burden of his guilt rolled away.

This turn in the poem has puzzled some readers, and some critics have mocked Coleridge for suggesting that the remedy for such a profound inward malady, as he describes, could be found by looking at water snakes; it smacks of witchcraft. But what Coleridge is suggesting is that the world of nature is the creation of the same God who is the author of our salvation, and that these creatures of nature, in the performance of their innocent ritual, are in their own way ministers of his saving grace; it was as he "bless'd them unaware" that he suddenly found himself in converse with God: "The self-same moment I could pray."[16]

Coleridge's claim to a unifying vision of the whole by means of the philosophic imagination was made in full recognition of the integrity and autonomy of science. As was already mentioned, he was a close student of science and he had a profound respect for the scientific achievements of men like Newton and his own friend, Humphry Davy. The scientific account of nature is important, but it is not sufficient. No one can live in the world which science describes; for it is an abstraction. There is need for a philosophy of nature, which is in no way prejudicial to science, but which enables us to see the facts, which science elicits from the study of nature, in a larger light. Such a philosophy, he insisted, is not an extravagance, but a necessity, if we are to live in the real world, to which we are related in ways more intimate than those adopted in scientific study.

There are original features to Coleridge's philosophy of nature, but it also embodies some that he inherited from the long tradition in which he stood; and two of these may be mentioned. The first is "the great chain of being," i.e., the conception that the world of nature exhibits a number of distinct levels of being which are arranged in an ascending scale. We are familiar with the evolutionary form of the conception as a temporal progression from the simplest to the most complex, highly organized forms of being. But what Darwin did was only, so to speak, to transpose the conception from a vertical to a horizontal axis and to amass the evidence for it—at least in the biological realm. Long before Darwin it had been observed that the contents of the world do not represent a heterogenous accumulation of odds and ends, but a number of different kinds of being arranged in a series ascending from matter through life to consciousness and spirit. It is reflected in the creation story in Genesis 1, in which creation is described as a process beginning with the mineral, next the vegetable, then the animal order, and culminating in man, who shares the sixth day of creation with the animals, but who is distinguished from the animals by being created in the image of God. It is present also in the discourse of the archangel Raphael, when he was sent to Eden to instruct Adam on the responsibilities and perils of his place in the created scheme of things; these are the opening lines:

> O Adam, one Almighty is, from whom
> All things proceed, and up to him return,
> If not depraved from good, created all
> Such to perfection; one first matter all,
> Endued with various forms, various degrees
> Of substance, and, in things that live of life;
> But more refined, more spirituous and pure,
> As nearer to him placed or nearer tending
> Each in their several active spheres assigned,
> Till body up to spirit works in bounds
> Proportioned to each kind.[17]

Coleridge also saw in nature a graduated series of levels and a tendency of the lower to rise to the higher. He emphasized particularly what he called "the tendency to individuation," meaning by that the striving of the inorganic toward the organic, as it is exemplified preeminently in life and consciousness. His conception of nature is close to being evolutionary, though he rejected the theory, which had apparently been advanced by his time, that man is descended from the ape. Nevertheless, he held that there is a continuity between them—that nature in some unexplained way makes a leap: "All things strive to ascend, and ascend in their striving."[18]

The second feature of Coleridge's philosophy of nature, which is deserving of notice, is also one with a long history; indeed it goes back to the first beginnings of Western philosophy. One feature of the world of nature, which, as we noted before, excited the wonder of the ancient sages, is the pervasiveness of order in the midst of change. Two different accounts of this phenomenon were given by two of the leading figures of the age.

Parmenides propounded the doctrine that being alone is real, i.e., eternal, changeless being, and change is only appearance, which deceives men into erroneous opinions. This seems an extreme, even drastic solution to the problem; but it sowed the seed which came to flower in Plato's doctrine of the two worlds. Heraclitus took a different view. He stressed the pervasive reality of change: *panta rhei,* all things are in flux, nothing abides, you cannot step into the same river twice. But this constant changefulness does not lead to chaos, it has a pattern to it; it is actuated by the interaction of opposites, and it is regulated by a transcendent principle or law, which Heraclitus sometimes calls God. He found the strife of opposites exemplified in a wide variety of things, day and night, up and down, drawing together and falling apart, sleeping and waking, slaves and free, gods and men. Heraclitus reproached Homer for wishing that strife would cease among gods and men, for, if that were to happen, everything would come to a standstill. It is strife, or war *(polemos)* that makes the world go round. But over all the strife there reigns harmony (*harmonia,* Heraclitus invented the word), which he sometimes pictures in juridical terms as justice administered in a divine court of law.[19]

Coleridge found the thought of Heraclitus congenial. In a letter to a friend he referred to his own philosophical project as *Heraclitus redivivus.* He believed that the science of his time had confirmed Heraclitus' principle of the harmony of opposites and furnished many additional examples of it. All matter he found to be a copula of "opposite energies," and the two principal energies or powers, which interact according to "the universal law of Polarity," are light and gravitation, which are associated with expansion and attraction and with form and formlessness. Like many another, he was fascinated with the statement in Genesis that God divided the light from the darkness, and he explained this to mean that God established the universe as a structure with two poles which have a tendency to unite; and he related these to the persons of the Trinity, gravitation to God the Father as the center, and light to his only-begotten Son who proceeds from the Father.

There is an interesting resemblance between the thought of Coleridge on this matter and that of Simone Weil. Like Coleridge (with whose work she shows no evidence of having been acquainted), she deplored the compartmentalization of knowledge into narrow specialisms, which she regarded as the curse of modern thought, and she demanded a comprehensive vision of the whole. She drew on her extensive knowledge of mathematics and the sciences for analogies, or analogous expressions, of what she considered to be the basic principle of reality, and she made much of light and gravitation—though she employed them in a more "existential" way than Coleridge. She observed that the light of the sun supplies chlorophyll which enables plants to grow upward and thus to defy the pull of gravity, and she applied this to the relationship between man and God; gravity represents that in man which pulls him away from God, light the grace that comes from God and enables man to grow toward him; thus she thought light a peculiarly appropriate image of Christ.[20]

By far the most ambitious construction of a philosophy of nature ever attempted was that of Hegel. If I say that a brief reference may suffice for our present purpose, this does not imply any lack of respect for the greatness of Hegel's achievement; it is because Hegel thought he had gathered up in his philosophy the rich and varied harvest of all previous philosophies; and this is certainly true of his philosophy of nature, which contains clear echoes of Anaxagoras, Heraclitus, Plato, Aristotle, and Proclus. He agreed with Anaxagoras that the original principle of nature is to be found in mind rather than in matter, or, as he reworded it, in subject rather than in substance. But he developed this principle with a consistency which Anaxagoras, to the disappointment of Socrates, did not, and presented a rational, or idealist, view of nature as a whole. He agreed with Plato that the natural world is an expression of ideas, but he refused to rest content with a mythological account of the transition from the ideal to the real. Here he availed himself of the thought of Heraclitus, that the natural world exhibits a continuous process of the conflict and reconciliation of opposites, and he traced this back to an analogous process in the originative principle, which he called dialectic, and which, with some help from Proclus, he elaborated in his *Logic.* His most distinctive contribution was his renaming of the original principle as Spirit, by which he sought to express its essentially originative character and, with Aristotle, its teleological thrust. Spirit is something more than reason, or idea, which he found "inert." Spirit is rational, but it is active and creative in the expression of itself outside of itself. The world of nature was to Hegel such an external self-expression of Spirit, and in his philosophy of nature he tried, in the light of the science of his time (with which he was well acquainted), to present a comprehensive view of the structures and dynamics of the natural world in a manner corresponding to the dialectic of the idea.

Hegel's philosophy of nature has been regarded as the most presumptuous part of his system and has been severely attacked. It was thought by some that Hegel was attempting to deduce the actual contents of the world from the logic of the idea. Nietzsche spoke of Hegel's "Gothic heavenstorming."[21] Scholars sympathetic to Hegel have tended for the most part to dismiss it as negligible, "an excrescence of romanticism," one has called it.[22]

There are three main reasons for this adverse judgment. The first is that Hegel's philosophy of nature is articulated in terms of the scientific knowledge of his time, and as that has become outmoded, the philosophy built around it has been thought to be outmoded too. The second is that the advances of science since Hegel's time have given added strength to the belief that science alone is competent to give knowledge of nature, and have made the idea of a philosophy of nature redundant. The third is that a philosophy of nature has almost invariably theological overtones and tends to evolve into a theology of nature. This clearly was the case with Coleridge, and barely less so with Hegel. Hegel's concept of Spirit is derived from the Bible, and while he presents his thought in philosophical language, he can on occasion transpose it into the representational language of religion. Hegel offered his system as a substitute for theology, not because he wished to abolish theology, but because he thought theology had fallen down on its essential task. Whether in so doing he transformed theology beyond recognition, as many critics have charged,[23] whether the Absolute is a replacement for God, or God attired in an academic robe—these are questions to be considered in a later chapter.

The possibility of a philosophy of nature, separate from and independent of a theology of nature, is suggested by Teilhard de Chardin. That his own vision of the whole is profoundly theological is beyond question, but in his first publication to appear in English he relegated the theological aspect to an Epilogue and presented his main thesis in ostensibly scientific terms in a manner that might be persuasive to anyone without theological commitment, and in fact his book was introduced to English readers with a warm endorsement by an eminent scientist who is an unbeliever. On the other hand, it was violently attacked by another scientist who said that the alleged science was "tricked out by a variety of metaphysical conceits." This is rough language; but it certainly seems to the ordinary reader that what Teilhard was doing all the time was something more than science, whether it be called metaphysics, or poetry, or theology. And this points to the question: What is the vantage point which affords the best and most comprehensive view of nature?

Chapter 5

The Science of Nature

The progress of science in the last four centuries is without doubt the greatest success story in the intellectual history of humanity; and its practical applications have done more to revolutionize the conditions of human existence than all the political revolutions put together. The world we live in today has been shaped almost entirely by the application of scientific discoveries and inventions to our domestic life: transportation, communication, medicine, and many other things, not forgetting the means of making war. The transformation that has taken place within the present century has outpaced that of all previous history; and the world in which I was born and brought up would seem as remote to my grandchildren as the Middle Ages does to me. It is no wonder that science, the means that has brought these enormous changes, has come to be regarded as an omnicompetent instrument and as the model and criterion of all true knowledge—not merely one way of acquiring knowledge of the world, but the only way of acquiring knowledge that is accurate, objective, reliable, and useful. All problems, it is widely believed, are soluble by science (in principle), and if there are some that remain unsolved, it is only a question of finding the appropriate scientific procedure.

The claim for the omnicompetence of science has sometimes been expressed in intemperate language, especially in the nineteenth century (e.g., by Herbert Spencer), but it is not invalidated by pointing to the excesses of scientific positivism. Science discovered in the twentieth century that its method had from the beginning of the modern era a built-in principle of self-criticism and self-correction which gave it a new flexibility and enlarged the range of its competence. The prestige of science has, if anything, been enhanced by its greater modesty; and it is still believed by the majority of people that what science tells us is true and reliable.

The question that keeps coming up in various ways is whether science tells us the whole story. Does science tell us all that we know about nature—and all that we need to know? While we accept the validity of the knowledge that science gives us, are there other questions we may ask, questions that science not only does not answer but does not ask? Is there, in other words, something in science, in scientific method and procedure, something that acts as a limiting factor on the knowledge it provides? It is certainly a paradoxical question to ask when we consider to what an extent science has enlarged the frontiers of human knowledge. But has this enlargement been purchased by the adoption of restrictive practices? Let me pursue this question in two or three directions.

First, science resembles a monastic order. It imposes an astringent discipline on those who practice it. They are required to take a vow of intellectual restraint, which forbids them to accept as fact anything that cannot be vouched for by sufficient evidence. It is not an easy rule to keep, and there is probably no scientist, however devoted, who does not at times chafe under the restriction. The temptation to transgress is exceedingly powerful. Even Newton, who proudly affirmed, "I do not frame hypotheses," went on to frame one of the most unscientific hypotheses ever heard of. But a more striking example of this is to be seen in Kant. Kant was not a scientist in the modern sense of the word; but his main concern was to determine the validity of scientific knowledge, and his answer was that scientific knowledge is valid so long as it confines itself within a certain restricted area; if it strays beyond that area, it falls into a morass of illusion. But the strange thing is that, for all his emphasis on the limits of scientific knowledge, Kant could not resist the temptation to look beyond them and to play with the possibility of a knowledge that goes beyond them. An example of this ambivalence may be seen in his treatment of teleology. After rejecting the teleological argument for the existence of God on the ground that the principle of teleology (design) cannot be established by induction from the data of experience, he concedes that the evidence is impressive enough to carry conviction to many people; later, in the third Critique, he goes further and allows that teleology, though it is not a matter of scientific knowledge, can assist in the pursuit of scientific knowledge, if it is used as a working hypothesis in the study of living things. For example, the evidence does not entitle us to say that the eye was designed for the purpose of seeing; but the whole science of ophthalmology is based on the assumption that the eye is for seeing and all the efforts of the ophthalmologist are directed to promoting that end.

If scientists sometimes chafe at the restraints on knowledge they are required to observe, the general public do so even more. This is very evident in the contemporary scene. There is a marked and rapidly widening interest in subjects which lie on, or beyond, the frontiers of ascertainable scientific knowledge. The best known of these is astrology; and some figures from a recent newspaper article show the amazing growth of its following. According to a recent poll, 32 million adult Americans believe in astrology, and 1,250 newspapers in the country, about two thirds of them, carry daily horoscopes, whereas only about 100 did so a generation ago. Interest has also greatly increased in paranormal phenomena of various kinds: ESP, exorcism, UFO's, the Bermuda Triangle, close encounters, and the like. The proponents of these interests maintain that they are not fads, but facts, deserving of scientific attention and susceptible of investigation under strict scientific conditions. And they have persuaded so many members of the public that some members of the scientific community have become alarmed, and they have lately founded a journal called *The Zetetic* (from the Greek word for "to investigate") for the purpose of exposing and refuting what they regard as pseudoscientific claims.[1] There is no doubt that from the orthodox scientific viewpoint, the phenomenon looks suspiciously like a reversion to magic, and the scientists, who remember that the rejection of magic was a prime condition of the rise of true science, are understandably alarmed. But, on the other hand, the current wave of pseudoscience (if that is what it should be called) reflects, not so much a distrust of science as a feeling that science, despite the vast range of its competence, does tend to be hamstrung by its own self-imposed restraints.

This is, I think, the dilemma of science, and it manifests itself in one or two features of scientific method, to which I want to refer.

I have spoken of the science of nature, in the singular, but there is no such thing. There is a multiplicity of sciences that direct their investigations to different parts of the totality we call nature: there is physics, the study of matter and energy; there is chemistry, the study of the composition and properties of substances; there is biology, the study of living organisms; there is psychology, the study of behavior of living beings; and a host of others. This partition of nature into a plurality of parts, each the province of a special science, is one main factor behind the success of modern science, in contrast to the comparative failure of science among the ancient Greeks; for the Greeks, despite the genius they displayed in the initiation of the scientific inquiry, failed to advance, and the reason is that they attempted to advance on too broad a front. They framed their questions in too general terms, they sought for principles that would explain all phenomena, and they did not address themselves to the investigation of particulars. This is not to say that the Greeks did not make important scientific discoveries in specific fields. Eratosthenes' calculation of the circumference of the earth by a carefully planned experiment ranks as a superb scientific achievement by modern standards, and the researches of Aristotle in a wide range of fields, from botany to zoology were so impressive that they were accepted as definitive for almost two millennia after his death. But these were the exceptions. The bent of the Greek mind was toward theoretical generalization, and experimental investigation savored too much of manual labor, which was beneath the dignity of a free man. They wanted to mount up on wings as eagles, but they did not learn to walk and not faint.

I have just referred to the other feature of scientific method, where we may also be caught in a dilemma. This is the empirical method, the method of observation and experiment. To find out about things, the way is to look at them, observe how they behave, and confirm your observations by testing them. It is so obvious, so self-evident, that it is hard for us to imagine how anyone ever supposed there was any other way of doing it.

The empirical method has proved to be the most effective tool in the hands of modern science, and there is no need for me to enlarge on what has been accomplished by means of it. It has, however, two consequences, or implications, which it is important to note.

The first is functionalism, i.e., concentration on how things function, or behave, rather than on what things are. This is one of the main shifts that took place in the transition from medieval to modern science. In medieval science, the endeavor had been to discover what things are, their essences, because it was believed that, if the essence of a thing could be determined, its behavior could be deduced. But the essence of a thing is not disclosed to observation; it has somehow to be intuited, or divined, and that is a hazardous operation. With the adoption of the empirical method, attention was focused exclusively on the behavior of things, which is all that they disclose to observation, and the question of essence was set aside.

The effect of this is seen best in what happened to the concept of the self. Under the empirical method, the concept of the self underwent a progressive attrition. It began with Descartes's famous experiment in methodical doubt; he wished to find out if it was possible by the empirical method to establish any incontestable certainty, and he found the answer in thinking; from his observation that there was thinking going on he reasoned to the existence of a subject who was doing the thinking. But was this inference justified —was it not, in fact, a relapse into the medieval idea that functions belong to essences? At all events, when Hume repeated the experiment, he observed only discrete pieces of thinking, but no evidence of a continuing subject or self that would bind them together into a unity. Finally, in the twentieth century, Gilbert Ryle maintained that the quest for some sort of entity behind the observable functions is like looking for "a ghost in a machine"[2]

The major casualty of the empirical method was teleology, i.e., the idea that the behavior of all things may be explained, in part at least, in terms of the purposes for which they were designed, on the analogy of human artifacts, or what Aristotle called final causes. On this view, the way things behave was explained by saying that that is the way they were meant to behave. But from the viewpoint of the empirical method this mode of explanation was tautological, because the empirical method is restricted to what may be observed, and purposes, if there are purposes in nature, are intrinsically unobservable. However, the methodological exclusion of teleology, however well justified, does not entail its ontological exclusion. The question whether there are purposes in nature is simply unanswerable by science, if the scientific canon of credibility rests on observation and experiment.

I wish to return to the reference made earlier in this chapter to the fragmentation of knowledge resulting from the specialization of the sciences, because it is here, I think, that the basic question arises for a theology of nature. The modern scientist has been described as a person who knows more and more about less and less; and the general public, who are dependent on the instructions of the scientists, are given many pieces of knowledge, but no knowledge of any way to bring them together into one package. Is there any such way?

There are some who say there is not. The success achieved by modern science through specialization has led to the belief that this is the only way in which knowledge can be obtained. This is the view that is held in the leading philosophical schools of the English-speaking world at the present time: according to Stuart Hampshire, "reality is accessible to human knowledge, only if it is divided into compartments, each marked and labeled. . . . For all genuine knowledge is specialized knowledge and cannot be anything else."[3] The quest for a comprehensive knowledge of reality as a whole—metaphysics in the traditional sense of the term—is dismissed as an impossible dream. Philosophers of this persuasion would agree with Paul when he said, "We know in part" (1 Cor. 13:12).

Is this a situation in which we can acquiesce? Must we resign ourselves to the fragmented knowledge provided by the special sciences and renounce all hope of advancing beyond that to a knowledge of the whole?

There are several angles from which this question can be approached. One is psychological. It is said that the quest for a knowledge, or understanding, of the world as a whole is rooted in the need of the self for significance and security. If I live in a world that is disjointed, and that does not make sense as a whole, how can I make sense of my own life? The question recalls the anguish of Pascal in the face of the Copernican revolution. But there are some who say that this applies only to the tender-minded, as William James called them; the tough-minded are able to accept the fragmentation of knowledge and are willing, as James was, to live in a pluralistic universe. But one wonders whether James's tough-mindedness was not conditioned in some degree by the temper of the time and place in which he lived, and how he would have felt in the Europe of the two world wars, when people were saying that the individual is thrown on his own resources in a world which is absurd—to create an island of meaning in an ocean of meaninglessness.

But the impulse to go beyond the parts and seek knowledge of the whole is more than psychological. It has logical roots, roots in the logic of science itself. Let me put it in a very simple way. Scientific explanation may be described, at its most elementary, as making connections—as, for example, when the Pythagoreans connected the pitch of a tone with the length of the string on which it is sounded, and when Sir Ronald Ross connected malaria with mosquitoes. But one connection leads inevitably to another, and to another, as both of these examples show. When the Pythagoreans went on from the particular mathematical connection they discovered and proclaimed that mathematics connects everything, they were too precipitate, though they were not entirely wrong. The discovery of the connection between malaria and mosquitoes led to the quest for antidotes and mosquito control measures, both of which involved a whole gamut of chemical connections. The question then is whether there is not a built-in drive in the logic of explanation that impels it to seek the connection that connects all the connections.

Something of the sort may be observed within the sciences themselves at the present time. There are within the sciences some evidences of a reversal of the trend toward ever-increasing specialization, which has been so conspicuous in the past.

This may be observed at several different levels. It has taken place on purely scientific grounds. For example, when I was a student, over fifty years ago, the curriculum of the university I attended contained courses in botany and zoology, and each of these subjects had a professor and other teaching personnel. The curriculum of Princeton University has no courses in botany or zoology, and there is no professor of either subject. When I first noted this, I was puzzled, but on closer examination I discovered that the subject matter of botany and zoology is included in what are called the biochemical sciences, which are concerned with the life processes in both plants and animals. These processes are of sufficient similarity, if not identity, to warrant their inclusion in a single discipline. It is also stated in the catalogue that a student entering the program in the biochemical sciences is required to have a specialized knowledge of biology or chemistry and advanced training in mathematics and physics. There has also been invented recently a new science called sociobiology, which is still in a highly controversial stage; it has been announced by one of its authors as a "new synthesis," and another has claimed that "sooner or later, political science, law, economics, psychology, psychiatry and anthropology will all be branches of sociobiology."[4]

The ecological situation is also a powerful factor in reversing the trend toward specialization. Indeed, the ecological crisis is itself in large measure a consequence of this specialization, inasmuch as it has led to the application of special scientific technologies without regard to their impact on the environment as a whole. The use of pesticides is the best-known example, and it was the central concern of Rachel Carson in her book *Silent Spring,* which probably did more than any other to make the general public aware of the dangers we faced, unless we could learn that all parts of nature are bound up together, and the use of any one part has effects on other parts, and ultimately on nature as a whole. Here is an example of such a chain reaction which occurred some years ago, and which was reported in an article in *Theology Today:* "It seems that the World Health Organization some years ago in Borneo used DDT to eliminate the mosquito. In the process, certain predatory wasps were also killed, and since the wasps kept the caterpillar population in control, the roofs of the houses began to collapse because they were eaten by the caterpillars. DDT was also used indoors to kill flies, which in turn were eaten by the gecko lizard, and they in turn by the cats. So the cats died from ingesting too much DDT, and then the rats began to multiply, and with them came the threat of plague. In order to restore some balance in this disrupted ecosystem, new cats were parachuted into the region"[5] The writer goes on to draw the conclusion: "Ecology speaks of the interdependency of organisms and things within the whole system. Entities in isolation do not exist. What seems to solve one problem may create another worse problem in another area. What affects one segment affects the whole system. Ecologists cannot afford the luxury of specialization; they must be generalists. So a new commitment and compulsion to systematics is upon us."

If the urge to generalization and system has been accented by the ecological crisis, there is another factor which has been moving the science of nature in this direction for more than a hundred years, something that has special importance for the theological problem.

The new factor in the situation is the increasing recognition within science itself that nature is historical. This took place in two stages, and it is important to distinguish them because of their effects on theology. The first was the discovery of evolution, which was made first in the geological field and then, with more dramatic effect, in the biological. The discovery was that the world and its contents did not always exist in their present forms, but came to their present forms through a continuous process of change that reaches back to the beginnings of time. The story is well known, but there is one thing I want to mention because it was destined to have theological repercussions. The initial shock of the Darwinian theory, as it applied to human beings, came from the feeling that it reduced man to his origins. In a way this was suggested by the title of the book in which Darwin set forth the application of his theory to the human species, *The Descent of Man;* he seemed to be saying it was a down-come for man, or at all events that is how people took it. Of course that is not what Darwin meant; he was using the word in a neutral way to denote man's family tree. But since he was showing that man's family tree was literally a tree, it was hard to think of it as other than a put-down. It came to be realized, however, before long, that there was another way of reading the story —not as the story of where man came from, but the story of how far he has come, and, if he has come so far, how much farther he might still have to go—in a word, not a story of a descent but of an ascent. *The Ascent of Man* is in fact the title of the last book of Henry Drummond, which was published in 1894 and contained the Lowell Lectures he had given at Harvard the previous year. This book had a great influence in changing the perspective on evolution and enabling people to view it as a vast process moving ever onward and upward toward "one far-off divine event, to which the whole creation moves." It is not necessary, for our present purpose, to review Drummond's argument, which shows many remarkable resemblances to that of Teilhard de Chardin. I mention it because it was the first of a series of attempts by scientists—scientists-turned-philosopher, like C. Lloyd Morgan, or scientists-cum-theologian, like Teilhard de Chardin—who felt constrained by their scientific studies to offer some account of the process as a whole, which carried them beyond the limits of ascertainable fact.

A similar urge to expand the conspectus of science, arising from within science itself, is to be observed in the field of astronomy. Evidence from their own scientific observations has led a large number of astronomers to the conclusion that the universe had a beginning and will have an end.

The scientific evidence for a beginning is derived from the expansion of the universe. It has been established by the "red shift," i.e., the fact that the light from distant galaxies is measured in the longer wave-lengths, which are in the red part of the spectrum, that the galaxies are receding from one another at a velocity which increases to about one seventh of the velocity of light. This observed fact has led some astronomers to form the theory that all the elements, of which the universe is composed, existed initially in an exceedingly dense concentration, which exploded, and the exploding matter eventually formed the stars. The proponents of this theory of a primordial explosion, commonly known as "the big bang theory," speak of it as creation, although the term does not carry any theological overtones for them—they use it only to describe an initial event, not an act, and they have certainly no thought of an agent who performs the act. And the same is true of the use of the term by those who hold an alternative theory, "the steady state theory" it is called—that the expansion of the universe can be accounted for by the regular addition of new matter; they speak of this as continuous creation, but, again, with no thought of a creator. The new matter simply appears from nowhere. It is more than *creatio ex nihilo,* it is *creatio a nemine.*

I am not faulting the astronomers for speaking of creation in this way. They are scientists, not theologians; and if they want to borrow a term from theology, theology can afford to make the loan—without interest. By that I mean, it is of minor interest to theology whether it can be established on scientific grounds that the world had a beginning. That is a cosmological question. The theological question is about God, and God's creation of the world. That is the question we shall have to examine.

But first let me refer briefly to the scientific evidence for the end of the world. It is based on the second law of thermodynamics. This law, which is sometimes referred to as entropy, was derived from the observation that in any system involving the conversion of heat into energy, there is always a certain loss, the potential cannot be fully realized, some of it is dissipated and cannot be recovered. To take an example from everyday life, only a fraction of the potential energy in gasoline is converted into mechanical energy in the engine of a car; the rest of it—in fact, the greater part of it—is lost to the cooling system and is carried away as heat from the exhaust gases and friction in the bearings. The efficiency of an engine is measured by the percentage of potential energy it converts into actual energy; and that is why increasing the efficiency of automobile engines is so important a factor in the conservation of energy. The process of the degradation of energy, as it is sometimes called, is going on throughout the universe continually, and eventually a state will be reached at which everything in the universe will be at the same temperature (thermodynamic equilibrium), and there will be no possibility of converting heat into energy. This eschatological prospect is sometimes referred to as the "heat death" of the universe—which is somewhat misleading if it calls to mind the cosmic conflagration of apocalyptic. The meaning is quite the opposite, it is the heat that will die, and with that, everything will come to a standstill.

The compulsion to systematize, however, even if it be seen as an inner necessity of science itself, does not bring with it the power to accomplish it. If the necessity is imposed by the ecosystem, it seems unlikely, in view of the enormous mass and variety of scientific knowledge, that any scientist, or group of scientists, will ever succeed in developing a superscience that connects the findings of all the separate sciences in one coherent whole. And there is still considerable opposition on the part of many scientists and philosophers, who, while they may admit the urge to go beyond the fragments and grasp the whole, regard it as a temptation we must resist —like a drug that gives us a "high" but takes us out of the real world. Questions that are concerned "not with any particular isolated problem or any particular aspect of our experience, but with experience, or life, or existence *as a whole*"[6] are called metaphysical; and in the climate of today anyone who asks such questions is regarded as an intellectual pariah.

But it has been pointed out that there are two kinds of metaphysics: transcendent and immanent. If metaphysics looks for principles which are explanatory of our experience of reality as a whole in some realm that is wholly transcendent to experience, like Plato's forms, its conclusions are, as Kant demonstrated, unverifiable, and as the analytical philosophers say, meaningless. If this world is confusing, to add another to it only makes the confusion worse confounded. But there is another kind of metaphysics, which seeks its explanatory principle(s), not in some realm beyond experience, but in some selected area or aspect of our experience. This has been called immanent metaphysics, but it might more appropriately be called metascience, since it is an extension, or extrapolation, of an accepted scientific method, the method of induction. This is the method by which science, from the study of a limited number of particular facts, draws general conclusions about all facts belonging to the same class.

It has been hard to find a logical justification for induction, but scientists have not been deterred by this difficulty, because it has worked so well in practice—at least in the natural sciences. Its employment in human affairs, in matters such as opinion research, has not been so successful. Since the inductive method has proved so useful in bringing great masses of data into comprehensible unities in the special sciences, it seems not illogical to suggest that its use be extended to bring the findings of the special sciences into some kind of comprehensible unity. This, I think, is what Whitehead attempted to do, and in his view we have no choice. If we wish to obtain a comprehensive view of things—and this is the ultimate objective of science—we have no choice but to take the explanatory principles that have been found effective in one area of scientific endeavor and see how far they can be applied to other areas as well. This is how both religion and philosophy work, according to Whitehead. "Religion claims that its concepts, though derived primarily from special experiences, are yet of universal validity, to be applied by faith to the ordering of all experience. Rational religion appeals to the direct intuition of special occasions, and to the elucidatory power of its concepts for all occasions."[7] We need only think of the place of the exodus in Jewish religion and of the story of Jesus Christ in Christian religion to see how true this is. Philosophy (speculative philosophy) proceeds in a similar manner by the imaginative extension of the method of induction, which Whitehead calls generalization, and which was described in the previous chapter[8] (p. 82).

Hegel shared with Whitehead the urge to seek a comprehensive and coherent understanding of the whole, and like Whitehead he thought to find the clue in some particular area of experience. He seems to have found it in the experience of self-realization, i.e., as one commentator has put it, "in the notion of a person's becoming more truly himself by triumphing over circumstances which at first seem alien to his personality, but are later seen to be necessary for its full development."[9] Hegel's model seems much too personal in character to be intelligibly applicable to these vast tracts of reality which exhibit nothing remotely resembling personal characteristics. Whitehead's model, on the other hand, has been charged with precisely the opposite defect; despite the fact that he described as "the reformed subjectivist principle," it is inadequate to the distinctive character of personal being.

These differences, however, do not concern us at present. What is common to Hegel and Whitehead, and many others besides, is the argument that the pursuit of a comprehensive and coherent view of reality as a whole leads to the thought of God. This is the question to which I want to refer briefly in conclusion. Does the science of nature lead necessarily to the thought of God?

The question takes two forms. The first concerns the traditional assumption of the uniformity of nature. Whatever modifications it may be necessary to make in this formula, it remains true that science, which is the quest for orderly relations between phenomena, presupposes the existence of a universal and intelligible order in the world. The word "universe," like the Greek *kosmos,* embodies this presupposition. Such a universal orderliness does not necessarily imply the existence of God. It may be taken as something that is just there and needs no explanation; or, as Hume suggested in one place, it may have evolved from a long process of trial and error. Nevertheless, the fact has so impressed the minds of some scientists that it has for them become invested with the attributes of God. It is well known how Einstein resisted the discovery of an element of indeterminacy in the behavior of elementary particles with the remark that "God would not play dice." And when I. I. Rabi, the physicist, was asked to comment on this in an interview, he said, "I think that 'God' is a very good heuristic principle, a standard by which you can judge things."[10] Such statements by scientists may be gratifying to theologians, but they are of questionable value.

A God who functions only as a heuristic principle may be nothing more than a scapegoat on which the scientist unloads an assumption for which he is unwilling to take responsibility himself. At all events, he is eminently expendable. Many scientists, perhaps most, are not only indifferent to the question of a philosophical or theological justification of the assumed orderliness of nature on which their work is based, they are unperturbed by the demonstration that any such justification is forthcoming—and in this, perhaps, they are like Hume himself; for his demonstration of the improbability of causality did not deter him from traveling from place to place in search of a cause that might effect a cure of the disease that caused his death.

The other way in which, it has been contended, the scientific study of nature implies the thought of God focuses on the fact that the order of the world is contingent. It has been argued by Whitehead, Michael Foster, and others that the recognition of this fact was a powerful factor in the rise of modern science. Contingency means that the order of the world is not inherent in the essence of things themselves in such a way that it can be deduced from it, but that it is imposed on them by the will of an omnipotent Creator, who acts according to his own counsel, and therefore it can only be discovered by actual observation. The argument has been succinctly stated by E. L. Mascall: "A world which is created by the Christian God will be both contingent and orderly. It will embody regularities and patterns, since its Maker is rational, but the particular regularities and patterns which it will embody cannot be predicted *a priori,* since he is free; they can be discovered only by examination. The world, as Christian theism conceives it, is thus an ideal field for the application of scientific method, with its twin techniques of observation and experiment."[11] The reference to the freedom of God in this passage is presumably intended to mean that God could have imposed a different order on things—that he could have chosen, for example, to make water freeze at some other temperature than 32 degrees Fahrenheit. Only we are assured that the choice he made—and this can only be found out by empirical investigation—will be found to be rational.

This argument is also open to question, both scientifically and theologically. If it has been found by empirical observation that water freezes at 32 degrees, in what sense is this rational? Would it be less rational if it froze at 31 degrees or 33? In a recent novel by Kurt Vonnegut, the scene is set at some future period, at which the power of gravitation varies from day to day; some days it is so strong that people can only move by crawling on all fours; on days when it is light, everybody—and everything—is erect. Of course, it is a fantasy; but would it be irrational if gravitation did in fact vary from day to day? The temperature varies, the atmospheric pressure varies, why should not gravitation vary also?

The theological weakness of the argument is more serious. If the rationality in the ordering of the world is wholly concealed within the will of God and can be discovered only by scientific investigation of the world, the rationality is, in the last analysis, a judgment of the scientist, and the invocation of God adds nothing to it. When Kepler said he was thinking the thoughts of God after him, he showed his piety, and we have no reason to doubt his sincerity; but we have only Kepler's version of the thoughts, and we have to make do with them. To refer them to God makes them no whit more intelligible. Whether or not science is impelled by an inner necessity to invoke supernatural sanction for itself, that does not transform it into a theology of nature. That is quite a different thing, as I hope to show in the next chapter.

PART II

THEOLOGY OF NATURE

Chapter 6

The Creation of Nature

The various perspectives on nature, which have been sketched in the preceding chapters, have shown that there is considerable variety in man's experience of nature and his relationship to nature.

The modern consciousness has been dominated by the objectification of nature in the natural sciences. In science, nature is a problem, i.e., *problēma,* something thrown in our path, an obstacle we have to overcome. The objectification of nature in science had its philosophical counterpart in the distinction between man and nature and the epistemological disjunction of subject and object. It had its theological consequence in the withdrawal of theology from nature as an object with which science alone was competent to deal, and its retiral into the realm of subjectivity. This was the theme of the first chapter.

But the objectification and problematization of nature has not gone unchallenged. It has been accompanied by a continuing undercurrent of protest against the disjunction of man from nature and a persistent quest for a union between them, which has been sought by means of romantic feeling, religious contemplation, and philosophical thought. This was the theme of the second, third, and fourth chapters.

Then the fifth chapter was devoted to developments within science itself, and new demands which are presented to science by the society it serves and which are forcing it to revise the compartmentalization, which has characterized its procedures hitherto, and seek ways and means to reach a more comprehensive understanding of the world as a whole. For the truth is being brought home to us in various ways that the world is a whole, and we can no longer enjoy the comfort of living in separate compartments, neither in science, nor in philosophy, nor in theology. Theology can no longer remain immured in the enclave of subjectivity; it must venture out into the world of nature. It must do this if it is to meet its responsibility as the interpreter of the word of God the Creator.

"We believe in one God the Father Almighty, Maker of heaven and earth, and of all things visible and invisible."

Thus states the first article of the Nicene Creed, the one truly ecumenical creed. It contains three affirmations about the meaning of faith in God: (1) it affirms the unity of God; (2) it affirms the duality of all reality other than God (we shall call it the world); and (3) it affirms that the world in its duality is to be referred to the one God as its creator.

It is the third of these affirmations that presents the most difficult problem for modern theology. How can the world in its duality be referred to God in his unity? Modern theology, as we have seen, has construed the meaning of faith in God primarily, if not exclusively, in terms of his relation to one half, or one side, of the world and neglected the other. We continue to profess our faith in God as creator of all things; but with one half of the things it has become an empty formality. According to the first article of the creed, this is heresy, in the basic sense of the word; for *hairesis* means selection, or partiality; it consists in taking a part for the whole. The real opposite of heresy is catholicity, in the sense of wholeness. And this is what the creed stresses when it describes God as maker of heaven and earth and of all things visible and invisible.

The terms used in the creed refer to a duality or diversity in the created world, and not to a distinction between this world and some supernatural or transcendent realm above this world. They express a clear awareness that this world, in which we live, has two sides to it, and that there are deep differences between them. Today our sense of the difference, or division, between the two sides of the world is even deeper, as the language in which we express it indicates: we draw the distinction between self and world, between thought and extension, between mind and matter, between subject and object, between spirit and nature. And it is our deepened sense of the difference between these two sides of the world that has forced us to articulate the meaning of faith in God in relation to the first term in each of these pairs, and to leave the second out of the picture.

When the creed asserts that all created being, in its duality and diversity, is to be referred to the unity of God as creator, it makes the unity of God equivalent to his universality. This is the meaning of the term *Pantokrator,* which is applied to God as creator. The customary English rendering, "Almighty," conveys a false impression. Pantocrator does not mean that God has so much power that he can do absolutely anything; it means that he is "ruler over all."

The inclusion of universality in the definition of God may reflect the influence of Greek thought on the Fathers who framed the creed, but it is also a faithful transcript of the Biblical understanding of God. In the Bible, however, the universality of God is presented in a peculiar, and paradoxical, relation with his particularity. And it is the particularity of God that has the priority in the Biblical understanding. It is a prime characteristic of the God of Biblical faith that he elects: he introduces himself and relates his action to particular persons and a particular people. But the election of the particular is from the first instrumental to the attainment of the universal; it is the method, or strategy, of God to begin with the particular and advance to the universal. The Old Testament clearly reflects this advance; the faith of the people of God is construed first in particular, not to say particularistic, terms, and only slowly did it grow to universal. The universality of God becomes articulate in the prophetic literature, and it received monumental documentation when the final collection of the literature of the peculiar people was prefaced with an account of God as universal creator and ruler over all.

The New Testament may seem to focus more narrowly on the action of God in the particular; in fact, the particularity of the action of God is now intensified to the point of "scandal" (1 Cor. 1:23). But here again, the particular is, paradoxically, integrated with the universal.

It was a matter of prime importance to the writers of the New Testament, as we can readily understand if we place ourselves in their historical situation, to assert that the particular occurrence, which they had witnessed, has universal dimensions, that what they had heard and seen with their eyes and touched with their hands is that which was from the beginning (1 Jn. 1:1). There are a number of passages in the New Testament which affirm that the one who was sent by God for the salvation of the world was present and active with God in the creation of the world, and will be so also in its consummation, and that the redemptive action in its particularity is integrally related to the creative and consummative in its universality. It is a great mistake to treat these passages, which are relatively few in number, as marginal speculations. It was central to the testimony of the New Testament that the particular event which occurred in Jesus Christ is coextensive with the work of God in creation and consummation.

The most explicit and elaborate statement of this thesis is found in the Prologue to the Gospel of John. In reading this, we tend to isolate the statement, which undoubtedly forms the climax, that the Word became flesh and dwelt among us (Jn. 1:14). But this statement must not be torn from its context, for the writer is saying something much more than that; he is saying that the Word *(Logos)* that became incarnate in Jesus Christ is identical with the Word by whom all things were made, that creation and incarnation are works of one and the same Logos, who was in the beginning, who was with God, and who was God. He is saying that Christ is the key to the meaning of creation.

This is a very difficult thesis to interpret. It will be useful to consider what has been made of it in Christian theology.

I. The Meaning of Creation

Why did God create the world? That he did create the world "in the beginning" (however that be understood) is the common faith of Jews, Christians, Moslems, and others. But if the question Why? is asked, there is no agreed answer, and often no answer at all.

The question may appear presumptuous to some.[1] And, indeed, there is a strain in the language of Scripture which suggests that the Creator-creature relationship precludes any interrogation of the former by the latter:

> Woe to him who strives with his Maker,
> an earthen vessel with the potter!
> Does the clay say to him who fashions it,
> "What are you making"?
> (Is. 45:9; cf. Job 9:12; Dan. 4:35)

It goes without saying that faith in God the Creator involves an element of mystery. But if the mystery is intensified to total ignorance, the confession of faith is reduced to a profession of agnosticism—as when the expression "God knows" is used in vulgar speech as a substitute for "No one knows." If faith in God as the creator of the world does not carry with it some understanding of creation that contains at least the possibility of an answer to the question Why? the confession is vacuous.

The question, however, is rarely asked in modern theology, partly for fear of trespassing the limits of inquiry into the mystery of "the depths of God" (1 Cor. 2:10), but chiefly because the whole subject of creation has become an apologetic problem, and the primary task of theology has been to establish the proposition that the world was created. This may be a reasonable proposition. There are certain features of the world which suggest, with some cogency, that its existence is not self-explanatory and that it is derived from some source or agency beyond itself. The elaboration of this line of thought has been the traditional subject matter of "natural theology," which received its classical expression from Thomas Aquinas. Aquinas identified five "ways" in which examination of the world as we know it leads us beyond the world to some power or cause that transcends it—"and this all men call God." It is of interest to note that investigation of the origin of the universe by modern astronomers has led some of them to propose creation as a serious hypothesis; but the term, as they use it, is divested of all theological connotation.

The proposition that the world was created by a power which may, or may not, be called God is, however well founded, far short of the confession of faith in God as the creator of the world. The latter is a theological statement, i.e., a statement about God, or, more specifically, about an act of God, and it raises the question why God should be understood to act in this way. Why did God create the world?

The answer most favored by theologians who have asked this question is one that was given, not by one of them, but by Plato. According to Plato, God is good, and the good is ever generous; it seeks to give, to impart itself to others. So God did not wish to enjoy a monopoly of reality; being good, he created a reality distinct from his own, in order that he might communicate his goodness to it. Creation, in a word, is the result of the overflowing goodness of God.[2] This thought of Plato's is echoed in numerous theologians. It may be sufficient to cite two. Karl Barth wrote:

> God did not remain satisfied with His own being in Himself. He reached out to something beyond, willing something more than His own being. He willed and posited the beginning of all things with Himself. But this decision can mean only an overflowing of His glory. It can consist only in a revelation and communication of the good which God has and also is in Himself.[3]

And Peter Brunner:

> God wills not to have the blessedness of his own intra-divine life for himself alone. In groundless love he wills to have creatures which shall share in his life within the limits of their creatureliness and which in such participation and fellowship shall be blessed, in that they receive his divine glory and as in a mirror reflect it back upon him.[4]

The conception of an overflowing goodness of God has its obverse in the thought of a deficiency in God, an incompleteness in his being that could only be filled by the creation of the world. Schiller put it in the lines:

> Friendless was the mighty Lord of worlds,
> Felt defect—therefore created spirits,
> Blessed mirrors of his blessedness.[5]

Whitehead also included an element of deficiency in his philosophical doctrine of God. He allowed a certain completeness to God in respect of his "primordial nature" as "the unlimited conceptual realization of the absolute wealth of potentiality," but he held that in this respect God is "deficiently actual," and the completion of his nature requires the creation of the world. If the world is not sufficient to itself without God, as natural theology maintains, then, in Whitehead's view, God is not sufficient to himself without the world.[6]

Christian theology, of course, has not been hospitable to the thought of a deficiency in God and has countered it with the Biblical notion of the "blessedness" of God, which it has equated with absolute self-sufficiency; as Paul said in his speech on the Areopagus, "The God who made the world and everything in it, being Lord of heaven and earth, . . . is not served by human hands, as though he needed anything, since he himself gives to all men life and breath and everything" (1 Tim. 6:15; Acts 17:24f.). The Platonic theory of the generosity of God seemed more consonant with this emphasis. But if the creation of the world is ascribed to an overflowing goodness in God, rather than a deficiency, is this not also to lay God under a necessity? If God created the world in order to relieve a superfluity in his being, this would seem to mean that he acted under necessity, just as much as if he created the world in order to repair a deficiency in his being. A river that overflows its banks is just as much out of control as one that runs dry.[7]

Christian theologians have sought to avoid this conclusion by stressing the freedom of God in creation; and in this they have relied heavily on the first account of creation in Genesis, which gives a strong impression that creation takes place at the divine word of command: "God said, 'Let there be light'; and there was light" (Gen. 1:3). It was so understood by the psalmist:

> For he spake and it was done;
> He commanded, and it stood fast.
> (Ps. 33:9)

It is also interpreted in this way, for the most part, by modern interpreters. To cite one of the most highly respected, von Rad writes: "This creative word is different from any human word; it is . . . powerful and of the highest creative potency."[8] It means, he explains, that the world is the creation of God's will, and he is its Lord. Christian theology too has, for the most part, adopted this view of creation as an act of the sovereign will of God, and has supported it with the argument that only in this way can creation be understood as a free act, an act to which God was in no wise constrained, but which he was free to do, or not, as he chose.[9] His choice was determined entirely by itself. Were it determined by any consideration extraneous to itself, this, it was felt, would be derogatory to the divine freedom.[10]

It is not surprising that philosophers who have sought to offer a rational account of the world have often rejected the idea of creation by divine fiat, on the ground that it contributes nothing to their purpose. The most vigorous was Fichte. He described the notion of a creation according to which the world proceeded from God by an act of absolute and arbitrary power as "the fundamental error of all false Metaphysics and Religion, and, in particular, as the radical principle of Judaism and Heathenism. . . . Of such a creation it is impossible even to conceive rightly in thought."[11] Whitehead was scarcely less vigorous; he frequently inveighed against "the doctrine of an aboriginal, eminently real, transcendent creator, at whose fiat the world came into being," describing it as "the fallacy, which has infused tragedy into the histories of Christianity and Mahometanism."[12]

Professor J. N. Findlay, who has undertaken the bold task of reinstating the Absolute in philosophy—meaning thereby "the notion of something having that indiscerptible unity, that necessity of existence and necessary possession of essential properties, which goes together with and totally explains the existence of all that exists finitely, contingently, empirically and separately"[13]— surveys a number of possible candidates for the role. Among them is the notion of "a Semitic Creator-God," but this he rejects on the ground that such a God is thought of as "able to create or not to create anything whatever," and thus is left as an Absolute, with "little or no explanatory work to do: the existence of the cosmos may depend on the Absolute, but the Absolute could equally well have given rise to no cosmos, or a very different one, and so explains little of cosmic being or structure."[14] Findlay thinks that if the world is taken as the creation of a "supercosmic" personal deity, the act of creation must be understood not only as free but "as in some manner gratuitous,"[15] and he assumes this to be the "Christian orthodox" view, which, he contends, must "be remedied by a more essentially Christian unorthodoxy."[16]

Findlay's objection to this view of creation as a gratuitous or arbitrary act of deity appears to have been shared by the Neoplatonists. According to A. E. Taylor, "unlike Christian theologians, Plotinus and Proclus do not represent the creative activity in which Goodness finds its outlet as one of 'free choice.' To them this would have implied that Goodness might conceivably not have imparted itself to anything, and therefore might not have been wholly good."[17] But Findlay is also dissatisfied with the Neoplatonic alternative of "emanation," which he compares contemptuously, and not very nicely, to "a sort of nocturnal emission."[18]

Martin Heidegger took a similar position. Holding that the first of all philosophical questions is, Why is there anything, rather than nothing? he refused to allow that the statement of Biblical faith, that God created the world, can serve as an answer to it; it merely forecloses the question. However, he did not contest the integrity of the confession of faith in its own place; and he thought that the believer, who takes his stand on the confession, was bound to regard the philosophical question as one that not only does not need an answer but one that it is foolish even to ask. It may be significant to note in this connection that Heidegger began his academic career with a dissertation on Duns Scotus.[19]

It has also been pointed out in a recent study by a group of Anglican theologians that "if creation is represented as resulting from an almost arbitrary act of will, so that it is a matter of indifference to God whether he creates or refrains from creating, then inevitably the created order is depreciated and deprived of intrinsic value. (This was the criticism of the biblical doctrine of creation propounded by Feuerbach.)"[20]

II. Freedom and Necessity in God

It has been thought by some to escape the dilemma of a necessity which detracts from the autarky, or self-sufficiency, of God, and a freedom which reduces creation to an arbitrary or contingent act of God, by seeking a reconciliation of necessity and freedom in the inner structure of the being of God. The doctrine of the Trinity clearly offers an inviting field for this endeavor; for the doctrine, viewed abstractly, is concerned with a distinction that is comprised in a unity. In this respect it may be treated as a question of what is called "the trinitarian principles" by Paul Tillich, who distinguishes it—and treats it separately—from the ecclesiastical doctrine of the Trinity as it was developed in the fourth century.[21]

The theme of the trinitarian principles resembles the ontological, or immanent, Trinity in the ecclesiastical doctrine, but it differs from it in that it is not informed to the same extent by the economic Trinity, i.e., the revelation of the triune God in the history of salvation. Rather, it takes the form of an attempted construction of the inner being of God on grounds that are considered to be intrinsic to it. In other words, the question it asks is: How does God come to be God?—not: How does God come to reveal himself as Father, Son, and Holy Spirit?

The question is one that obviously presents serious difficulties. It looks like an attempt to bypass the revelation of God in Christ and to pry into the inner being of God directly. The church first encountered the threat in Gnosticism, and since that time official theology has looked askance at all attempts to stray beyond the confines of revelation. Protestant theology has been particularly suspicious of all such ventures, which it has branded by various opprobrious names: speculation, mysticism, theosophy, and the like.[22] Luther was untiring in his condemnation of persons who wanted to climb up to heaven and scrutinize the majesty of God directly, as he put it, instead of receiving God where he has made himself accessible to us in the lowliness of Christ. And more recently Karl Barth assigned all attempts to bypass revelation to the category of natural theology, which he would have expelled root and branch from Christian theology.

Nevertheless, the question has refused to be silenced; it has continued to engage attention, usually within the most earnest and pious circles in Protestantism, and in fact responsible and respectable theologians will be found to be wrestling with it in their own way.

How does God come to be God? The question could be construed as one concerning the "origin" or "birth" of God, which is technically known as theogony.[23] Some Christian thinkers have felt free to use theogonic language. Jacob Boehme writes: "The whole or total God stands in seven species or kinds, or in a sevenfold form or generating; and if these births . . . were not, then there would be neither God, nor life, nor angel, nor any creature."[24] Schelling, who was deeply impressed by Boehme and described him as "a theogonic personality,"[25] adopted similar language: he spoke of "the longing which the Eternal one feels to give birth to itself."[26] Despite this language, however, neither Boehme nor Schelling can be charged with doing theogony in the strict sense of the term; for the theogonic question is, How does God come to be? or, How does God come into being? The question begins from absolute nothingness. But neither Boehme nor Schelling approaches the question in this way. For both, there is a given from which they start; for God cannot be born of nothing: "As there is nothing before or outside of God he must contain within himself the ground of his existence."[27] The ground of his existence, which is coeternal with God, is "that within God which is not *God Himself*"[28]—but it is only on this ground that God comes to be himself.

Schelling's endeavor was to articulate a concept of God as vital, dynamic, active, in contrast to the inert, unchanging essence of the classical metaphysical concept. "Nothing can be achieved at all by such attenuated conceptions of God as *actus purissimus* and similar notions which earlier philosophy set forth, or by such concepts as the newer thought constantly produces in its concern to separate God as far as possible from all of nature. God is more of a reality than is a mere moral world-order, and he has in him quite other and more vital activating powers than the barren subtlety of abstract idealists ascribes to him."[29] He followed Boehme in seeking to develop a concept of God involving a dynamic unity of two factors, one of which he described as a ground, a depth, or a nature, "which, though it belongs to him himself, is, nevertheless, different from him"[30]—and the other light, love, or reason.

Tillich's analysis of the "trinitarian principles" is a highly sophisticated rendering of the same pattern of thought found in Boehme and Schelling (for both of whom he expresses high regard).[31] He makes a distinction between two "principles," or elements, which are at the same time bound together in unity. He employs the apt figure of a polarity, and he speaks of the two principles as dynamics and form, with which he associates a number of other pairs: potentiality and actuality, vitality and intentionality, freedom and destiny, ultimate and concrete. The first term may be said to denote that which constitutes God's power to be, the second that which determines his being as God.

Barth's construction of the doctrine of God also follows a similar pattern. His concern, as he explains, is to develop a concept of God as being-in-act, and in order to do this he distinguishes two sides, one that relates primarily to the being of God, which he calls freedom, and one that relates primarily to the act of God, which he calls love. "God is who He is in the act of His revelation," and in that act he is revealed as the One who "loves in freedom."[32] Barth does not speak of two principles, nor does he use any of the other abstract terms Tillich associates with them; he prefers to retain the concrete terms, freedom and love, because he wishes to emphasize that God's freedom and God's loving are determined by their subject, God, and not by any abstract dialectic.[33] Only once, so far as I have observed, does Barth depart from this rule, when he speaks of freedom and love as "moments."[34]

When we compare the dynamic construction of the being of God, represented by these writers, with the older classical concept of God as an unchanging essence, the difference may be likened to that between an ellipse and a circle. The classical concept of God might be fittingly represented by a circle in which everything revolves around a single center and is determined by its relation to it. God's being is absolutely "simple": it has one center, and the relation of the center to the circumference is identical at every point. The figure of the ellipse can be described only in relation to two foci, which can never be resolved into one; thus it more fittingly represents a concept of God who has relatedness at the inmost core of his being and who is more readily conceivable in relative terms.

If the transition from a circular to an elliptical model of God may be said to be characteristic of recent theology, there is a curious parallel with what took place in modern astronomy. It was universally held until the time of Kepler that the planets moved in circular orbits—not on the grounds of observation, but on the ground that, since the circle was considered to be the perfect figure, God, being perfect, could not be conceived to have designed the orbits of the planets in any other way. When Kepler discovered that the planets move in elliptical orbits, he changed the shape of the astronomical universe.

III. Dynamics and Form in God

A

The statement of the problem in terms of a polarity is sufficient in itself to suggest the principal ways in which attempts to solve it tend to diverge. The most obvious is an emphasis on the distinction that drives the two elements so far apart as to endanger the possibility of their unification. Usually the emphasis has been on the first of the two elements in the being of God, the element of dynamics, or power, which is singled out as that which is primordial and distinctive in God. It is the "numinous" element, in Otto's term, the element which arouses dread. It appears also in the *potentia absoluta,* the interminate will, in Duns Scotus; in the terrifying majesty of the unrevealed God, in Luther; in the abyss, or fathomless depth *(Ungrund),* from which God seeks to bring himself forth, in Boehme; in the preconscious longing, or "will of the depth," which is the basis of God's existence, in Schelling. It is this element, according to Tillich, which constitutes "the basis of Godhead, that which makes God God," and to remove it is "to rob God of his divinity."[35]

This emphasis arises not merely from speculation of a gnostic or theosophical nature, but from religious experience of life and the world, which has sometimes a dark, mysterious, terrifying side to it. This is conspicuous in Boehme, who saw everywhere around him a conflict of opposites: yes and no, good and evil, love and wrath, light and darkness, life and death. It was his profound sense of the conflict of opposites that led him to a construction of the being of God which could account for it. There is a similarity in the experience of the mystics, which includes not only the bliss of union with God but the anguish of abandonment by God.

The dynamic, abysmal, pre-formal element in God, however it may be registered in experience, is incapable of being conceived or expressed, except in an indirect manner. Only that being which has form, which is actual and concrete, can be grasped by reason.[36] But form is manifest everywhere in human experience—and not least in the experience of being human, i.e., as something that comes to be. Hence the question arises of what it is that is antecedent to form and acquires form. And since only that which has form can be expressed, that which is prior to form can only be indicated indirectly by such cryptograms as the wilderness *(Wüste)* of Eckhart, the abyss *(Ungrund)* of Boehme, and the Indifference of Schelling.

The absolute indeterminateness of the abysmal element in God is stated by Boehme in uncompromising language: "For it cannot be said of God that he is this or that, evil or good, or that he has distinctions in himself, for he is in himself, natureless, passionless and creatureless. He has no tendency to anything, for there is nothing before him to which he could tend, neither evil nor good. . . . There is no quality nor pain *(Qual)* in him."[37] Schelling describes the indifference of the *Ungrund* in similar terms: "Indifference is not a product of antitheses, nor are they implicitly contained in it, but it is a unique being, apart from all antitheses, in which all distinctions break up. It is naught else than just their non-being, and therefore has no predicate except lack of predicates, without its being a naught or a nonentity."[38] But absolute indeterminateness, or indifference, seems indistinguishable from nothing, and it is hard to see how anything determinate can arise from it. Tillich replies that if it is equivalent to nothing, it is not absolute nothing, the nothing that simply is not *(nihil negativum);* it is *nihil privativum,* "the *me on,* the potentiality of being, which is nonbeing in contrast to things that have a form, and the power of being in contrast to pure nonbeing."[39] Despite the absence of determinate qualities in it, this element is not inert; it is dynamic, it is the potentiality of being.

It is this emphasis which is expressed in theological voluntarism, i.e., the position which asserts the primacy of the will over the intellect in God. Voluntarism, which came from the school of Duns Scotus, also provided a firmer basis for the freedom of God in creation. The Scotists asserted that the power of God embraces not only that which he has chosen to do *(potentia ordinata)* but also that which he has chosen not to do—or not chosen to do *(potentia absoluta):* God in his infinite power was free not to create the world, or to create a different kind of world.[40] Voluntarism took a more radical form in Ockham, and was inherited by Luther, who was enabled by it to discover the gospel of grace.[41] The primacy of the will was a decisive factor in the reformation of theology. It became deeply embedded in classical Protestantism, and it tends to reappear whenever Protestant theology seeks to return to its classical roots. It appears, for example, in the early work of Karl Barth; Barth explained that when he spoke of God as "wholly other," he meant God "as king, monarch, despot," and it is in this that he saw what is "essentially and specifically divine."[42]

When, however, the dynamic element is identified as will, the force of the distinction with form is reduced, since the concept of will, as distinct from that of power, implies form and determination. The notion of a will that is totally without form appears occasionally in Boehme and Schelling, but when they attempt to describe it, both men have recourse to figures in which some degree of determination is involved. Boehme calls it a "craving" *(Sucht)* and a "desire" *(Begierde):* "The will seeks itself, and its seeking is a desire and its finding is the essence of the desire, wherein the will finds itself."[43] "The nothing hungers after something, and the hunger is the desire. . . . For the desire has nothing that it is able to conceive. It conceives only itself, and draws itself to itself."[44] Schelling describes it in terms of what would now be called a biological drive: "It is not a conscious will, connected with reflection, but neither is it completely lacking in consciousness, moving in accordance with blind mechanical necessity. But it is of a middle nature, like desire or passion, and most readily comparable to the lovely urge of a developing being striving to unfold itself, whose inner actions are undeliberate (cannot be avoided) and yet involve no sense of compulsion."[45]

The emphasis on the dynamic element received its most extreme expression when it was removed from theology altogether and developed into a philosophy of will by Schopenhauer and Nietzsche. Schopenhauer's view of reality as the expression of a "will," not in the sense of something consciously and rationally directed, but in the sense of a blind, irrational force, marked the total isolation of the element of dynamics from that of form. He saw it exemplified preeminently in the biological drives of the animal world, such as that of the mole, which spends its life burrowing endlessly in the dark—and to what end?—and conspicuously in sex, which drives all creatures to continue life—and, again, to what end? This will has no end but itself, and it makes no sense. The path of wisdom is to resign ourselves to it.

Schopenhauer was led to his philosophy of will by reflection on the experience of the self as will. He held, with Kant, that the self, as knowing subject, can get no further than phenomena; it is in willing that the self encounters a resistance, and it recognizes in this resistance a reality comparable to itself. Objective reality, "the thing-in-itself," is not found by theoretical knowledge. The object *(Gegenstand)* is literally that which objects to me, withstands me; and thus it manifests itself as will.

Nietzsche, who was powerfully affected by Schopenhauer in his youth, proposed a reintegration of dynamics and form (or will and idea), by focusing on the human will and ascribing to it a formative function. He was not interested in Schopenhauer's metaphysic of the will and the attendant counsel of resignation, which he traced to a false set of values. He found in the human will a capacity to form a new set of values corresponding to its own nature as will, and this he called the will to power.[46]

Another nontheological version of this same doctrine is to be found in the Freudian psychology, according to which this element is the source of all vital and psychic energy in man. It is called the id, and it is described as "the dark, inaccessible part of our personality . . . a cauldron full of seething excitations." In Freud, of course, the id is not isolated (though it is certainly emphasized), but functions as a component part of the personality; the energy it supplies is given form and direction by the ego, with the assistance of the superego. Freud aptly compares the relation of the id to the ego with that of a horse to its rider: "The horse supplies the locomotive energy, while the rider has the privilege of deciding on the goal and of guiding the powerful animal's movement."[47] Max Scheler presented the same thesis in his philosophical anthropology. He held that though spirit is distinctive of man, it lacks an original energy of its own; all the energy in life and history is located in the basic drives, and spirit acquires energy only as it takes it from those drives and "sublimates" it.[48]

B

While the emphasis on the element of dynamics in God has been preponderant, there has also been an emphasis on the element of form. Negatively expressed, when the priority is given to the element of dynamics in the process of the divine life, the unexpressed assumption is that form, *logos,* intellect, as such, is devoid of dynamism, and thus, if there were nothing in God but *logos,* and his essential occupation were "the thinking of thought," God would be inert and unfree; he might serve as the goal toward which all things tend, but not as the source from which they proceed.[49]

Is this assumption justified? The question has a special and controversial relevance to Plato's philosophy of forms (or ideas). According to one view, there is a radical separation *(chōrismos)* between the forms and the perceptible objects of ordinary experience which resemble them. The resemblance may be described as imitation *(mimēsis),* or as participation *(methexis),* but no more; the forms and the objects remain apart. But there are some scholars who maintain that Plato ascribed to the forms a causative function and gave them an ontological as well as an epistemological significance, so that they are "causes or givers of being, in some sense, to the things of this world" as well as "causes of true knowledge in our minds."[50] Failure to recognize "the causality of the Forms" has been traced to Aristotle's obtuseness about Plato's doctrine, although it is conceded by the writer who makes this charge that causality is a "quality which Plato only half-heartedly attributed to his Forms."[51] If it is argued in opposition to this view that in the account of the creation of the world, which Plato gives in the *Timaeus,* the forms are inert until the Craftsman puts them to work, the radical Platonists point to the special character of this account, which is avowedly mythical, and they contend that the Craftsman should be demythicized and interpreted as "the Ideas conceived as agency."[52]

However that may be, the Logos of the Prologue to the Fourth Gospel offers a clearer example. Reference was made earlier to the general impression, received from the Genesis narrative and other passages in the Old Testament, that creation took place at the divine word of command, and the general acceptance of this view in theology. It is a question, however, whether the intention of the writer is correctly understood in this way. If we read the narrative as a whole, it becomes clear that what the writer is portraying is not the production of the world and its contents by a series of divine fiats, but the design of the world as an ordered structure, in which everything is assigned to its proper place and furnished with its proper endowments, and the whole culminates in the creation of man and woman, in whom the Logos of creation becomes articulate. When we turn to the Prologue to the Fourth Gospel, it is unmistakably clear that the Logos here means something other than a word of Command; for if it were a word of command, it could not sustain the argument that there is an internal relationship between creation and incarnation, that creation and incarnation are informed with one single thought, meaning, or intent, and the Logos is the bearer of that meaning. The Logos is the bearer of that meaning which was with God in the beginning and informs all his works from beginning to end.

The emphasis on the logical, as distinct from the imperative, character of the word in creation is not original with the Fourth Evangelist. It is clearly anticipated in the Wisdom literature, both canonical and apocryphal. There Wisdom appears as the divine agent in creation; "The LORD by wisdom founded the earth" (Prov. 3:19); Wisdom was created by the Lord "at the beginning of his work," and that means "at the first, before the beginning of the earth" (Prov. 8:22f.); Wisdom stood at his side "like a master workman" (or as "his darling and delight," NEB) "when he marked out the foundations of the earth" (Prov. 8:29f.). But the creation of Wisdom is "from eternity" (Sir. 24:9); and as such it is more than creation: Wisdom "came forth from the mouth of the Most High" (Sir. 24:3); it is "a pure emanation of the glory of the Almighty . . . a reflection of eternal light . . . and an image of his goodness" (Wis. 7:25f.). Moreover, it is by the presence and action of wisdom in creation that all things are ordered "by measure and number and weight" (Wis. 11:20). Echoes of this language are to be heard in the New Testament descriptions of Christ as "the first-born of all creation" (Col.

1:15) and "the effulgence of God's splendour" (Heb. 1:3, NEB).

It is Philo of Alexandria who first recognized the affinity and the possibility of a synthesis between the Greek idea of the Logos and the Judaic notion of Wisdom. Philo continued to use the concept of the Logos, which has, of course, firm roots in the Bible, but he shows a distinct shift of emphasis from the Biblical, or Old Testament, notion of the Logos as the instrument of power, to the more Greek understanding of it as the vehicle of thought. For Philo the creation of the world is not just an arbitrary act of divine omnipotence but an expression of the mind of God, and so, in a sense, of God himself, as is clearly shown in the following excerpt from his account of creation in his treatise on the subject:

> God assuming, as God would assume that a beautiful copy could never come into existence without a beautiful model . . . , when he willed to create this visible world, first blocked out *(proexetypou)* the intelligible world, in order that using an incorporeal and godlike model he might make the corporeal world a younger image of the elder, containing as many sensible genera as the other contained intelligible. The world consisting of ideas must not be spoken or thought of as being in space. Where it exists we shall know by using a familiar illustration. When a city is being founded . . . sometimes there comes forward a man trained as an architect, and after surveying the favorable features of the site, he first makes an outline in his mind *(diagraphei prōton en heautō)* of almost all the parts of the city that is to be built—temples, gymnasia, council-chambers, markets, harbors, docks, alleys, the structure of the walls, the plan of the houses and public buildings. Then, receiving an impression of each of them in his soul, as if in wax, he models a city of the mind *(noētēn polin)*. . . . Looking to this model he proceeds to construct the city of stone and wood, making the corporeal substances resemble each of the incorporeal ideas. In like manner we must think of God. When he decided to found the great city, he first conceived its types, and from them conceived a world of the mind *(kosmon noēton)* and then using it as a model completed the world of the senses.[53]

Radical Platonism is said to have attained its highest fulfillment in Hegel, whose "*Begriff* has . . . all the causative dynamic quality which Plato only half-heartedly attributed to his Forms."[54] Hegel saw no need to invoke a distinct, dynamic element, he ascribed to the logos all the power necessary to effect the existence of the world; for while the divine is logos, and nothing but logos, it is not without polarity; only, the polarity is between the inner and the outer logos, the logos as it is *in itself* and the logos as it is *for itself.* The "depth" of God is not an abyss or an indifference,[55] it is the idea; and it is the idea that is actualized in the logos of his being and the logos of creation. There is nothing in God, neither in the process of his own being nor in his work of creation, that is to be ascribed to an unfathomable, inscrutable, indeterminate exercise of power; all that God is and does is "logical."[56]

The sovereign place that Hegel assigns to the logos in the being of God—it has been called panlogism—has long been regarded as the most vulnerable feature of his system. It has been subjected to a variety of criticisms.

1. It has often been charged that Hegel is not able to offer a plausible account of the dynamism of the logos. The point in the system at which he sets forth the transition of the idea into nature has often been considered the most obscure and the weakest in it. Findlay, who claims to find "nothing but the utmost intellectual sobriety in Hegel's transition from the Idea to Nature," concedes that it is wrapped up in "much quasi-theological mystification."[57] Schelling, Hegel's erstwhile friend and colleague, suggested more unkindly that it was boredom with mere logical being that prompted the idea to pass over into nature.[58]

2. It has been charged that Hegel's panlogism is prejudicial to the freedom of God. If the dynamism of the divine action resides wholly in the logos, the effect, it is argued, is to make God subject to necessity. This charge is made by Karl Barth with special reference to God's act of revelation. If it is the essence of a logical being, a mind, or spirit, to

reveal, or utter, itself, then, says Barth, "Revelation can now no longer be a free act of God; God, rather, must function as we see him function in revelation. It is necessary to him to reveal himself." God is thus "his own Prisoner."[59]

3. What many have felt to be the most damaging consequence of Hegel's panlogism is the fact that it entails an explanation of evil, which, in effect, explains it away. If everything is logical, if everything that exists has a fitting place in the system, then evil loses its radical character as that which has no such place, and it is transfigured into a strategic device employed by Reason in the pursuit of its rational end. Evil then becomes a necessary "moment" in the dialectic process of reality, a fortunate event, like the fall of Adam (and Hegel sometimes speaks of the world as an *Abfall,* or falling away, from the idea), a *felix culpa,* which was instrumental in bringing the Redeemer.

4. The major theological difficulty of Hegel's system arises in connection with the doctrine of creation. When the logos is assigned the sovereign role in the being of God, all his acts are traced to attributes which are essential and eternal. Creation is the expression of a creativity which belongs to the being of God, and cannot, therefore, be understood as an event in time; and the question of whether it is necessary or contingent becomes irrelevant.[60] The problem of conceiving creation as a temporal act, which was first raised by Origen, and which was keenly felt by Aquinas, has in recent theology been broadened to cover any thought of an act of God in time.[61]

C

It is of equal importance to those who distinguish two elements in the structure of the being of God to offer an account of their unification. If we agree with Tillich that the theme concerns "trinitarian principles," trinitarian thought has as much to do with the unity as with the diversity in God. And if we find that there has been in some instances an emphasis so strong on one or other of the discrete elements as to make the thought of their unification problematical, we find also in some an emphasis on the unity, or unification, of the discrete elements, which is so strong as virtually to obliterate the distinction between them. The latter of these tendencies is to be found in both Tillich and Barth.

Tillich strives to maintain an even balance between the unification of the two principles in God and the preservation of the distinction between them; but he uses such a variety of language that his precise meaning is hard to determine. Sometimes he speaks of dynamics and form: "The polar character of the ontological elements is rooted in the divine life, but the divine life is not subject to this polarity." If we wonder how this is possible, an answer is suggested in the sentence that follows immediately: "Within the divine life, every ontological element includes its polar element completely, without tension and without the threat of dissolution."[62] In another place, where he is speaking of the polarity of freedom and destiny, he appears to assert that one eliminates the other: "Only he who has freedom has a destiny. Things have no destiny because they have no freedom. God has no destiny because he *is* freedom."[63] In most cases, however, he is at pains to maintain the integrity of each of the polar elements, and also to accord a certain priority to the first as relating more to the subjective side of the polarity, which corresponds to the self-world structure of existence.[64] In yet another place he expresses the unification in terms of a complete coincidence, or interpenetration, of the discrete elements: "The ground is not only an abyss in which every form disappears; it also is the source from which every form emerges. The ground of being has the character of self-manifestation; it has *logos* character. This is not something added to the divine life; it is the divine life itself. In spite of its abysmal character the ground of being is 'logical'; it includes its own *logos*."[65] It resembles the *communicatio idiomatum* of Lutheran Christology: each nature retains its identity, but at the same time it possesses the properties of the other.

In Barth, the emphasis on the unification of the discrete elements, which he calls freedom and love, is, if anything, more extreme. While the distinction between them is essential to the dynamism of the reality of God, which combines being and action, the unity between them is given in the reality of the revelation of God; so, if we hold to that, as it is given in Scripture, "the unity of God must be understood as this unity of His love and freedom which is dynamic and, to that extent, diverse."[66] Barth's doctrine of God differs from Tillich's in that it *follows* the doctrine of the Trinity, and, therefore, the "trinitarian principles" employed are in fact trinitarian and not ontological. The doctrine of the Trinity itself is for Barth an implicate of revelation; it is an attempt to determine the conditions of the possibility of revelation, and the point of entry to the problem is always the reality of the revelation of God in Christ. The doctrine of God is a variation on the same theme, and it pursues basically the same approaches. If the doctrine be described as an exploration of the depths of God (as Barth is prepared to do), this depth must be sought in the actual decision of the divine will which was fulfilled in Jesus Christ, and to look beyond that "to a supposedly greater depth in God" (such as an absolutely arbitrary freedom) is to look "to the depth of Satan."[67] However deeply we probe into the depths of God, we can discover nothing other than what is manifested at the surface. So, although the distinction between freedom and love is essential to the dynamics of the freedom of God, there seems to be no place for diversity.

Chapter 7

The Role of the Spirit

There is one feature of the attempts we have reviewed to establish a ground for creation in a construction of the inner being of God that calls for special attention. We have to examine what role is ascribed to the Spirit in this context; then, in a later chapter, we shall ask how this accords with the Biblical doctrine of the Spirit.

While Barth's construction of the doctrine of God is professedly informed by the doctrine of the Trinity, as was noted at the end of the previous chapter, there is one respect in which it is less faithful to the trinitarian pattern than that of Tillich: it has no distinctive role in it for the Spirit. The "trinitarian principles," on which Barth bases his doctrine of God, are in fact binitarian: it is the relationship of the Father and the Son that forms the framework for the dipolarity of freedom and love. Tillich assigns a distinctive role to spirit among the trinitarian principles: spirit (which he spells with a lowercase *s,* to distinguish it from the Holy Spirit in the ecclesiastical doctrine of the Trinity), he says, is the unity of the ontological elements of power and meaning.[1] Here he follows Boehme and Schelling.

In Boehme's inspired, visionary speculation there is much that defies interpretation, but the broad outline of his picture of God is fairly clear. In his account of God's coming-to-be (theogony) there is a powerful emphasis on the diverse elements involved in the birth of God, from the dark, fathomless, unknowing, indeterminate *Ungrund,* to his manifestation and expression in creation; and the Spirit plays a large role in the process of unification. To match the seven stages he distinguishes in God's coming-to-be, Boehme has recourse to the seven spirits of God mentioned in Rev. 1:4, etc., and to each of them he assigns a distinctive function in the process. It is needless to rehearse them in detail; it is sufficient to note that some of these functions are related to the internal dynamics of the divine life, others to the outgoing *(Ausgang),* or emanation, of God into the world.[2]

Schelling virtually reproduces the thought of Boehme, but in much less colorful language. Like Boehme, he distinguishes the ground of God's existence,[3] for which he sometimes uses Boehme's term *Ungrund,*[4] and the God who has come to full self-realization as love; and to each he assigns a will—to one the will of the ground, or the depth,[5] which is less than a conscious will,[6] and more in the nature of a primal longing or instinctive drive,[7] to the other a will of love, which is manifest in revelation and creation. Each of these wills retains its integrity, yet they can never come into conflict: "God as spirit (the eternal nexus of the two) is purest love. . . . But God himself requires a foundation in order that he may be; only this is not outside him, but within him; and he has in himself a *nature* which, though it belongs to him himself, is, nonetheless, different from him. The will of love and the will of the basis *(Grund)* are two different wills, each existing by itself; but the will of love cannot withstand the will of the basis, nor can it elevate the latter, since in that case it would have to strive against itself."[8] But the Spirit not only brings the primal longing in God to rational expression and God to recognition of himself in his own image; the Spirit also brings the union of longing and reason to utterance outside of God in nature: "There is born in God himself an inward, imaginative response, corresponding to this longing, which is the first stirring of divine Being in its still, dark depths. Through this response, God sees himself in his own image, since his imagination can have no other object than himself. This image is the first in which God, viewed absolutely, is realised, though only in himself; it is in the beginning in God, and is the God-begotten God himself. This image is at one and the same time reason—the logic of that longing, and the eternal Spirit which feels within it the logos and the everlasting longing. This Spirit, moved by that love which it itself is, utters the Word which then becomes creative and omnipotent Will combining reason and longing, and which informs nature, at first unruly, as its own element or instrument."[9]

The Spirit in Trinitarian Theology

There is, however, a critical question that has to be asked concerning the introduction of the concept of spirit in the context of a discussion of the trinitarian principles. It is an arresting fact that, while the distinguishable elements are designated by abstract terms—dynamics and form, power and meaning, vitality and intentionality, etc.—spirit appears, so to speak, *in propria persona* (apart from the decapitalization of the initial). Tillich is at pains to assert that spirit is "a significant philosophical term," and this is certainly true of the particular philosophical tradition to which he himself was related.[10] But he does not pause to inquire whether it has its deepest roots in Biblical and theological discourse, and whether its relative absence from English (and some German) philosophy is due to the suspicion that a philosophy of spirit is a "theology in disguise" *(verkappte Theologie).* The question, in other words, is whether the concept of spirit in the context of the trinitarian principles is not silently (or not so silently) infiltrated with material drawn from the Biblical revelation. The dual connotation of the term "spirit," which Tillich notes, points to this: "The third principle is in a way the whole (God *is* Spirit), and in a way it is a special principle (God *has* the Spirit as he has the *logos).* It is the Spirit in whom God 'goes out from' himself."[11] This bland statement glosses over the question of how the two senses of Spirit are related—or how (to use the language of the classical trinitarian theology) the *mission* of the Spirit "out from"

God is related to the *procession* of the Spirit as an element in the inner process of the divine life. That there must be correspondence between them has been a fundamental principle of trinitarian theology from Augustine to Barth and Rahner. But the application of this principle to the doctrine of the Spirit presents peculiar problems, and this is well illustrated in Augustine's treatise on the Trinity. Augustine's method (which resembles that of the other two theologians named) may be described as Kantian; he himself described it as an advance from *scientia* to *sapientia.*[12] According to this method, he starts from the "empirical"[13] data of Scripture, which are, for the most part, and particularly as regards the Spirit, occupied with the divine operations *ad extra,* and he then proceeds to inquire what are the internal structures of the divine being which form "the conditions of the possibility" of the external operations. Thus in his treatment of the Spirit he sets out from the basic fact of revelation, that the Spirit is the *gift* of God *(munus, donum);* he then asks what it is in the being of God in which the giveability of the Spirit is rooted. He finds the answer in the thought of the Spirit as "person" who proceeds from the Father to the Son, and from the Son to the Father, and unites them in love.[14]

There are several difficulties here. One, of which Augustine was aware, is the difficulty of relating a gift, given by God to others, to a giveability, when the latter is understood as an internal relation in the being of God.[15] What is the logical connection between the internal function of the Spirit in the being of God and the external operation of the Spirit? Closely related to this is the difficulty, not peculiar to Augustine, of the whole concept of the "procession" of the spirit as an intratrinitarian relation, in contrast with the "mission" of the Spirit as an extratrinitarian operation. The designation of the term "procession" for this special purpose in trinitarian theology was a desperate attempt to find a Biblical basis for the doctrine of the internal relations, and it involves a distortion of the Biblical sense of the term. The term, which occurs only once with reference to the Spirit (*ekporeuetai,* Jn. 15:26), clearly refers to that movement "out from God," which was for Paul the defining characteristic of the Spirit (the Spirit which is *from* God, 1 Cor. 2:12; it is translated "issues" in the NEB).[16] The use of the term for an intradivine function is not justified by appealing to 2 Cor. 2:10–16, for the intradivine function of the spirit, of which Paul speaks there, is not the precondition of the gift of the Spirit, which is a gift of grace (v. 12). There is, finally, the difficulty involved in the doctrine of the "double procession," which has caused so much controversy between the Eastern and Western churches, and, more specifically, the interpretation of "double" as bidirectional—from the Father to the Son and from the Son to the Father. Aquinas states it succinctly: "From the fact that the Father and the Son mutually love each other, it necessarily follows that this mutual love, the Holy Spirit, proceeds from both."[17] The interpretation of the double procession in terms of a mutual love between the "persons" of the Trinity intensifies the difficulty of the Augustinian project; for it reinforces the notion of the self-sufficiency of God and provides no foundation for an extension of that love "out from God."

It should be added that the attempt to undergird the formal bridge from procession to mission by means of the more substantial concept of love involves a change in the meaning of love, which can barely be concealed by the use of the same term. In modern theology much has been made of the difference between *eros* and *agape.* But even in earlier times, when only one word was in use, the need for discrimination was felt; Hegel, for example, who used only the one word, often spoke of the love between the persons of the ontological Trinity as a play of love, "love disporting with itself," and he characterized as "serious" the love which "goes out" into the world to endure suffering and death.[18] The transition, however, is not made easier by this means. The blissful play of love, the more blissful it is, would seem to act as a barrier, rather than a springboard, for the serious love that goes out to suffer loss. The structure is the same, but this is not sufficient to account for the difference in the quality of the love that takes place.

It is evidently a sense of this difficulty that lies behind Barth's attempt to read some of the quality of the economic love back into the structure of the ontological Trinity. There is a significant difference between his earlier and later treatments of the doctrine. In his earlier treatment the ontological Trinity is based on the structure disclosed in the self-revelation of God; and this structure is formal.[19] But when he came to reexamine the doctrine in the light of the doctrines of creation and reconciliation, he saw that if these acts are to be traced to "a possibility grounded in the being of God,"[20] no such ground can be found in the traditional doctrine of "the second person of the Trinity" as the discarnate Logos. Barth conceded that this is "a necessary and important concept in trinitarian doctrine,"[21] but in effect he set it aside and replaced it with a concept of the Logos eternally bearing the lineaments of the incarnate and suffering Christ, "One who in the eternal sight of God has already taken upon Himself our human nature, i.e., not of a formless Christ who might well be a Christ-principle or something of that kind, but of Jesus the Christ."[22] "The meaning of His deity . . . can be learned only from what took place in Christ."[23] He then proceeded to reformulate the doctrine of the Trinity in a manner which corresponds more closely to the pattern of the revelation and which admits of difference of above and below, majesty and humility, authority and obedience, and the like, in the structure of the being of God.[24] But even if we accept his claim that such differences are not incompatible with the homoousia of the classical doctrine, it is still not evident how this structure, however "dynamic and living,"[25] can be the condition of the possibility of divine activities outward. Whenever it comes to the question of relating the actuality to the potentiality, Barth falls back on an undefined concept of freedom, which, despite his disclaimer, is indistinguishable from caprice.[26] This is conspicuous in his treatment of creation. He grounds the possibility of creation in an eternal self-other structure in God. Thus the relationship of God to the world as a reality other than himself does not involve a radical change in his situation; for the otherness the world offers to him he already has as "the original and essential determination of His being and life as God."[27] But by the same token, the possession by God of an otherness in himself makes the projection of this otherness to a reality outside of himself superfluous, and Barth can only ascribe it to freedom. There is a structural correspondence between the relationship between God and the world and the self-other relationship in the intra-trinitarian being of God; one is a "reflection"[28] of the other, but it is not derivable from it.

The problem of the role of the Spirit in creation may be approached from the other side by an examination of the doctrine of creation and the models that have been employed in the effort to make it intelligible. This will be the theme of the following chapter.

Chapter 8
Models of Creation

It may be of some help in seeking an answer to the question, Why God created the world, to consider the question, How God created the world. This question has also been held to be impermissible by some, but not so much on grounds of piety as of epistemology; for the act of creation is unique and beyond the bounds of our experience; it is not an object of our experience, but the precondition of all our experience.

The incomprehensibility of creation is associated particularly with the idea of creation out of nothing *(creatio ex nihilo);* for comprehension means grasping the relationship between something and its antecedent cause or ground, and *creatio ex nihilo* appears to assert that creation has no antecedent. The difficulty is aggravated if creation is taken as an act in time, and it is this difficulty that led Fichte to declare that "creation is simply unthinkable."[1]

If, however, creation is completely incomprehensible, its ascription to God, however pious in intent, is a blind act, and faith in God is vacuous. Nevertheless, theologians continue to make this assertion. Thus, for example, Barth declares that "we have no analogy on the basis of which the nature and being of God as Creator can be accessible to us," and he bases this statement expressly on the idea of *creatio ex nihilo,* of which he says that "within the sphere of the ideas possible to us *creatio ex nihilo* can appear only as an absurdity."[2] This is surely an absurd statement; for it would have the effect of equating faith in God as creator with assent to an absurdity. This conclusion would be inevitable if it is true that we have no analogy to creation. Is it true? It is surprising to encounter such a statement in Barth, in view of his predilection for analogies in theology; and it may be that he was here led into a verbal lapse by his profound regard for the uniqueness of the divine creation. Creation out of nothing is indeed something of which we have no exact equivalent; but if we have no analogies to it, it would be totally incomprehensible to us. Analogies, of course, cannot make it totally comprehensible, they can take us only part of the way; but without analogies we can go no part of the way at all.

The truth is that we do have a number of analogies to creation, and no one has ever developed a doctrine of creation without some dependence on one or more of them. Moreover, many of them have some foothold in the Bible itself.

The emphasis on the uniqueness of the divine act of creation has often been supported by the fact that the Hebrew verb *barah* ("to create") is predicated exclusively of God. That is certainly significant, but it should not be overlooked that the word is relatively rare in the Old Testament and it is frequently replaced (or paralleled) by words that are applicable to human activities. Even that profound and precise theologian who composed the first account of creation in Genesis felt no impropriety in using the ordinary verb "make" for several of the creative acts of God,[3] and the author of the second account speaks of all the acts of God as "forming" and "making," and does not use the verb "create" at all. Moreover, these acts are not only named by these common verbs, but described in ways that correspond to the human acts to which the verbs are ordinarily applied.

There are five modes of origination which are familiar in human experience and which have been used as models or analogies of the divine act of creation. None of them is identical with it; but severally and together they may serve to illumine some aspects of it and so make possible a measure of understanding.

1. Generation. The most venerable of the models of creation is generation. It can be readily understood how at the

earliest stages of human life, when man was wholly dependent for his livelihood on the products of nature, the process by which these products were brought forth assumed a supreme importance for him and acquired a divine status.[4] Many of the oldest cults centered on the process of generation and they involved rites which were felt to be appropriate modes of participation in the great mystery. For great mystery it is, and it is not surprising that it should have acquired a high place as a model of creation. Perhaps some sense of this is reflected in the use of the English word "procreation" for the generative function.

The model of generation is also to be found in the Bible, not in the creation narratives (which follow other models, as we shall see shortly), but in the ascription to God of the name of Father. When this name is given to God in the Old Testament, the reference is not primarily to his disposition, but to his role as the originator of Israel's existence; and it becomes prominent (surprisingly, or not surprisingly?) in Deutero-Isaiah and postexilic prophecy. It is in Second Isaiah that the thought of God as creator first comes to expression, not out of an independent interest in the origin of the world, but as an extrapolation of God's direction of history through the destiny of Israel; God's use of Israel as the instrument of his purpose points to his relationship to Israel as its creator:

> Yet, O Lord, thou art our Father;
> we are the clay, and thou art our potter;
> we are all the work of thy hand.
> (Is. 64:8)

It is plain, however, from the mixture of metaphors in this passage that the fatherhood of God was not intended in a literal sense. And there is a passage in Jeremiah where it clearly bears an adoptive sense:

> I thought
> how I would set you among my sons. . . .
> And I thought you would call me, My Father.
> (Jer. 3:19)

Some vestige of the literal meaning of the term may cling to the appellation of God as Father in the words of Jesus (e.g., Matt. 5:48; 11:25); at all events, it is used to express his own personal relationship to God. And in the later Christological controversies it was decided that the concept of generation is applicable only to the relationship between God the Father and the Son: only the Son is begotten of the Father, all others are created or made.

2. Fabrication. This term is used in the broadest sense to cover all the productive activities of man as *homo faber,* which are commonly expressed by the verb "make."[5] It is used of the creative activity of God in the P narrative of creation (as was noted above) and with great frequency throughout the Bible. It is used also in the first article of both the Apostles' and the Nicene Creeds, where God is described as *poiētēs, factor,* "maker," and not as creator, *ktistēs,* which occurs only once in the New Testament (1 Pet. 4:19). The connotation of the term is so broad and general that its application to God would seem to obscure the difference between his creative activity and that of his creatures, especially with regard to *creatio ex nihilo;*[6] the human maker cannot make anything out of nothing, he always makes with material which he has not himself made. And on this account it can be described more specifically by the term "formation."

3. Formation. Human making consists in forming material into an object. The stock example of formation in the Bible is the potter with his clay, and it is clearly in this role that God is pictured in the second creation narrative, where we are told "the LORD God formed *(yatsar)* man of dust from the ground" (Gen. 2:7; cf. Is. 64:8). The concept of formation adds two things to that of fabrication:

a. It directs attention to the order and structure of the things which God has created. This aspect of the world is conspicuous in the P narrative of creation, though the author does not in fact employ the verb; the created world, as he describes it, is a world of order, a world in which everything has a definite nature and a definite place in the scheme of things, a *kosmos* in the Greek sense of the term.[7] The verb "form" occurs first at the creation of man in Gen. 2:7, and it may reflect a sense that the human frame presents a signal example of the formative element in creation, as it is celebrated by the psalmist:

> For thou didst form my inward parts,
> thou didst knit me together in my mother's womb. . . .
> My frame was not hidden from thee,
> when I was being made in secret,
> intricately wrought in the depths of the earth.
> Thy eyes beheld my unformed substance;[8]
> in thy book were written, every one of them,
> the days (limbs, NEB) that were formed for me,
> when as yet there was none of them.
>
> (Ps. 139:13, 15–16)

It is this aspect of the world, the manifold evidence of orderly arrangement in things, and not least in the organic structure of the human body, that forms the foundation of the cosmological argument. The Bible itself does not develop the argument;[9] it does not contend, for example, that so complex and intricate a structure as the eye can only have been designed by a supreme intelligence, but it does suggest that if so wonderful a faculty as vision exists in the creature, it can hardly be lacking in the Creator: "He who formed the eye, does he not see?" (Ps. 94:9).

b. The potter at his wheel turned out vessels for practical use; though some were designed for more "honorable" uses than others (Rom. 9:21, KJV), utility was the governing aim. But the potter discovered—or those who used his products discovered—that the process might produce something more than utility, a "surplus value" of another kind. The vessels that he made of clay were not only useful for holding wine; they could give pleasure to the eye; people could find a delight in the mere beholding of them, which was different from the delight of drinking their contents. This delight, which is called beauty, came from their form.[10]

c. There is a third element in formation which leads onto another model of creation. The formation of an article, whether for utility or beauty, implies a prior plan or design in the mind of the agent. When the psalmist celebrates the formation of the embryo in the womb, he envisages a kind of blueprint, or handbook, of anatomy, which God has before him as he knits the limbs together. More commonly we think of the design as an idea, or conception, in the mind of the agent. And it serves as a contributory factor in the production of the object; the idea of the pot in the mind of the potter is the formal cause, as Aristotle called it, to which he gives objective form in the clay, the material cause. Formation in this sense suggests another model of creation, which may be called expression, and which merits consideration by itself. But before we do that, it will be better to glance at another model, of which we may discern traces in the Bible.

4. Conflict. In an ancient Babylonian myth the story of creation is told in terms of a cosmic struggle between a primeval monster representing the forces of darkness and chaos, and a god representing the power of light and order. The creation of the world is accomplished when the hero slays the monster and cuts her body in two parts, one to form the sky with the waters above, and the other the ocean with the waters below. Traces of this myth are clearly to be seen in the Old Testament, in allusions to the primeval monster which appears under the names of Leviathan, Rahab, and the dragon (Is. 27:1; 51:9; Ps. 74:14; 89:10); and probably also, in demythologized form, in the chaotic waters and the primeval darkness, which represent the first obstacle to be overcome in the process of creation in Genesis 1. It may also be a more complete demythologization and a more sophisticated reinterpretation of the same myth that is found in the thought of Heraclitus, one of the towering figures among the Ionian pioneers of Greek philosophy. To the question, to which all the Ionian philosophers addressed themselves, and which may be formulated in broad terms as: What is it that makes the world what it is? Heraclitus gave a distinctive

answer. He replied that it is the conflict of opposites. It may be that the thought of Heraclitus goes back to some physical observation of the sort that is supposed to lie behind the Babylonian myth of creation, such as the yearly struggle of land and water which was a familiar occurrence in the Mesopotamian plain. At all events, Heraclitus broadened it to a universal principle applicable to the process of reality as a whole. He did not, to be sure, apply it to creation, which, in fact, he denied. But everywhere he looked he saw the same pattern, and sometimes he called it God: "God is day–night, winter–summer, war–peace, surfeit–hunger,"[11] and sometimes he spoke of it more abstractly as war or strife: "War is father and king of all. Some he makes gods, others men. Some he makes slaves, others free."[12] The universal struggle of opposites, however, does not result in chance, but in harmony *(harmonia).* It is the harmonious interaction of opposites that makes the world what it is; and both the opposition and the harmony are necessary. Heraclitus reproached Homer for expressing the wish that strife would cease among gods and among men; for if that were to happen, he felt, everything would come to a standstill.[13]

A remarkable parallel to the thought of Heraclitus is to be found in the ancient Chinese doctrine of yang and yin, which developed in roughly the same period and in very similar circumstances. Greek philosophical thought, and particularly philosophical theology, arose in part as a revolt against the popular religion of the Olympian gods and its mythological crudities, and its program may be described as one of demythologization. The description would be more patently applicable to the Chinese movement of enlightenment and rational criticism, which occurred in the fifth century B.C. The two principal gods of the traditional religion, Shang-ti, the god of heaven, and Hon-t'u, the god of earth, were demythologized and transmuted into two impersonal principles: Yang, the active, male principle, and Yin, the passive, female principle, from the interaction of which all things originated. It is reported by Aristotle that Heraclitus also cited the relationship of the sexes as an illustration of his thesis;[14] and if that is correct, the opposition is equivalent to what would now be called complementarity, and the supervening harmony is the more important factor.[15]

5. Expression may be described in general terms as the giving of outward, objective form to something that had originally an inward subjective existence. The most familiar example of it is the utterance in speech of a thought that was originally conceived in the mind. The Greeks, as is well known, used one and the same term, *logos,* for the spoken word and for the inner thought from which it springs, and they distinguished them only by attaching qualifying adjectives to the noun. It was the identity of the *logos* in both thought and speech that came first for them; the idea of a *logos* that does not come to articulate expression would have seemed strange to them. When they defined man as a being possessed of *logos,* they meant not only that he was capable of performing rational processes in his mind but also that he was capable of articulating them in speech.[16]

It is Herder who is credited with first having brought out the significance of expression as the distinctive mark of persons. Sir Isaiah Berlin has called it "Expressionism" and described it as "the doctrine that human activity in general, and art in particular, expresses the entire personality of the individual or the group, and are intelligible only to the degree to which they do so . . . and that self-expression is part of the essence of human beings as such." It differs from fabrication; for it "claims that all the works of men . . . are not objects detached from their makers."[17] It is much closer to generation; for it is a way in which a person reproduces himself. It is significant that in English we apply the terms "conceive" and "conception" both to the generation of a child in the womb and to the formation of a thought in the mind.

Although speech is the most elementary form of expression, there are other forms,[18] and of these art in particular, as Berlin notes, is a better example, and it has often been employed as a model of creation.[19] It is in the context of art that words such as "create," "creation," "creative" are most often heard. There are several features of artistic work which illustrate the resemblance.

a. A work of art is the expression of an idea that was originally conceived in the mind of the artist. The manner of the original conception is a fascinating subject of inquiry, but it is not necessary for our present purpose to pursue it—except, perhaps, to note two things. (1) When the artist ascribes the conception to inspiration, he sees himself as the agent of a power that operates mysteriously at, or beyond, the limits of the human (whatever the ratio of inspiration to perspiration may be). (2) The conception often takes place in an instantaneous manner, while the execution of it takes time. There is a letter by Mozart in which he gives an account of the process of musical composition, as he experienced it. The idea would come to him in a flash, and the whole piece would take shape in his mind in an instant, so that he could hear it in an inner ear in a single instant, though the work of transcribing it onto paper might take days or weeks.[20]

b. A work of art is more than the expression of an idea in the mind of the artist. In great art, at least, it is an expression of the artist himself; and in this respect art may be more expressive than speech. We speak of a person expressing himself, when he speaks, but generally we mean no more than that he is expressing what is in his own mind. It can take place in a more profound and revealing way in a work of art; for here the artist may express aspects of himself of which he was not aware and which are barely expressible in speech. Thus his work may be a means by which the artist comes to a knowledge of himself.

c. As the conception of a child in the womb is the initiation of a process that presses toward completion in the emergence of a separate existence, the conception of an idea in the mind is accompanied by a pressure toward external expression in a form that is relatively independent of its origin. Expression is spontaneous and urgent; and it is this important aspect of it that was enshrined in the concept of emanation. The relationship of this concept to that of creation raises such profound and complex questions that it requires more extended consideration, which it will be appropriate to defer to the end of the present section, after we have noted several other aspects of the analogy between art and creation.

d. A work of art comes closer than anything to *creatio ex nihilo.* Of course, it cannot reach it; no human work can. The artist can work only with a material that is not of his creation; the potter needs the clay, the painter the pigment, the poet the language, the musician the sound, etc. But the artist, in giving form to the material, so transforms it that the result is like a new creation. In fabrication, by contrast, the properties of the material remain intact; they are merely ordered or arranged, that they can be made to serve specific purposes. But it is the genius of the musician that, in the words of Browning, "out of three sounds he frame, not a fourth sound, but a star." The model of artistic creation appears especially apposite in a world that is understood to be in a process of evolution, marked by the emergence of novelty.

e. The expression of the artist takes place in a medium other than the self of the artist. What has the clay in common with the potter? What has matter in common with mind? The latter question has been a main staple of philosophical discussion for centuries, but it has seldom been noted in the course of the discussion that art builds a bridge between mind and matter, and may even be said to consist in doing so. However incongruous the clay and the potter may be, the latter by his art communicates something of himself to the former.

f. The products of artistic creation tend to become independent of their creator and to acquire a life of their own. They communicate with those who view them—and not merely as bearers of communications from their creators; they can communicate with their creators themselves. The artist who has completed his painting and stands back to view it may find that the finished work reveals to him elements that were not consciously present in his original conception, and that it may thus enlarge his knowledge of himself. The most familiar example is to be found in the work of the novelist. The novelist creates his characters, but the better he is at doing this, the more the characters tend to acquire identities of their own and to work out their own destinies. The writer who makes his characters act like puppets that he dangles on a string is an inferior artist. In art there is two-way communication, both from the artist to his work, and from his work to him (to say nothing, of course, of the communication from the work to other people). In this connection it is interesting to recall the Biblical figure of the potter and the clay, and the ways in which it is used—for it is, in fact, used in two different ways. In Isaiah and Paul it is used to express the absolute power of the potter over the clay, his power to dispose of it as he will; neither of them can tolerate the thought that the clay should speak back to the potter. But when Jeremiah went down to the potter's shop to observe him at his work, this is not what he saw—rather, the opposite; he saw that there was a kind of dialogue going on between the potter and the clay, and when the clay protested to the potter about what he had made of it, he listened and responded. The lesson that Jeremiah drew from his observation of the potter at work was that the Creator (to change the metaphor) does not treat his creatures as if they were helpless pawns on the chessboard, he meets them as players, and he makes his moves in response to theirs (Jer. 18:1–11). The fabricator makes objects for utility or for pleasure; the artist creates objects with which there is some possibility of communication. We might say that the ultimate aim of art is communion.

6. It was suggested above that it is the spontaneity and urgency of artistic expression that is reflected in the concept of emanation. This is the concept in which the thought of Plato was crystallized by his later successors. The term *aporroia* applies originally to the emission of light and heat by the sun[21]—"radiation" would be a more intelligible translation to modern ears than "emanation," which applies originally to the flowing of water from a spring. It came to play a central

role in the cosmology of Neoplatonism, in which it was used to describe the derivation of the many from the One.[22] It found its way into Christian theology through the work of Pseudo-Dionysius the Areopagite and his Western translator and interpreter, John Scotus Eriugena, and it attracted a number of bolder spirits; but these were always a minority, and they were viewed with suspicion by their orthodox colleagues, who considered that emanation is totally incompatible with creation and cannot serve as a model of it.

Christian theologians have rejected emanation as a model of creation principally for three reasons.

a. Emanation denotes an impersonal process, and an impersonal process, it is thought, cannot serve as a model for a personal act. Schelling voiced the general objection when he said, "No matter how one pictures to oneself the procession of creatures from God, it can never be a mechanical production."[23] And contemporary philosopher condemns it in even harsher terms, because it reduces creation to an involuntary act of deity.[24] Against this objection, however, it should be noted that the figure (not the term) was first used by Plato to illustrate the doing of good by the good, which he describes in purely personal terms without recourse to the illustration.[25] It is the spontaneity of the process he wished to bring out; just as it is the nature of the sun to put forth light, so it is the nature of the good to put forth goodness.

b. The second objection follows closely from the first. It has been alleged by theologians that emanation makes creation a necessity for God and thus violates his freedom. They have considered it essential to maintain that creation was a free act of God, and they have interpreted this to mean that God was free to create, or not to create, according to his good pleasure. The contingency of the world was correlated with this conception of the divine freedom. It is noteworthy, however, that Aquinas, though he based one of his five arguments for the existence of God on the contingency of the world, was not happy with the implied conception of the freedom of God in creation. To refer the existence of the world to an arbitrary motion of the divine will was to refer one contingency to another and was therefore devoid of explanatory value. Dionysius the Areopagite and John Scotus Eriugena had already appropriated the concern of Neoplatonism to make the existence of the world intelligible by relating it to the being of the One from whom it took its origin, and they sought to revise the Christian understanding of creation in the light of it. Aquinas pursued their endeavor with greater circumspection but with clear acknowledgment of the source of their inspiration. He introduces the topic of creation under the general title of "the procession of the creatures from God"[26]: he felt no impropriety in using the same term, "procession," of the internal relations of the persons of the Trinity and the external action of God; rather, it underscored his contention that the former are the *rationes* of the latter, and thus "to create is proper to God according to his being."[27] He also used the term "emanation" as synonymous with "creation." This teaching laid him open to the charge of making creation a necessity for God rather than a free act of his will; and his efforts to avoid this conclusion led him, according to one sympathetic interpreter, "into very deep waters."[28] The issue came to a head in connection with the idea of creation as an act in time. If creativity belongs to the nature of God (which is unchangeable), why should the world not have been created from all eternity? Aquinas could think of no reason why not, and he saw no difficulty in the idea of an eternal creation, despite the objection of some that the idea is self-contradictory. He accepted the notion of a temporal beginning of creation solely on the authority of the Biblical revelation. Copleston raises the question whether Aquinas would not have solved his problems, particularly the problem of free creation, if he had adopted some form of pantheism. This points forward to the third main objection to the concept of emanation, which will be considered shortly. The question at issue for Aquinas was rather, it seems to me, whether the freedom of God in creation is adequately understood as freedom to choose whether to create or not. It was probably as a preferable alternative to such an equation of freedom with arbitrary choice that the Neoplatonic concept of emanation appealed to him. According to one eminent authority, it was precisely for this reason that the successors of Plato adopted the term to describe the action of the One, from whom all things derive their being, in preference to "creation."[29] If the contingent existence of the world can only be referred to a contingent act of the divine will, there can hardly be a doctrine of creation; we are left with an equation of two unknown quantities and no means of assigning a value to either.

c. The most serious objection to the concept of emanation from the viewpoint of Christian orthodoxy is that in its original usage it implies a continuity of being, or nature, between the original source and that which emanates from it, and thus obliterates, or weakens, the radical distinction between the Creator and the creature, which is held to be indigenous to Biblical faith. Emanation comes close to the concept of generation—it may be said to be the equivalent in the inorganic realm of generation in the organic. And in fact the original model of emanation, viz., the derivation of light from a luminary, was frequently used in the Christological debates of the early church as an illustration of the generation of the Son (in contradistinction to the making of a creature), and it eventually found its way into the Nicene Creed in the phrase "light from light" *(phōs ek phōtos)* which was set alongside "God from God" *(theon ek theou).* The point was that that which is derived from God by generation, like that which is derived from a luminary by emanation, is the "same-in-being" *(homoousios)* as its source; that which is created is "of another substance or being" *(ex heteras hypostaseōs ē ousias).*[30]

It should be noted, however, that the use of the figure of emanation as an (illustrative) equivalent of generation differs in an important way from the usage of the Neoplatonists; for the process of emanation, in the Neoplatonic world scheme, does not result in an identity of being between the emanant and its source, but in a diminution, or dilution, which progresses as the emanant moves farther from its source, until it reaches the nadir of nothingness.[31] Thus light, to take the original example, diminishes in intensity as it becomes more distant from its source, and at length it is extinguished altogether—a fact which suggests that the figure of "light from light" in the creed might have been thought more appropriate to the Arian position.

While the concept of emanation as the emission of light by a luminary is not present in the Bible, its attraction for theologians is readily understandable in view of the place that light holds in Biblical thought. That light is associated with God is suggested on the first page of the Bible, where light is introduced as the first thing to be created by God—not merely as first in a series, but first in a preeminent sense as the element in which all the following acts of creation (including that of the sun and the moon, Gen. 1:14–19) take place. Light is the sphere of form, while in darkness all things are formless.[32] Therefore, the creation of light at the beginning is an intimation that the world to be created will be a world of form and order.[33] Though this primal light is a creature, it is peculiarly akin to God (Ps. 36:9); it is the element in which he dwells (Ps. 104:2; 1 Tim. 6:16).[34] The Old Testament does not go so far as to say, with the New, that "God *is* light" (1 Jn. 1:5), but it comes close to it when it says that where God is present, light is present also (Ps. 139:12), and this light is the medium of true vision (Ps. 36:9). Moreover, the Old Testament promises the day in which the light of the sun and the moon will be superseded by the light which is in God himself (Is. 60:19f.; cf. Rev. 22:15).[35]

A note may here be added on the relationship of the Biblical and Platonic views of light to the science of light. The Neoplatonic concept of radiation was not, of course, based on scientific study—although it may not unfairly be described as a speculative extrapolation from phenomena observed by Plato—but it does anticipate in a remarkable way the findings of modern science regarding the pervasive role of radiation in the constitution of the physical universe. A popular scientific writer of some decades ago wrote: "The tendency of modern physics is to resolve the whole material universe into waves, and nothing but waves. These waves are of two kinds: bottled-up waves, which we call matter, and unbottled waves, which we call radiation or light. If annihilation of matter occurs, the process is merely that of unbottling imprisoned wave energy and setting it free to travel through space. These concepts reduce the whole universe to a world of light, potential or existent, so that the whole story of its creation can be told with perfect accuracy and completeness in the six words: "God said, 'Let there be light.' "[36]

Chapter 9

Creator Spirit

Of the models of creation surveyed in the preceding chapter expression seems to be the most adequate and to accord most closely with the way in which creation is presented in the Bible by means of the concepts of Word and Spirit. As we noted earlier, it was a matter of fundamental importance to the writers of the New Testament to affirm the coherence of incarnation and creation. The *Logos* incarnate, they maintained, is the key to the meaning of creation, which is the work of the same *Logos.* But this thesis raises several very difficult questions.

One of the difficulties lies at the heart of the controversy that broke out between Lutheran and Calvinist Christologies. It may be described as a question of the parameters of the *Logos.* Both sides were in agreement on the affirmation of the New Testament, that the *Logos* who became incarnate in Christ is identical with the *Logos* through whom all things were made, but they disagreed as to how these two aspects of the *Logos,* the unique and the universal, were united. Luther took the view that the universal was coincident, or coterminous, with the Unique. It is an index of Luther's intense feeling for the reality and integrity of the incarnation of God in Christ that he felt bound to ascribe the universal functions of the *Logos* to the Christ in whom the *Logos* was uniquely present. He expressed it vividly in one of his Christmas hymns:

He whom the worlds cannot enclose
In Mary's bosom doth repose.
To be a little child he deigns,
Who all things by himself sustains.[1]

But it has always been extraordinarily difficult to conceive how the cosmic functions of the *Logos* could be exercised by the child in Mary's bosom.

Calvin removed this particular difficulty by teaching that while the *Logos* is indeed uniquely present in Christ, he is also present and active outside of Christ in the universe at large: "For even if the Word *(Logos)* in his immeasurable essence united with the nature of man into one person, we do not imagine that he was confined therein. Here is something marvelous: the Son of God descended from heaven in such a way that, without leaving heaven, he willed to be borne in the virgin's womb, to go about the earth, and to hang upon the cross; yet he continuously filled the world even as he had done from the beginning."[2] This conception of a presence and activity of the *Logos* outside of Christ *(extra Christum)* as well as in the person of Christ was called the *Extra Calvinisticum* by the Lutherans, although it has the support of the majority of the church fathers. But it also has its difficulty: while it recognizes the diversity of the two spheres in which the *Logos* is present and active, it shows no convincing reason why the activities in these so diverse spheres are to be ascribed to the same *Logos.*

This difficulty goes back to the New Testament itself. The passages, previously cited, which affirm the cosmic parameter of Christology, do not themselves go beyond mere affirmation of the fact; they do not spell out the connection between the unique and the Universal. There are, however, a number of passages in which Christology, the *Logos* of Christ, is described in some detail, and these may furnish a clue. The most important of these are the early Christological hymn in Phil. 2:5–11 and the Christological disquisitions which form the core of the Fourth Gospel. The conspicuous feature of these passages is that the Christological question is posed, not in the terms in which it was answered at Nicaea and Chalcedon, but in terms of a sequence of two movements. This appears most clearly in the disputation between Jesus and the Jews in the Fourth Gospel; the question, Who is this man? is regularly resolved into the two questions, Where does he come from? (Jn. 7:27) and, Where is he going? (Jn. 7:33–35). These questions recur again and again, and significantly it is in terms of them that Jesus makes his definitive disclosure to his disciples: I came from the Father and have come into the world; again, I am leaving the world and going to the Father (Jn. 16:28).[3] It is this movement also which forms the main theme of the Prologue to the Fourth Gospel: it is not just the fact that the *Logos* was in the beginning, was with God, and was God; it is that this was really the beginning—the beginning of a movement, which is in God himself, and in which he moves out from himself to the creation of the world, and in incarnation to restore it to himself. The light of the world is the light that was in the *Logos,* and this light has not been extinguished by the darkness in which it has been shrouded; and thus the coming of the light in the *Logos* incarnate was a coming to his own, and by his coming the world, which was from God, was restored to God. The Evangelist focuses on the restoration of this relationship in those who are enabled to perceive and recognize the light of the *Logos.* But it is not restricted to them. This is the paradigm of all the acts of God; this is the shape of all reality, as it is expressed in the Pauline doxology: From God, through God, to God are all things (Rom. 11:36).

The Evangelist affirms the identity of the *Logos* incarnate and the Creator *Logos,* but he gives little help in tracing the connection between the unique and the universal. This is one of the problems that the New Testament bequeathed to the church of a later time and that led to the formation of the doctrine of the Trinity. It is not necessary for our present purpose to go into that doctrine in detail. If we bear in mind that the fundamental purpose of the doctrine is to affirm the unity, or identity, of God in all his manifestations of himself, it is possible to focus on the problem raised by the Evangelist.

The problem, simply stated, is that, though the Evangelist ascribes the activities of creation and incarnation to the *Logos,* there is no inherent dynamism in the concept of the Logos as such. The *Logos* expresses admirably the thought or purpose that informs all the works of God, but it does not indicate why those works are done. The concept of the Spirit, especially as it is used in the Old Testament, seemed eminently suited for this purpose; for the Spirit expresses the dynamism or energy which is characteristic of God in action. Moreover, the connection between the incarnation of the *Logos* and the mission of the Spirit as its sequel and complement provided an additional link to the coherence of creation and incarnation.

It was the view of Hegel that the most profound truth of the Christian faith is enshrined in the doctrine of the Trinity, and he complained of the neglect of the doctrine in the theology of his time. He traced this neglect, in part, to the fact that the theologians were too locked up in the language of the Bible and popular piety, and he contended that the doctrine could not be made intelligible unless it is translated out of that language, which is pictorial and representational, into the conceptuality of pure thought. Hegel's contention was rejected by a majority of theologians, who feared that he was subverting the faith. But in point of fact, he was only continuing a practice that had been going on in Trinitarian theology from the beginning (though he may have carried it farther than anyone earlier)—the practice of seeking models of intelligibility for the doctrine. Indeed, one of the most popular models found its way into the Nicene Creed, no less: when the relationship of the Son to the Father is described in the phrase "light from light" *(phōs ek phōtos;* the current translation, "light of light," obscures the point, which is the sameness of light with the luminary from which it is derived), this is one of the most venerable models, or analogies, employed to make the language of the Bible more intelligible. The most famous exponent of this practice was Augustine, who devoted a great part of his treatise on the Trinity to the quest for models of intelligibility; he found several, but the best known is probably the analogy of love, which, as he saw it, entails three—one who loves, another who is loved, and the love that binds the one to the other. Anselm of Canterbury was a devoted student of Augustine, and in his *Monologium*, which is a meditation on the being of God, and particularly the triune being of God, he asks the reader to compare his (Anselm's) work with that of Augustine and to judge it accordingly. But he makes one significant change: he uses the concept of the Spirit as his model for the understanding for the triune being of God, and he subsumes the analogy of love under it. One of the strange things about Augustine is that he does not appear to have been arrested by the Biblical statement that God is spirit (Jn. 4:24); so far as I know, he makes only a casual reference to this text. Of course, he treats extensively of the Spirit as the third person of the Trinity, and he describes the Spirit as the bond of union between the Father and the Son, in terms of the analogy of love. In that analogy love serves as the principle of distinction between the Father and the Son, as well as of the union between them. Anselm ascribed this dual role to the Spirit. The essence of Spirit is self-expression, and the self-expression of Spirit is the creative Word (Anselm, *Monologium* 27–32); at the same time, the expression of the Spirit is united with the self of the Spirit in love (*Monologium* 49–63).

Hegel's thought on the doctrine of the Trinity is marked by a progression from the Augustinian analogy of love to the Anselmian analogy of spirit. In his earlier work he described the inner triune love of God as love at play with itself, but in his mature work he replaced this with the dialectic of Spirit. And the reason is plain. The analogy of love, if it is taken to mean the play of love with itself, may serve to illuminate the ontological Trinity, but it sheds no light on the economic. On the contrary, it tends to point up the self-sufficiency of God, the absence in him of any need of another to be the object of his love. The analogy of Spirit provides a bridge from the ontological to the economic, since it is the essence of Spirit, as Anselm noted, to express itself outwardly, without losing its identity with itself. And it is much closer to Biblical thought, where the preponderant emphasis is on the activity of the Spirit in the economic order.

It is the concept of God as Spirit which best enables us to grasp, in some measure at least, the identity of the *Logos* in incarnation and creation, on which the New Testament lays stress.

The role of the Spirit in the incarnation is plain in the New Testament, and it has come to be recognized more and more in Christology. Indeed, the earliest attempts at Christological construction were made in terms of Spirit, and there are some theologians today who think it would have been better if the church had stuck with this approach instead of turning in the direction that led to Nicaea and Chalcedon.[4] Be that as it may, there are several features of the activity of the Spirit which are exhibited in incarnation and creation alike.

1. The incarnation of the *Logos* is initiated by the Spirit. This is the main point of the Nativity stories in the Gospels of Matthew and Luke; and it was rightly given the first place in the second article of the Creed: the incarnate Son was "conceived by the Holy Spirit." The virgin birth, which has received so much more attention, is the obverse of the conception by the Spirit. Now the term for conception in the Nativity stories refers solely to the biological formation of a babe in the womb, and it is not, like its English equivalent, applicable also to the formation of a thought in the mind. Nevertheless, it is significant that in the Lucan story the conception is initiated by annunciation, and it is consummated, so to speak, by Mary's humble acceptance of the word (Lk. 1:38).[5] The first characteristic of Spirit, which we may note here, then, is utterance. I am using the word, not solely with reference to speech, though that is included, but in the broader sense indicated in the etymology of the word which is derived from "outer," i.e., to put out.[6] It is the prime

characteristic of the Spirit to go out, to "proceed," as Jesus put it in one of the Paraclete sayings (Jn. 15:26). This thought was picked up in the third article of the Nicene Creed, which describes the Spirit as proceeding from the Father (and the Son). When Paul speaks of the Spirit which is *from* God (1 Cor. 2:12), he also points to utterance as the prime characteristic of Spirit. And if we may transfer this to God as Spirit, we may speak, with Hegel, of self-externalization, or self-utterance, as the primary act of the being of God. It is of the essence of God as Spirit to go out from himself.[7]

2. The second characteristic of Spirit is embodiment. This is probably the point at which our prevailing mode of thought is most at variance with the thought of the Bible. But it is not only a prejudice of modern times. There was, from the beginning, a reluctance to accept the embodiment of Spirit, as affirmed in the incarnation, and many sought to avoid it by reducing it from reality to appearance. But Spirit and body are not antithetical in the thought of the Bible. The antithesis of Spirit is flesh, and flesh is not un-spirited body; it is body in-spirited by another spirit, "the spirit of the world," as Paul calls it (1 Cor. 2:12). Of course, the Bible recognizes the difference between Spirit and body; but its central message is the embodiment of Spirit. Of this the incarnation is the paradigm:

> When Christ came into the world, he said,
> "Sacrifices and offerings thou hast not desired,
> but a body hast thou prepared for me."
> (Heb. 10:5)

It has its replica in the church, which is the body of Christ: those who are called into the fellowship of Christ are not called into a purely spiritual fellowship (whatever, if anything, that might be); it is spiritual, but it is bodily. "For by one Spirit we were all baptized into one body" (1 Cor. 12:13). And it has its cosmic parameter in the creation of the world, which is introduced, in the first account, by the moving of the Spirit over the face of the waters—to stress the fact that what follows is not an extrinsic or contingent act of God, but one in which the being of God as Spirit is invested.[8]

The thought of the Bible on the relationship of Spirit and body is more akin to that of Aristotle than that of Plato, and the same is true of the thought of Hegel. There are two features of the thought of Hegel that have caused needless offense to theologians through failure to recognize the Aristotelean—and Biblical—pattern of his thought. One is the statement of Hegel that "without the world God is not God."[9] With this he seemed to be saying that the world is necessary to God, and thus to infringe the freedom of God, which has been taken by theologians to mean his freedom to be God with, or without, the world. But Hegel's statement is merely the negative form of his positive point, that it is of the essence of God as Spirit to create the world. Then if we speak of the world as the embodiment of the Spirit of God, this sounds like pantheism, and the charge of pantheism has frequently been brought against Hegel. But this is to overlook a third characteristic of Spirit, which is exhibited paradigmatically in the incarnation, and which Hegel sought to express in his own distinctive way.

3. It is characteristic of Spirit, or of God as Spirit, not only to utter himself and to become embodied but to go to the uttermost extremity of bodiliness in separation, dereliction, and death. Here too Hegel caused much bafflement when he spoke of Spirit positing its opposite in order to be itself. But it is clear from his allusion to the death of God that he was thinking of the kenosis, or exinanition, of Spirit in the *Logos* incarnate and seeking its counterpart in the Spirit of the *Logos* in creation. At Golgotha "there was darkness over the whole land" (Mk. 15:33), just as "darkness was upon the face of the deep; and the Spirit of God was moving over the face of the waters" (Gen. 1:2).

When Karl Barth described the dual movement of the *Logos* incarnate in Christ, he put it under two captions: *(a)* "The Way of the Son of God Into the Far Country" and *(b)* "The Homecoming of the Son of Man."[10] This was a startling way to put it; for these captions are obviously taken from the story of the son who took his substance from the father and went off to the far country to waste it in riotous living, until in his extremity he resolved to return to his father's house and seek forgiveness and reconciliation. How can such language be applied to the only Son, "who is in the bosom of the Father" (Jn. 1:18)? By this bold transfer Barth pointed up the full measure of the "utterance" that took place, when the eternal Son went out from the Father's house and identified himself with those who were exiles there, even to the point of death, and then from that far country he came home again as the leader of the returning exiles.

The mystery of nature is then to be understood according to the same dual movement of the *Logos,* since it is by the same Logos that all things were made, and without him was nothing made that was made. It is the mystery of Spirit that it loses itself in its opposite, and fulfills itself by bringing its opposite to fulfillment in itself. In order to accept this mystery it is not necessary to pretend that anything is other than it is. The world of nature is a world of matter and energy, force and gravity, space and time, contingency and irrationality, frustration and futility. It has been felt by many that the world of nature, being what it is, is the most conclusive argument against the existence of God; for if God created the world, why, it is asked, did he create it so different from all that he himself is believed to be? But if we look at the *Logos* incarnate as paradigm of the Spirit, we can see it is not the character of Spirit either to keep itself to itself or to replicate itself, but to go out from itself, to embody itself, to lose itself in that which is remotest from itself, in order to unite that other with itself.

The Neoplatonists, who in their own way discerned the pattern of the process, thought of the Spirit (though that is not the term they used) in its procession as all but extinguished except for a feeble spark left smoldering in the human soul, so that the human soul alone could make the return journey to its source, "the flight of the alone to the

Alone," as Plotinus called it. And it is to be feared that many Christians, past and present, have taken a similar view of redemption. But the promise of Christ is not redemption *from* the world, it is the redemption *of* the world. And the role of the children of God is to march in the vanguard of the whole creation as it moves toward its eternal destiny in God, as Paul states in Rom. 8:19–23, and according to that same passage, the prime role of the Spirit is not to endow us with a mode of speech that sets us apart from our fellow human beings, but one that brings us into concert with the inarticulate groanings that pervade the whole created world.

It may be appropriate to conclude this chapter by calling attention to certain features of the creation narratives in Genesis, which may illustrate what has been said. At the time when the ecological crisis was first brought to public attention several years ago, much publicity was given to an essay by the historian, Lynn White, in which he charged that the original root of the crisis is to be found in the Biblical injunction to man to subdue the earth and have dominion over its contents (Gen. 1:28), which has been taken as a warrant for unrestricted exploitation of the world of nature for the satisfaction of human need and human greed.[11] But to expand this into a general indictment of the Biblical attitude toward nature betrays an extremely limited acquaintance with the Bible, which for many people, I fear, extends no farther than its first page.

If we turn to the second account of creation, which is given in Genesis 2, we find quite a different picture—here, in fact, the roles of man and nature are reversed. Whereas, in the first account, man is appointed lord of nature, in the second he is its servant; indeed, it is for the service of the ground that he is himself formed of the substance of the ground. And there is another important difference between the two accounts. Whereas in the first account it is man who is distinguished as the bearer of the image of God (which we may interpret as that part of creation in which the purpose of the whole is brought to a focus, or that part in which creation, so to speak, responds to its Creator), in the second, it is a part of the ground that is designated as the point where God initiates his purpose with the whole, and from this point, as a center, there flow out the four rivers of paradise to bear its promise to the four corners of the earth.[12]

Apart from these specific differences, there is a broader difference which may be observed if we place the two accounts side by side. The first account, which depicts the process of creation as beginning at the bottom, with the mineral order, and ascending by orderly stages through the vegetable and the animal to the human, may be said to portray the creation in its upward striving toward its Creator. The second, although in it the levels of reality are less precisely articulated, clearly portrays creation in its movement forth from God, as the four rivers of paradise carry his blessing from the center to the periphery, and man plays less than a central role. In the juxtaposition of the two accounts —if I am not reading too much into it—we have a vivid representation of the Biblical view of the world as having its being in a dual movement, from God and to God, and thus as being a work of the same *Logos* who became incarnate in the Son, who came forth from the Father and who returned to the Father. It is in this dual movement *(itus, reditus)* that all things have their unity.

In recent and contemporary theology there has been a notable quickening of interest in the return side of this movement, and various attempts have been made to interpret the ultimate unification of all things in God. The revival of eschatology at the turn of the century, the development of the historical consciousness, and the discovery that nature itself has a "history," a history of slow advance from lower to higher forms of being, from the inorganic, through the organic, to life, consciousness, and self-transcending spirit—all these things have combined to reorient the quest for unity toward the future. This is evident in the thought of Alfred North Whitehead, in which many theologians have found inspiration, and also in that of Pierre Teilhard de Chardin.

According to Whitehead, reality is a process that is proceeding toward ultimate unification in God, but God does not create the world, except in a sense in which the world creates him.[13] Likewise the dominant theme in Teilhard de Chardin is the convergence of all things toward the unity of the Omega point. The best-known example of this new direction in contemporary theology is Moltmann's theology of hope, which stands under the aegis of Bloch's description of God as one "whose essential attribute is futurity."

There is no doubt that this direction appeals strongly to the modern mind, which, as Langdon Gilkey has remarked, looks to history as the arena of meaning, and is thus oriented to the future with its open possibilities, not backward to the past and its determinate structures.[14]

But now we must ask, What is it that elevates hope from a principle to a faith? What is the ground of the assurance that all things are moving toward Omega, toward ultimate unification in God? In Biblical faith this assurance does not stand alone, it is not grounded solely on the perception of the ongoing work of God in history and in nature; it is bound up with the assurance that all things have come from God, that they have their primordial unity in God.[15] For God is not merely the Omega, toward whom all things tend, he is also the Alpha from whom all things proceed. He is the first and the last, the beginning and the end. He is the Creator and the Redeemer.

> For from him and through him and to him are all things.
> To him be glory for ever.
> (Rom. 11:36)

PART III

THE PERCEPTION OF NATURE

Chapter 10

The Whole Realm of Nature

If there is any validity to the theological account of nature that was offered in the preceding chapter, it remains to be asked how this may affect our faith. It is the ecological problem, as we noted at the beginning, that has forced the problem of nature on our attention, and while the immediate response to the problem is the taking of measures to protect the world of nature from further misuse, the problem raises questions about the world of nature that go beyond the ecological concern. It may be that the ecological concern, urgent and unavoidable as it is, runs some risk of aggravating the misuse of nature, if it is pursued on the assumption that the world of nature exists solely for the purpose of providing an *oikos* (*oikos,* meaning a house or habitat, is the root of the "eco-" in "ecology") for human beings. This, of course, it is. But the question is whether this is *all* that it is. And this is a question which theology has to ask. We want to ask how nature is to be viewed from the perspective of a theological doctrine of the world as God's creation. It may be called a question of perception.[1] We have seen in previous chapters that nature is perceived differently as it is viewed from different perspectives. It is the question of a theological perception of nature that this chapter will attempt to explore.[2]

We observed in the first chapter that theology, as the doctrine of God, may be done in one or more of three parameters, which we described as the cosmological, the political, and the psychological. The concept of nature can also be understood in three parameters, which correspond roughly to the three parameters of theology: (1) it may be used to denote the entire universe, the sum total of the reality which surrounds us; (2) it may be used in a narrower sense to refer to this world; (3) it may be restricted in scope to so much of nature as is accessible to us within the range of our experience of life. Let us consider how our perception of nature in each of these parameters is, or may be, affected by faith.

Nature in the broadest, cosmological sense has become a prominent theme in contemporary scientific research. The frontiers of astronomical investigation have been pushed to the utmost limits of what is observable by the most refined instruments, and questions about the beginning and the end of the universe are being vigorously debated. Opinion is divided among three views: the first, that the universe had a beginning and will have an end (popularly known as "the big bang theory," because it ascribes the beginning of the universe to an enormous explosion of matter that had been condensed into an extremely small space); the second, that the universe exists eternally in virtue of a continuous creation of new matter ("the steady-state theory"); and the third, that the universe exists in a state of alternating expansion and contraction ("the oscillating universe"). There appears to be a mounting weight of evidence in favor of the first view, so far as a layman can gather from the reading of popular reports; and this has led some to see the possibility of a rapprochement between science and Biblical faith. It is not the literal veracity of the Biblical record that is at issue now, as it was in the controversies of the past, but rather the broad fact of creation, to which the Biblical record bears witness in its own "mythological" way. Is Christian faith committed to the proposition that the created universe had a beginning? There are many who hold that it is. To cite only one, Stanley L. Jaki, one of the most learned scholars in the area of dialogue between theology and science, maintains that the cosmos becomes a meaningless treadmill unless it has an absolute origin and an absolute end, and that the whole scientific enterprise depends on this belief: "Science owes its only viable birth to a faith, according to which the world is a created entity, that is contingent in every respect of its existence on the creative act of God, and that its existence has an absolute origin in time, majestically called 'in the beginning.' "[3] But not all theologians attach the same importance to a beginning in time; some, indeed, have seen it as an embarrassment to theology, since it raises the question of what God was doing before he created the world,[4] and others have been impressed by the apparent lack of evidence. Aquinas, as is well known, saw nothing in the world to suggest that it had not existed from all eternity, and he accepted the belief that it had a beginning solely on the authority of the Biblical record.[5] Kant also was able to hold on to a faith in God as "the cause (and consequently the author) of nature," while maintaining that the question of whether the world had a beginning in time or not is one that cannot be answered.[6]

Kant's attitude to the question of a beginning, which was tied up with his view that our knowledge cannot be extended beyond the limits of actual or possible experience, was a potent factor in turning modern theology away from the cosmological parameter, as we saw in the first chapter. The new direction appears very clearly in the man who pioneered it. Schleiermacher accepted the Kantian principle that significance depends on the relationship of concepts to experience, and he applied this to theology, making the significance of doctrines dependent on their relationship to religious experience, the basic form of which he described as "the feeling of absolute dependence." But this feeling can arise only in relation to the divine preservation of the world, not to its creation, which is beyond the reach of all experience, and Schleiermacher argued accordingly that in separating the doctrines of creation and preservation theology effectively took the former out of the sphere of faith into that of (speculative) knowledge: "In general the question of the origin of all finite being is raised not in the interest of piety but in that of curiosity, hence it can only be answered by such means as curiosity offers. Piety can never show more than an indirect interest in it."[7] Schleiermacher was able to retain the doctrine of creation in his theology only by assigning it an auxiliary role in relation to the doctrine of preservation; it is there that we have to do with "the positive development" of the feeling of absolute dependence, but this feeling, he adds, "could have no truth even in relation to ourselves" if all things were not dependent on God for their origination as well as their preservation,"[8] and thus "creation is complementary to the idea of preservation."[9]

It is interesting—and ironical—to observe that Barth, despite his difference from Schleiermacher, gave the doctrine of creation a similar place in his theology. He declares, formally, that it is a matter of faith. But it is not the heart of faith. The heart of faith is Jesus Christ, and faith in God as Creator is more precisely an "insight" which is derived from faith in Christ, a "knowledge" which faith "contains within itself," a truth which the man who confesses his faith in Christ "takes seriously."[10]

The question, which both Schleiermacher and Barth point up, is how the perception of nature on the cosmic scale can be affected by a faith that is articulated within a political or psychological framework. The cosmic process (assuming it is a process) is so incommensurate with human history and human existence that it is hard to see how it can come within the compass of human perception, any more than the procession of the seasons can come into the perception of a mayfly. If it cannot exactly be described, in the Kantian phrase, as beyond the limits of possible experience, inasmuch as it is constructed by extrapolation from scientific observation, it is nevertheless so far beyond the limits of actual experience that it can hardly affect anyone's actual perception of nature.

But it would be wrong to dismiss the cosmic dimension of nature from the purview of faith. The Old Testament shows a pervasive consciousness of the cosmos as the place in which man has been set by his Creator and in which his relationship to his Creator has to be worked out; and in several places it suggests that the cosmos may serve to arouse in man that awe and reverence which are properly shown to the Creator. If "the starry heaven above," to use Kant's phrase, raises questions that are beyond our capacity to answer, it is one of the two things that "fill the mind with ever new and increasing admiration and awe, the oftener and more steadily we reflect on them."[11] The Bible, particularly the Old Testament, abounds in expressions of this sentiment toward the created world. Despite the strong emphasis on the fact that the world is created by God and as such is something other than God, nevertheless the sublime qualities with which it has been endowed are such as to elevate the minds of those who contemplate it to the praise of the Creator. This is the theme of the so-called Nature Psalms, which comprise a sizable group in the Psalter.[12]

If we describe the theme as wonder at the works of God —and the Bible frequently uses language of this kind; examples are Ps. 40:5; 107:8—we are reminded of the fact that Greek philosophy began, and according to Aristotle, always begins, in wonder.[13] But if the wonder of the Greeks moved them to the investigations that eventually developed into "science," the wonder of the Bible remained more contemplative. Such contemplative wonder is a distinctive feature of the perception of the world as God's creation, and thus an ingredient of faith.[14]

The sense of wonder at the contemplation of the created cosmos, as it is expressed in the Bible, is aroused by several features of it, of which two may be mentioned. One of them is the sheer vastness of the universe. It is commonly believed that this is a discovery of modern times and that the people of the Bible thought of themselves as living in what was little more than an enlarged three-story house, in which they occupied a place of central significance. The people of the Bible certainly did not share our modern knowledge of the extent of the universe, but they knew enough of it to recognize that it dwarfed them into comparative insignificance:

When I look at thy heavens, the work
of thy fingers,
the moon and the stars which thou
hast established;
what is man that thou art mindful
of him,
and the son of man that thou dost
care for him?

(Ps. 8:3f.)

Behold, the nations are like a drop
from a bucket,
and are accounted as the dust
on the scales;
behold, he takes up the isles
like fine dust.

(Is. 40:15)

When the new insights of the Copernican revolution led some bolder spirits, like Giordano Bruno, to assert that the universe is infinite, this was rightly felt to be a violation of Biblical theology, which reserves the attribute of infinity for God alone. But if the universe is not infinite, it is certainly immense, and the modern believer, who is acquainted with the discoveries of modern astronomy, can hardly fail to be stirred to wonder as he contemplates the magnitude of the Creator's work.[15]

It may be objected by some that quantitative magnitude is not in itself something to be admired; and this objection gains force when it is remembered that the magnitude of the universe is largely a magnitude of emptiness. It is the vast expanses of empty space that struck dismay into the heart of Pascal. The reply to this objection is, I think, that the magnitude of the cosmos has the ambivalent character of the numinous—it is *mysterium tremendum et fascinans,* it is both ravishing and daunting, it exercises an irresistible attraction and it fills us with dread.[16]

The second feature of the created cosmos that aroused the wonder of the people of the Bible and may still do so in people who contemplate it with informed eyes is the orderliness of its contents and arrangements. It has already been pointed out that in the Biblical treatment of creation it is not merely the fact that the world has been brought into existence by a sovereign act of divine power that is celebrated, but the fact that it is an orderly world, in which everything occupies its proper place in relation to everything else. When the prophet declared that the Lord "who formed the earth and made it, he established it, he did not create a chaos, he formed it to be inhabited" (Is. 45:8), he expressed a sentiment which is echoed many times in the Old Testament.[17] This world is a place of order, which is evidently the work of a supreme intelligence—a thought that found expression in the later literature in the elevation of wisdom to the role of an (hypostatized) architect (Prov. 8:22–31). The general verdict of the Old Testament on the created world is that "he has made everything beautiful in its time" (Eccl. 3:11).

It is this aspect of the world that was developed into the teleological argument, of which we may hear a distant echo in Rom. 1:20, and which, despite the criticisms to which it has been subjected, remains impressive, as Kant, one of its leading critics, confessed.[18] Kant's criticism was based on logical or epistemological grounds, but criticism of the argument is more frequently based on the empirical fact of disorder in the structure and processes of the world and its malign effects on the lives of human beings and other living creatures. The presence of evil in a world that was created by a good God and was pronounced good at its creation is a sore trial for faith, and it presents a problem to which no one has found the solution. But one thing may be said: the disorder in the world, which is the cause of so much suffering, becomes problematical only because it stands out from the order, which is the cause of well-being. It is the pervasive presence of order in the structure and workings of the world that throws the fact of disorder into relief; it is the exception to the rule, if not the exception that proves the rule. Measured dispassionately, the amount of disorder in the world is small in proportion to the amount of order. Doubtless the suggestion of such a dispassionate measurement of the proportions of order and disorder will seem intolerable to some, if not, in fact, a contradiction in terms. It would certainly be inhuman to seek to console the victims of cancer with the reflection that the majority of their fellow beings are exempt from it. But the fact remains that if there is a problem of evil, there is also a problem of good, and one cannot be isolated from the other. Both are recognized in the Bible, and if no resolution of the conflict between them is offered, this is not to be ascribed to a lack of sensitivity, but rather to a sense that, if the universe around us is God's creation, its structure is not to be judged solely by the impact of its workings upon us.[19] As someone has put it, we have no grounds for the assumption that God created the heavens and the earth and all that is in them solely in order that at the end of the day it might be said, "A good time was had by all."

The sense of wonder has also been aroused in some people by reflection on the contingency of the world, i.e., on the bare fact that the world—or anything at all—exists. Why is there anything at all, and not rather nothing? This question, first formulated (so far as I know) by Leibniz,[20] was declared by Heidegger to be the first question of metaphysics[21] and, although, like other metaphysical questions, it has been dismissed as meaningless or unintelligible by philosophers of the modern analytical school, it has been allowed even among them as an expression of wonder at the mystery of existence. Wittgenstein is reported to have said "that he sometimes had a certain experience which could best be described by saying 'that when I have it *I wonder at the existence of the world.* And I am then inclined to use such phrases as How extraordinary that anything should exist, or How extraordinary that the world should exist.' "[22] Whether the fact of existence can excite wonder apart from the question of possible non-existence is questionable. At all events, the question never crosses the horizon of Biblical faith; the Bible expresses wonder at the continuance of created things, but not at their having been created in the first place; it marvels at God's providential sustenance of his creatures, but not at his creation of them (Ps. 75:3; Job 34:34). It is perhaps an index of the integrity, or intensity, of Biblical faith in God as the creator of all things that it does not seek to penetrate the mind of God behind creation (Rom. 11:34; Is. 40:12ff.). If the formula *creatio ex nihilo* conveys (among other things) the suggestion of an alternative, it is, perhaps, significant that it is not found in canonical Scripture.

The metaphysical question cannot be dismissed as meaningless, but it is one that can be asked only by a sophisticated mind capable of a level of detachment never attained by the Biblical writers.[23]

When we turn to nature in the more restricted reference to this world and its historical development and ask how our perception of nature is affected by faith, we meet some of the same difficulties. That the nature of the world is a developing process is a conclusion which has been established beyond a reasonable doubt by scientific investigation, elaborated in philosophical systems, and accepted by most Christian theologians as compatible with Christian faith. But the rate of this process is so slow in comparison with the course of human life that it barely enters the field of human perception. There is perceptible evidence for the process of evolution, both geological and biological, but the actual process is never perceived—a fact that lends ammunition to the diminishing remnant who reject the theory of evolution altogether. And if the majority of believers accept the theory of evolution on the basis of the evidence, it is a question of whether the theory has been integrated with their faith, or whether the two things are held together in their minds in a state of peaceful co-existence.

If the theory of evolution is to be integrated with faith, the first thing that is called for is not so much a new perception of nature as a new perception of ourselves, of our human nature. It is in this area, as is well known, that the impact of the theory was most acutely felt at its first publication. But while most people have learned to accept the fact that the human race is descended from prehuman, or subhuman, ancestors, it is doubtful if many have realized the full implications of this for faith.

There are two principal ways in which our perception of ourselves may be affected when we view ourselves in the context of an evolving nature. The first is that we may be led to a deeper recognition of the continuity, or unity, between man and the rest of nature. Traditionally, theology has stressed the uniqueness of man in the scheme of creation, the unbridgeable difference between man and the rest of nature. It has recognized the continuity between man and nature at the physical level, but it has always found in man something distinctive—call it mind, or spirit—which is altogether peculiar to him and which sets him over against the world of nature as something alien to him, at best a means or instrument for him to use as he works out his own destiny. Evolutionary theory, of course, does not deny the distinctiveness of man; rather, it sees it as one instance of a feature of the process, which from time to time takes a "leap" to a higher level, at which something new and unprecedented emerges. But the more it adheres to strictly scientific method, the more it tends to stress the continuity of the process; emphasis on the novelty of the new is more often to be found among persons who are not practicing scientists, but who reflect philosophically, or theologically, on what scientists have brought to light.[24] The two emphases tend to become polarized, and Christian believers tend to side with those who exalt human nature above the rest of nature. The balance needs to be redressed. A reconsideration of the relationship of the human to the rest of nature is important, not only in the interest of human integrity but also because of the ecological problem, which is in large measure the consequence of man's arrogant exaltation of himself over nature. We shall take up this theme in the next section.

Our perception of ourselves in the context of an evolving nature may also be integrated with our faith as it brings us to a deeper recognition of the fact that we and nature are involved in a common history. Traditional theology has regarded the order of nature, which God established at creation, as fixed and unalterable—this was one of the main causes of the strife between theology and evolutionary theory in the nineteenth century—and likewise the nature of man, who, it was thought, had been endowed with all human excellencies. Man had fallen from his high estate, and his nature had become de-natured. The restoration of man to his pristine condition was the object of God's work of redemption. This work was accomplished in a history, which is recorded in the Bible. But it is only here that history was given a place in theology. It was, moreover, a subordinate or instrumental place; for when its purpose had been accomplished, all things would return to the condition in which they had been created and would continue unchanged in that condition for all eternity.

There were some in the early church, however, who saw an essential role for history in the life of man from the beginning. While the conservative view had been that man was originally created perfect, so that, as it was put by a noted seventeenth-century preacher, "an Aristotle was but the rubbish of an Adam, and Athens but the rudiments of Paradise,"[25] there was an alternative view, reaching back at least as far as Irenaeus, according to which Adam, at his creation, was thought of as an infant, ignorant, immature, imperfect, but with the potentiality of developing into a mature human being. Irenaeus was led to this view by two things. One was the simple observation that the normal course of human life is from infancy to maturity. So, while God could conceivably have made man perfect from the beginning, such a man would have been so different from man as we know him as to be unrecognizable:

> For as it is certainly in the power of a mother to give strong food to her infant (but she does not do so), as the child is not yet able to receive more substantial nourishment; so also it was possible

> for God himself to have made man perfect from the beginning; but man could not receive this (perfection), being as yet an infant.[26]

The other thing of great importance for Irenaeus is the parallelism between Adam and Christ, first propounded by Paul in Romans 5: the purpose of the mission of Christ was to repair the damage done by Adam, and the method, as he saw it, was to "recapitulate" the course of Adam's life, to retrace his steps and to "reverse the reversal" which he had made at each critical turn. One feature of the parallelism, which Irenaeus delighted to trace in detail, was the infancy:

> It was for this reason that the Son of God, although he was perfect, passed through the state of infancy in common with the rest of mankind, partaking of it thus not for his own benefit, but for that of the infantile stage of man's existence, in order that man might be able to receive him.[27]

The theme was reintroduced and pressed with vigor and sophistication in the Middle Ages by Duns Scotus, who taught that the purpose of God for man involved from the beginning his development from an immature to a mature state, and that the primary purpose of the incarnation was to further this development and not merely to save man from sin.

It has thus become possible for us to recognize that human life and the world of nature are involved in a common history. Nature and history are no longer to be thought of as the coordinates of a stage on which the drama of our human existence, which alone has significance, is played. Rather, nature and history are like the hull and the deck of a ship, of which we are the crew, and which it is our responsibility to navigate to its destination. The historification of reality has brought it back to a unity under God; but it has shifted the focus from the beginning at which all things have their unity by derivation from one God who is Creator of all, to the end toward which all things are moving in his eternal purpose. To the eye of Christians, who see in Christ the one through whom God's purpose for his creation is being brought to its consummation, the world of nature will thus appear primarily in the light of its destiny; and while this does not in any way abrogate from the importance of creation, it means that creation itself at the beginning cannot be properly comprehended except in the light of the consummation.

Viewed in itself, without regard to its destiny, the world of nature presents an aspect of futility or frustration; it appears as an endless repetition of the same processes, a treadmill which continues to turn but gets nowhere:

> The sun rises and the sun goes down,
> and hastens to the place where it rises.
> The wind blows to the south,
> and goes round to the north;
> round and round goes the wind,
> and on its circuits the wind returns.
> All streams run to the sea,
> but the sea is not full;
> to the place where the streams flow,
> there they flow again.
>
> (Eccl. 1:5–7)

The fact that such a report on the course of the world is included in the Bible is an indication that there is a measure of truth in it. The Bible as a whole, and the New Testament more explicitly than the Old Testament, asserts that the world of nature is included in the purpose of God, which embraces all his creation; but it recognizes the contrary aspect of nature presented in the passage just quoted.

The contrariety recalls a question whether it is legitimate to speak of a fallen nature, or even of a fallen world. The Bible records that when God looked upon the world that he had created, he saw that it was "very good." Is this judgment applicable to the world as we know it? Is the world in which we live the same good world that God is said to have created, or has it fallen from its prime condition?

Christian theology, especially in the Western church, has

taken a grave view of the consequences of sin, but it has, for the most part, restricted these consequences to human nature. It is man that is responsible for sin, and it is man's nature that has been corrupted by it.[28]

This was made possible by an exaggerated view of the uniqueness of man in creation, one consequence of which was that the connection of sin and death, which is copiously attested in the Bible, was discussed exclusively in the context of human existence, and the relationship of human death to the universal phenomenon of death in the world of nature was not considered. Biblical faith, especially that of the Old Testament, tended to focus on the providential aspect of the world, as it had been designed by a beneficent creator for the sustenance of human life. The providential arrangement of nature for the good of human life is celebrated in many of the psalms.

But the Bible does not confine itself to this point of view. There are a number of passages in which it is clearly suggested that, while human sin is the source of evil, its effects extend beyond the human existence in which it was committed to the world of nature as a whole. The best known is the classical account of the Fall in Genesis 3. As we have previously noted, both accounts of creation in the opening chapters of Genesis present the creation of man in an integral relationship with the world, and it is entirely consonant with this view that the consequences of sin fall not only on the man and the woman who committed it but also on the rest of the created world. When man falls out with God, the whole world is thrown out of joint.

Precisely how the "fall" of nature is to be understood is a question to which we have no explicit answer, only a few suggestive allusions. One of these is contained in the passage in Colossians, where the purpose of the incarnation of God in Christ is said to be "through him to reconcile to himself all things, whether on earth or in heaven, making peace by the blood of his cross" (Col. 1:20).[29] Here it is indicated that it is not merely the sinful human race that is in a state of estrangement from God but the whole created universe, and the language used earlier in the passage suggests that the universe was conceived as the sphere of transcendent powers which are in insurrection against God; the work of Christ is to put an end to the hostility between God and his creation and so to make universal peace (Col. 1:13ff.).

Another suggestion regarding the evil that has pervaded the world of nature may be seen in the different verb that is used in the reproduction of the same thought in the parallel passage in Ephesians, viz., "to gather together in one," as the KJV renders the rather rare Greek word *anakephalaiōsasthai* (Eph. 1:10). This term indicates that the state of things which called for the action of God in Christ is one of disintegration, of "things falling apart"; and this state of things is also attributed to transcendent powers which have been subdued (proleptically?) by Christ.

The modern reader may tend to regard these conceptions as mythological; but if he has learned that the mythological is not something to be dismissed out of hand, but something to be interpreted, he may be able to find elements of them reflected in his experience of nature. And he may find assistance in a study of The Book of Job. The problem with which this book deals consists in large part in the dislocation between human life and the course of nature, between the moral order and the natural order, or, in Kantian language, between virtue and happiness. Job does not teach a doctrine of total depravity, which might be taken to explain the discord; it does, indeed, recognize human frailty and fallibility, but it assumes the possibility of human virtue; and the major premise of the argument between Job and his friends is that all the arrangements of the world are (or should be) conducive to the good of the virtuous man (however that good be conceived).[30] Job himself appears to have believed that if a man is fully dedicated to the will of the Creator, all the powers in creation will be cooperative with him, and he was encouraged in this belief by his friends. Eliphaz the Temanite said to him that if he were really right with God,

You shall be in league with the stones
of the field,
and the beasts of the field shall be at peace
with you.
(Job 5:23)

But when Job is at last granted the audience he so greatly desired, God said to him:

"Where were you when I laid the foundation of the earth? . . .
when the morning stars sang together,
and all the sons of God shouted for joy?
(Job 38:4, 7)

—as if to say, Do you suppose that this whole universe, with all its immensities and depths, time and space, light and darkness, land and sea, Pleiades and Orion, behemoth and leviathan, was created simply for your sake? The "postulate" of an ultimate resolution of the discord between the life of man and the order of nature nowhere comes into view, even where the latter is held to bear testimony to the wisdom of the Creator, as it is in the great poem on wisdom which forms the twenty-eighth chapter. This poem, which is certainly a superb literary production, is considered by most interpreters to be a later insertion in the original (whatever that may have been), since it bears no evident relationship to what precedes and what follows. Barth suggests that since its theme, as he reads it, is the total inaccessibility of wisdom to all save God alone, the redactor, who inserted it at this point, may have considered it an appropriate prelude to the final confrontation between Job and God—assuming, as Barth does, that v. 28 is a pious gloss by a timid scribe, somewhat like the concluding words of Ecclesiastes.[31] But this interpretation is inconsistent with the final section of the poem, which celebrates the wisdom of God in creation. This wisdom is not inaccessible, for it is present in the cosmos, and God has "declared" it. If, however, man fails to find it there—and the possibility of such failure is recognized in the literature of wisdom[32]—he is not totally bereft of it; the last verse reminds him that there *is* a place where wisdom may be found: the timid scribe, if such he was, was a Kantian before Kant; not doubting that the wisdom of God is displayed in "the starry heaven above," but unable to lay hold of it there, he turned to "the moral law within," availing himself of the option, which Kant allowed, of taking it as a divine command:

> And [God] said to man,
> "Behold, the fear of the Lord, that is wisdom;
> and to depart from evil is understanding."
> (Job 28:28)

Perhaps the most profound and suggestive allusion to the state of the world of nature in this time in which man still awaits his redemption is to be found in Rom. 8:20, where Paul says that the creation (and the context shows that the reference is to the nonhuman part of creation) was made subject to "futility" (RSV; "frustration," NEB), but in hope, and this not by its own choice, but by God (for though the author of the subjection is not named, and the subjection to futility might conceivably be ascribed to Adam or the devil, the subjection in hope could hardly be other than the work of God). The "futility" recalls the doleful dirge of Ecclesiastes on the "vanity" of all things, but, while he sees all things condemned to a repetitious and wearisome routine, and ends on a note of unrelieved gloom, Paul sees a light beyond the darkness and asserts the eventual inclusion of the created world in the purpose of God. In so doing, however, he accepts the word of Ecclesiastes as a true, provisional judgment on the present aspect of things, and by ascribing it to God he has been taken to mean that "futility" (or something of the kind) is built into the condition of creaturely being as such. Some interpreters have found support for this view in the *tohuwabohu* ("without form and void") of Gen. 1:2. According to Peter Brunner: "The creation-narrative in Genesis 1 indicates that the creature, in the leap from nonbeing to being, must pass through an extreme limit of potential being, which stands in the closest proximity to nothing.

The creature, when it is called out of nothing, must pass through the *tohuwabohu* of primeval chaos, and it remains marked by this passage. This mysterious, dark underground of its luminous being remains somehow associated with it as its lowest possibility in this age. We may perhaps venture to say: In the measure in which the creature revolts against the limits of its creaturely being, which has been given to it and set for it by the Creator's word, and thereby comes under judgment, it comes near to this uncanny underground of its being. The assumption of creaturely autonomy, therefore, always includes the relapse into the chaotic. The creature cannot indeed of itself cross the line to nothing. The leap from being to nonbeing is beyond its power as much as the leap from nothing to being. The striving toward nothing is therefore the opposite of a redemptive movement; it is a never-ending self-contradiction and therefore a never-ending torment."[33]

The question that arises is whether the fallenness of nature is "only" a theological proposition, however well grounded it may be, or whether it also registers in our perception of nature. This is a question that may best be examined when we proceed to consider our perception of nature as it encounters us within the range of our existence. And in this context we may also find the best vantage point from which to consider the redemption and fulfillment of nature.

Chapter 11

Nature Lost and Nature Found

If a theology of nature is to have any effect on our perception of nature, this can be expected to occur initially within the restricted range of nature, with which human existence is coextensive. It is true, of course, that the human observer will quickly realize—without the help of the natural sciences—that nature far exceeds his own existence in duration and scope; and this may instill in him a salutary sense of his place in the scheme of things.

If man has been disposed to assign himself a high place in the scheme of things, this may be fairly attributed to the Bible; for the first creation narrative in Genesis portrays man as the crown of creation, and in the New Testament God's purpose with his whole creation is said to hinge on man (Rom. 8:19f.). At the same time, however, the Bible recognizes that there are dimensions to creation which are superior to man. When God is called the Creator of the heavens and the earth, an important distinction is intended:

> The heavens are the LORD's heavens,
> but the earth he has given to the sons
> of men.
>
> (Ps. 115:16)

And, however it may stand with the belief in angels, the belief that God has at his service beings of a higher order than man attests a reluctance on man's part to regard himself as the apex of the Creator's work. It may be added that in the historic idea of "the great chain of being" man's place, though certainly significant, was in the middle.[1]

It was noted in the previous chapter that a primary effect of a theology of nature on our perception of nature should be a deepened recognition of the relationship between human life and the world of nature. That there is an organic relationship between them is generally recognized, and it seems to be indicated in the second (and older) account of creation in Genesis, where man is said to have been formed of the dust of the ground. But if this is now generally recognized, it is due to scientific discovery rather than to reflection on the doctrine of creation; and there is an important difference between them. The concept of nature, employed in modern science, refers to the world as an object which is susceptible of investigation by itself, without reference to a transcendent Creator. The concept is of Greek origin; it appears nowhere in the Old Testament, and only marginally in the New Testament. Fundamentally it denotes that which grows by itself. But it is not necessarily incompatible with the concept of creation, as its admittance into the New Testament shows. If all reference to a transcendent Creator is excluded, or "bracketed out" from the concept of nature, the exclusion may be methodological, not ontological: i.e., it may be intended, not as a denial of the existence of God, but as an objection to the introduction of God into scientific inquiry as an explanatory principle or hypothesis. The introduction of God as a *deus ex machina,* or "God of the gaps" (which has been done by some of the most eminent scientists, from Newton to Einstein), is now generally condemned, not on the basis of atheism, but as a violation of the integrity of the scientific enterprise.

Science proceeds on the basis of the assumption of a divorce between the concepts of nature and creation, or, to speak more exactly, a separation. But if there are good grounds for the separation—and the success of the scientific enterprise which has been conducted on the basis of it is chief among them—it cannot be made absolute. There comes a point at which the question of a reconciliation, or reunion, between them arises. It arises in the context of the current ecological problem. The ruthless exploitation of nature and its resources, which has been traced by Lynn White to the Biblical doctrine of creation, is in fact the result of a substitution of nature for creation, which made the world the property of man and not of God. But the reintegration of nature and creation presents difficult problems, such as occur when questions arise regarding the preservation of endangered species when that involves some cost to human interests.[2]

Modern science has been a main factor in effecting a dissociation between man and the world of nature, because it has advanced by the objectification of nature over against man, the knowing subject. As Hannah Arendt has said, "It is in the nature of the human surveying capacity that it can function only if man disentangles himself from all involvement in and concern with the close at hand and withdraws himself to a distance from everything near him."[3] The modern consciousness has been determined by the stance of science. Modern man does not look on nature as the mother in whose womb he is formed, at whose breasts he is nourished, and in whose bosom he finally comes to rest; nature has become an object which lies before him and which is to be investigated, weighed and measured by his analytic intelligence. Since it is by objectifying nature in this way that science has achieved its successes and conferred so many benefits on mankind, we can readily understand how the majority of people are well satisfied with science and pin to science their hopes for further improvement of the human condition. But the pragmatic triumph of science has been purchased at the price of an alienation of man from nature, which has been accompanied by a loss of reality as a whole and an increasing immurement of man in the subjectivity of his own mind. The new method of science received its philosophical codification in Descartes's method of doubt, which, as Hannah Arendt has pointed out,[4] had the nightmare effect of destroying any hope of finding an Archimedean point, from which the truth of the world as a whole could be grasped, and driving man back on his own mental processes. Of these the most admired has been the mathematical, and the responsiveness of nature to mathematical scrutiny has led some scientists to praise the Creator as a mathematician.[5] But the possibility that the mathematical structure of the world is only a construction of our minds and a reflection of their pattern only intensifies the isolation and alienation of man from the world.

It is a feature of the present time that increasing numbers of people in the Western world are turning their eyes toward the East. The eastward turn in its varied manifestations is sometimes regarded as a fad that attracts people who are unable to fit into contemporary Western society. But its roots go deeper; it springs from the malaise of alienation from the world of nature, which is indigenous to Western scientific civilization but is unknown in the East. According to one eminent authority, "Unlike Western man, who believed himself to be situated somewhere between God and the world of nature, Eastern man has always accepted the humble role of being a part of nature. This does not mean that man as man has no value. Man has value, but in himself he has no separate destiny apart from nature. Man in the East has never been regarded as a sojourner in this world; he is certainly not the master of the world, nor is he an intruder or a guest. Man is an integral part of the cosmos with its seasons and changes. Thus the inner fabric of Eastern religions is characterised by the belief in the inseparability of man and nature."[6]

It is extremely difficult, and probably impossible, for people in the West to divest themselves of all the traces of the culture by which they have been conditioned. Westerners can never become wholly Eastern. But there are some ways in which, perhaps, they can assimilate the wisdom of the East, and one of these might be a reappraisal of the place of the senses.

Here we may have something to learn from Goethe (who

was versed in the knowledge of the East which was reaching Europe in his time), if we can separate the wheat from the chaff. Goethe was a diligent student of nature, especially of those areas which are the subject matter of physics, botany, and zoology. But he became disenchanted with the mathematical method that was employed in these areas in the science of his time, and that abstracted from the sensuous qualities of the objects studied. He argued that a better insight into nature is to be obtained by an approach from immediate sensuous experience, more akin to that of art. Goethe alienated much support he might have received, and finally drove himself to despair, by the mistaken assumption that the immediate apprehension of nature is incompatible with the mathematical analysis of nature—that it is impossible to enjoy the light of the sun in the manner of the Biblical writers (Eccl. 11:7), and at the same time to accept Newton's theory of the composition of light. It may, indeed, be difficult to do both, but it is not impossible; and it is the merit of Goethe that he recalls us to a relationship to nature, which is as real and important as that of the scientific intelligence. It has been doubted whether Goethe could be regarded as a Christian, but it is noteworthy that when the varied phenomena of nature are celebrated in the Prologue in Heaven, in *Faust,* it is because they are "glorious as on the first day." It is the sense of creaturehood in nature that underlies its affinity with man.

Very unlike Goethe in many respects, but like him in his sense of oneness with everything that God has created, is Francis of Assisi. To Assisi the whole created world was one family, and in his famous *Canticle* he hailed the earth as his mother, the sun as his brother, the moon as his sister, and even death as a "most kind and gentle" host who was waiting to receive him.[7]

A similar attitude to nature is found in many poets, both sacred and profane. I cite only the Scottish poet Robert Burns because, while he was certainly profane, the theological background is apparent in his "Address to a Mouse":

> I'm truly sorry man's dominion
> Has broken Nature's social union,
> An' justifies that ill opinion
> Which makes thee startle
> At me, thy poor earth-born companion,
> An' fellow mortal!

Are such expressions of human oneness with nature sentimental, poetic fancies? One thing that makes us suspicious of them is their obvious selectivity. We can empathize with Burns's address to a mouse—but if it had been a rat that he encountered, we wonder if he would have expressed the same sentiments. And it is not merely that the mouse is so "wee"; nature abounds in creatures infinitely smaller than the mouse, with which it would be extremely difficult to fraternize. One would be the liver fluke, which is the cause of "sheep-rot"; its life cycle is described by Sherrington as "a story of securing existence to a worm at cost of lives superior to it in the scale of life as humanly reckoned."[8] In propounding his doctrine of reverence for life, Schweitzer recommended that a truly ethical man, "when working by lamplight on a summer night . . . would rather keep the windows closed and breathe stuffy air than see insect after insect fall on the table with wings that are singed."[9] But if he were working in a malaria-infested area, would he extend the same protection to mosquitoes?

Perhaps, however, the question is not one of a specific sentiment, but rather of a deep sense, to which the sentiment is incidental. Thus the sense of oneness between human beings and other living creatures is not derived from the fact that some animals are capable of various degrees of domestication. Rather, the relationship that develops between human beings and their domestic animals is a special expression of a sense that human beings and all living creatures are common participants in the gift of life (however the giving of the gift be understood).[10]

A sense of oneness between human being and inanimate nature appears to have undergone considerable attenuation.

It is this aspect of the relationship that was uppermost in the minds of the poets and other writers of the Romantic age: it is the hills, the lakes, the flowers, the sea, etc., that figure most prominently in Wordsworth's verse, and the interminable descriptions of natural scenes that abound in Scott's novels seem to be intended by the author, not as gratuitous embellishment, but as essential to the context in which the action of the human characters is to be understood.[11]

An interesting suggestion of a relationship between human beings and inanimate nature is to be found in Martin Buber. This is somewhat surprising, since it was Buber's main purpose to bring out the full depth of what is involved in relationships between persons. It was to this end that he developed his famous distinction between I-Thou and I-It. But Buber did not intend to say that these two relationships are strictly divided between the two principal classes of objects that compose our world, viz., persons and things. The distinction is not so much one that applies to the contents of the world as to two different ways in which the self can be engaged with the world. In other words, the difference is not merely between Thou and It; there is a difference between the I of I-Thou and the I of I-It, and, by the same token, between the hyphen of I-Thou and the hyphen of I-It—in the former it designates a relationship, in the latter an experience, and Buber draws a sharp distinction between them. A relationship can exist only between one subject and another, who can be present with, and enter into dialogue with the first; an It is an object that can be there before the subject (*vorhanden,* in Heidegger's term), but not present in the proper sense of the word, and there can be no dialogue between them. The subject experiences the object, and the experience is monological.

These latter aspects of the distinction are the important ones for Buber, and they can, so to speak, override the distinction between persons and things. When he said, "All real life is meeting,"[12] he did not confine this to meeting "between man and man"; he saw the possibility of a relationship of the

I-Thou type with the world of nature, although the world of nature is in general a field of experience. Buber illustrates this in a striking passage about a tree. A tree is an object of experience which I can examine and classify and study scientifically, but at the same time, by virtue of what he calls "grace," the relationship may change: the tree becomes a presence "and has to do with me, as I with it," in a mutual relationship. In order for this to happen, Buber emphasizes, it is not necessary for me to give up my experiential knowledge of the tree; but my experiential attitude to the tree can by "grace" be transfigured, or transformed into a relationship in which the tree "meets" me, not indeed as another self (for Buber rejects panpsychism), but as a presence[13] with which I enter into (silent) dialogue.

Buber does not make it clear how this relationship takes form, or, if the relationship may be construed as a silent dialogue, what the tree says to me.[14] He seems to treat it, rather, as a kind of Platonic recollection of a primitive state,[15] in which man enjoyed this kind of relationship with the world as a whole and his knowledge of it was immediate. The kind of knowledge, for which the subject-object relation is fundamental, and which is exemplified preeminently in scientific knowledge of the I-It type, marks a kind of epistemological fall, "an expulsion from the paradise of primitive relation."[16] If I could really hear what the tree is saying to me in that silent dialogue, I should be hearing an echo of Eden.

Buber's piece on the tree has been described as a prose poem.[17] But there is a poetical poem on the same theme by the English poet Francis Thompson in which the philosophico-theological presuppositions are indicated somewhat more clearly.[18] In "A Fallen Yew" he writes of a yew tree that had stood for ages, and seemed immortal, but had eventually fallen. He recalls how boys had climbed it, and birds had nested in it, but he reflects—and this is his central theme—that neither birds nor boys had ever penetrated to the heart of the tree; for in the tree, as in every human being, there is an inmost core, which is impenetrable to all, save only God:

The sweetest wife on sweetest marriage-day,—
  Their souls at grapple in mid-way,
    Sweet to her sweet may say:

"I take you to my inmost heart, my true!"
  Ah, fool! but there is one heart you
    Shall never take him to!
The hold that falls not when the town is got,
  The heart's heart, whose immured plot
    Hath keys yourself keep not!
. . . .
Its keys are at the cincture hung of God;
  Its gates are trepidant to His nod;
    By him its floors are trod.

Such expressions of communion with a natural object such as a tree are, of course, poetical, and many people will be disposed to ascribe them to poetic license. But they have a philosophical counterpart in the recurrent efforts to overcome, or modify, the deep-seated dichotomies—between mind and matter, subject and object, person and thing, inward and outward—which have been characteristic of modern thought. The ascription of some kind of sensitivity, or inwardness, or subjectivity, to what would ordinarily be regarded as inanimate objects, is to be found in Leibniz, Whitehead, and Teilhard de Chardin; and if Buber is to be included in this group, there can be little doubt that his immediate inspiration was Hegel, whose language he clearly echoes when he writes, "Spirit appears in time as a product—even as a by-product of nature, yet it is in spirit that nature is timelessly enveloped."[19] When he opposes those "who see in the spirit —confusing it with their intellect—a parasite of nature, when it is rather (though exposed to diverse illnesses) nature's best flower,"[20] he might have been describing, in anticipation, the existentialist position which Sartre propounded twenty years later, and which he in like manner illustrated by an experience with a tree.

In his novel *Nausea,* Sartre describes how Roquentin sits

on a bench in a park and gazes at a tree; but what is disclosed to him in this experience is not the "presence" of something "spiritual" behind the mystery of being; it is the sheer absurdity of being, and it arouses in him a feeling of disgust.

There are several aspects to the contrast between these two encounters with a tree. One is that while Buber considers the tree in the fullness of its being, not merely as a perceived object of shape and color but also with a knowledge of its vegetative life and growth (which is not so different from one's own), Sartre's hero ignores the spreading branches and the foliage and the floral flambeaux (for the tree was a chestnut) and focuses exclusively on the roots that sprawl around the base of the tree like serpents. Sartre's attitude may seem narrow and perverse, but at the same time it reminds us that all natural beings (including human beings) have their *pudenda*—and much better examples could be found than the exposed roots of a chestnut tree: "a swarm of maggots feeding on carrion" was, I believe, William James's favorite example. Sartre's intention, however, was not merely to counter a romantic idealization of nature by calling attention to its seamy side, it was meant to support his main thesis, that the objective world as it exists in itself *(en-soi)* marks the absurdity of existence, and that consciousness *(pour-soi)* is an errant and unauthorized intruder in this world—a kind of bad dream which disturbs the sleep of being. Compared to the solid fabric of being, consciousness is a negation, and its emergence marks the supreme absurdity.[21]

The contrast may also be interpreted in the light of the two ways of perceiving the created world, which are implied in the great passage in Romans 8 which was discussed earlier. As was noted then, the distinction that Paul indicates is basically one between the present aspect and the future prospect of the created world. The world, when we focus on its present condition, presents an aspect of futility and corruption, which might well arouse in us a feeling of disgust and despair. But when, as Christians, who have the Spirit, we perceive the world in the light of its destiny, the symptoms of its present condition become harbingers of hope. In his comment on Romans 8:19, Luther wrote: "The apostle philosophizes and thinks about the things of the world in another way than the philosophers and metaphysicians do, and he understands them differently from the way they do. For the philosophers are so deeply engaged in studying the present state of things that they explore only what and of what kind they are, but the apostle turns our attention away from the consideration of things as they are now, and from what they are as to essence and accidents, and directs us to regard them in terms of what they will be. He does not speak of the 'essence' of the creature, and of the way it 'operates,' or of its 'action' or 'inaction,' and 'motion,' but, using a new and strange theological word, he speaks of 'the expectation of the creature.' By virtue of the fact that his soul has the power of hearing the creature waiting, he no longer directs his inquiry toward the creature as such but to what it waits for. . . . So then, you will be the best philosophers and the best explorers of nature if you learn from the apostle to consider the whole creature as it waits, groans, and travails in pain, i.e., as it turns with disgust from what now is and yearns for what is to come. Then the science of the essence of things and of their accidental qualities and differences will soon become worthless. . . . Would it, then, not be sheer madness on our part to sing the praises of philosophy? For is it not so that, while we think highly of the science of the essences and actions and inactions of things, the things themselves loathe their essences and their actions and inactions and groan under them? We take pleasure and we glory in our knowledge of the created world and yet it mourns over itself and is dissatisfied with itself! . . . We conclude, therefore, that anyone who searches into the essences and functionings of the creatures rather than into their sighings and earnest expectations is certainly foolish and blind. He does not know that also the creatures are created for an end."[22] Neither Paul nor Luther is speaking of a choice between two mutually exclusive ways of perceiving the created world. They are speaking of two aspects of the world which point to a profound inner tension in it but which must be brought together to form a true picture of it.[23] The sighs and groans of creation, which express the futility and corruption to which it is subject, point also to the expectation and glorious destiny for which it has been created.[24]

It is important to note how Paul coordinates the role of Christians with the predestination of the created world. Christians are distinguished from the rest of the created world by the fact that they have received the Spirit. But while their having the Spirit directs them beyond the world to that "absolute transcendence,"[25] for which Paul's symbol is glory, it brings them into a deeper sympathy with the world and unites them with it in a universal symphony of groaning (*symphōnōs stenazei,* Theodore of Mopsuestia). Paul sees a profound analogy between the destiny of Christians and that of creation. The destiny of Christians (which is called their glory) is here defined as manifested sonship to God, and it is equated with a redeemed form of bodily existence. Thus it preserves the distinction between them and God. Whatever Paul means in I Cor. 15:28, here he views the final destiny of the redeemed in terms of adoption and liberation, not identification or dissolution. The alternative to sonship is not equation with God, but enslavement; though Paul does not here develop the meaning of human enslavement and enslavement to sin, as he does elsewhere in this Letter (Rom. 6:12–23), it has its counterpart in the enslavement of the created world to futility and corruption. But neither the liberation of the world nor that of Christians involves the abolition of subjection as such. Subjection is common to both states of the creature (see especially Rom. 6:13, 16–19); the contrast is between a subjection that spells slavery and a subjection that spells liberty.

The most difficult feature of Paul's thought in this passage is the suggestion that the liberation of Christians to sonship is the model or paradigm of the liberation of all creation. How can the created world, which does not have the Spirit, participate in the destiny of these creatures who have the Spirit as a presage of it? How can the world of nature be redeemed from the futility, to which it has been subjected? Isaiah pictures the age of the coming of the Messiah as one in which:

> The wolf shall dwell with the lamb,
> and the leopard shall lie down with the kid,
> and the calf and the lion and the fatling together,
> and a little child shall lead them.
> The cow and the bear shall feed;
> their young shall lie down together.
> (Is. 11:6f.)[26]

It is an idyllic picture, but it is impossible to conceive what a transformation of human nature is envisaged in God's purpose for his human creation: "Eye hath not seen, nor ear heard, neither have entered into the heart of man, the things which God hath prepared for them that love him" (1 Cor. 2:9).[27]

Paul acknowledges this indirectly in the section in which he speaks of the predicament and the promise of prayer in the Spirit. Here as elsewhere Paul sees in prayer a characteristic manifestation of the presence of the Spirit. To have the Spirit is to be drawn beyond what we have and what we are—in the language of this passage, to join in concert with the longing of the whole creation—but this beyond is not something alien to what we have and what we are, it is the destiny which God has set for us as his sons, and of which the Spirit is the pledge and foretaste; the Spirit in us is the lure by which God draws us toward it. Prayer in the Spirit is, in the basic sense of the word, extravagant; it is not, as has often been supposed, a withdrawal into the inward privacy of the individual soul; prayer gives voice to the striving of all creation toward its goal; for creation is not condemned to an endless round of futility, it too is embraced in the purpose of God.

But we do not pretend to comprehend God's universal purpose, not even in prayer. When it comes to the question of what to pray for, we can only stammer incoherently, but as our incoherent stammerings are the work of the Spirit in us, they are translated by the Spirit into requests appropriate to the purpose of God.[28] However, while the nature of God's purpose for his creation exceeds our comprehension, and our hope of it exceeds our sight, it is not groundless; the experience of the Spirit in us who have the Spirit brings us the assurance of the fulfillment of God's purpose for ourselves, and since at the same time it brings us into tune with the basic thrust of all things, we *know* that *all things* converge on God's purpose for those who love him (Rom. 8:28).[29]

Paul's hope for the created world is expressed in ecstatic language which might seem to take it out of the realm of sober consideration. Yet it is concerned with a question that has exercised the minds of thoughtful people for at least two millennia—it is the place and scope of purpose in the world. So long as people were able to believe that they lived in a world that is purposively ordered (whether by a transcendent Creator or by some immanent principle), they were not troubled by the question of the purposiveness of their own lives. But when that belief was lost, as in ancient Gnosticism, or shaken, as it was by the Copernican revolution and subsequent scientific developments, the question of the purpose of human life was thrown into relief. Can meaning and purpose for human life be retrieved in a world from which they have vanished?

The urgency and complexity of the question may best be seen in the light of Nietzsche's sustained wrestlings with it in the latter part of the nineteenth century. The crisis was precipitated for Nietzsche by Darwin, who had a profound influence on him in his early years (though later, as his manner was, he turned against Darwin and became contemptuous of him, and of Englishmen in general). As Walter Kaufmann has said, "Nietzsche was aroused from his dogmatic slumber by Darwin as Kant had been by Hume a century earlier."[30] He saw that the Darwinian theory, which demonstrated the continuity between animal and human life and explained the process in naturalistic terms, destroyed the basis on which the significance of the world as a whole had previously been understood from the unique position of man as the instrument of God's purpose. Viewed as the end product of the evolutionary process, man could hardly justify this position, since in most cases he is barely distinguished from the animals. But "man is something that shall be overcome,"[31] and the occurrence of higher specimens suggested to Nietzsche the possibility of a higher type of man, which should come into being, not by a natural process, but by deliberate self-creation on a model radically different from the traditional Christian ideal. To call for this higher type of man, the overman, or superman, became the mission to which Nietzsche devoted his life, and which he pursued with such passionate intensity that it burned out his mind.

Nietzsche's animosity toward Christianity is notorious. But, while his philosophy was offered as a radical antithesis to Christianity, Christianity is, so to speak, the shell from which it emerged, and in its earlier expression it shows fragments of the shell adhering to it. There is a remarkable passage in his *Untimely Meditation* on "Schopenhauer as Educator," in which nature is portrayed as a blind and meaningless process, but as one that leads toward man as the being through whom she should be redeemed from her bondage and attain to her real significance; only, the man to whom nature looks for redemption is not the man we are, but a higher type of man, to which we must be elevated. "If universal nature leads up to man, it is to show us that he is necessary to redeem her from the curse of the beast's life, and that in him existence can find a mirror of itself wherein life appears, no longer blind, but in its real metaphysical significance. But we should consider where the beast ends and the man begins —the man, the one concern of nature. . . . It is so with us all, for the greater part of our lives. We do not shake off the beast but are beasts ourselves, suffering we know not what.

"But there are moments when we do know; and then the clouds break, and we see how, with the rest of nature, we are striving toward the man that stands high above us . . .

"But we feel as well that we are too weak to endure long those intimate moments, and that we are not the men to whom universal nature looks as her redeemers. It is something to be able to raise our heads but for a moment and see the stream in which we are sunk so deep. . . . We must be lifted up, and who are they that will lift us up?"[32] The passage is a blend of Darwin, Hegel—and Paul. That is not surprising in the son and grandson of Lutheran pastors; indeed, it reads almost like a meditation on Rom. 8:18–23. If Nietzsche himself was unaware of the parallel, this was due, no doubt, to his belief that Christianity had abandoned the world of nature, together with the body, and concentrated on the salvation of the soul in an "afterworld."[33] But if this was true of the Christianity of his time, it is not true of the Christianity of the New Testament; and when Nietzsche had Zarathustra call on his disciples to "remain faithful to the earth,"[34] he was more in tune with the New Testament than he supposed. It is in line with the New Testament also that he pins his hope for the earth on the appearance of a higher type of man, whom he outdoes the New Testament in calling "redeemer."[35] If "the overman is the meaning of the earth," it is not because he forms an isolated island of meaning in an absurd world (Zarathustra is not an existentialist in that sense), but because he replenishes the earth with meaning: "Verily, the earth shall yet become a site of recovery. And even now a new fragrance surrounds it, bringing salvation—and a new hope."[36] Who can fail to hear in this an echo of Paul's word: "The creation itself will be set free from its bondage to decay and obtain the glorious liberty of the children of God" (Rom. 8:21)?

The final point to be considered in this passage concerns the pivotal role of man in connection with the purpose of God for the whole creation. If we ask what bearing this may have on our perception of nature, two things may be said.

The primary or most intimate effect is on our perception of ourselves, for it enlarges the responsibility that rests upon us. The "glory," for which we are destined, is not for ourselves alone, nor can it be pursued by monastic or ascetic concentration on ourselves. "It shines forth so powerfully . . . that everything waits on it and longs for it. Looking and striving toward it is the basic movement of creaturely life. . . . For everything creaturely, up to man himself, is drawn into the destiny of man and into his freedom."[37] Of course, it has to be pursued; for we are called to this "glory" (1 Pet. 5:10), and to this call we must respond. In the Romans passage Paul concentrates on the expression of this response in hope and prayer, which reflect the divine authorship of our predestination to glory. But those things do not preclude response in ethical action, by which we have to "become what we are."[38]

There is, however, another side to our involvement in the destiny of nature, to which Nietzsche may again be called as a special, if unwitting, witness. It was his view, as we have just seen, that nature looks to man as the instrument of her redemption, but that hope of redemption lies, not in the generality of men, who do not rise above the animals, but in the higher specimens, whom Nietzsche identified at this stage in his thought as the philosopher, the artist, and the saint. It is, he says, the "single task before each of us to bring the philosopher, the artist and the saint, within and without us, to the light, and to strive thereby for the completion of Nature. For Nature needs the artist, as she needs the philosopher, for a metaphysical end, the explanation of herself, whereby she may have a clear and sharp picture of what she only saw dimly in the troubled period of transition—and so may reach self-consciousness."[39] This trio echoes Hegel's doctrine of art, religion, and philosophy as the three forms of Absolute Spirit,[40] and Nietzsche speaks as an idealist when he ascribes to philosophy and art the function of bringing nature to self-consciousness. But, while Hegel interpreted religion from his idealist perspective as an inferior form of philosophy, Nietzsche saw it in a more romantic light, and by locating it at the end of the series he appeared to accord it the highest place: "Finally, Nature needs the saint. In him the ego has melted away, and the suffering of his life is, practically, no longer felt as an individual, but as the spring of the deepest sympathy and intimacy with all living creatures: he sees the wonderful transformation scene that the comedy of becoming never reaches, the attainment of the high state of man after which all Nature is striving, that she may be delivered from herself. Without doubt, we all stand in close relation to him, as well as to the philosopher and the artist: there are moments, sparks from the clear fire of love, in whose light we understand the word 'I' no longer; there is something beyond our being that comes, for those moments, to the hither side of it: and this is why we long in our hearts for a bridge from here to there."[41] Theologians will hear in this an echo of Schleiermacher's romantic description of religion in the second of his *Speeches,*[42] though the source of Nietzsche's inspiration was more probably Emerson.[43] What is common to them is the notion of a relation to nature, which is not a mode of consciousness, but a feeling—and a feeling of unity with nature in which the sense of separate selfhood in the individual is transcended. But what is different in Nietzsche is his characterization of this feeling as suffering. This is absent in Schleiermacher and Emerson, but, again, it is something that Nietzsche has in common with Paul, who "with his sharp apostolic eyes descried the dear, holy cross in all creatures" (Luther).

Chapter 12

The Destiny of Nature

The truth of Christ, who is the light of the world, has the form not of an idea or principle but of a history or drama, of which the climactic elements and the pervasive theme are death and resurrection.[1] When people become Christians by participation in Christ (as Calvin loved to put it), it is by the assimilation of their lives to this recurrent pattern, which is sealed upon them in their baptism; in their baptism they are conformed to Christ in the sequence of his death and resurrection (Rom. 6:3ff.). And as the death and resurrection of Christ form the paradigm of all Christian living, it is so also with the vicarious power which proceeds from them. There is both a centripetal and a centrifugal movement in the process. On the one hand, Paul seeks for himself to "gain Christ and be found in him, . . . that I may know him and the power of his resurrection, and may share his sufferings, becoming like him in his death, that if possible I may attain the resurrection from the dead" (Phil. 3:8–11). On the other hand, he rejoices in his participation in the sufferings of Christ, because he knows that he is extending those sufferings in their vicarious power (Col. 1:24). Participation in Christ in this double sense is the *syllogismus practicus;* for "to know Christ," in Paul's phrase (Phil. 3:8), is to know ourselves included in the circle of which he forms the center, from which the power of his death and resurrection proceeds. The church, or the body of Christ, which Paul has in view and to which he extends the sufferings of Christ, forms the immediate or inner circle around the center. But there is also an outer circle, and to this too the truth that is revealed at the center applies. Christ is not only the truth for his disciples or for humanity at large, he is the truth for all creation (Eph. 3:10).

It is a vision of the created world in the light of Christ that Paul presents in Rom. 8:18–23. Here he offers us a guide to a Christian perception of nature. There are three main elements in it, and we may offer some brief comments on them in conclusion.

1. The first is sympathy, community with nature in its suffering. The community between man and nature, of which Paul speaks here, would have been readily understandable in the world of his time, which had been taught by Stoicism of a unity that pervades the entire cosmos and establishes a correspondence between the larger, physical cosmos (macrocosm) and the smaller, human cosmos (microcosm). This view of the relationship between man and nature, as we have already had occasion to note, was destroyed by the advent of modern science, which set man as knowing subject over against nature as object. But the desire for a closer union persisted, and it found expression in the Romantic movement, which turned from knowledge to feeling, and in idealism, which, at its loftiest, saw in human consciousness the attainment by nature to consciousness of itself.[2] When Paul speaks of Christians having the Spirit, he is referring to the knowledge they have through the Spirit that their lives are involved in the process of death and resurrection, which has its paradigm in Christ, and which is being reproduced in the world of nature. Christians, therefore, will look on the world with sympathy, not as a slave at their disposal, but as a partner with them in the purpose of God which embraces all his creatures, and more particularly as one which is participant with them in the suffering which is the reflex of the cross of Christ.

The term "sympathy," which was used by the Stoics for the unity embracing the cosmos in all its parts, more perfectly expresses the thought of Paul (though he does not use the word[3]) than that of the Stoics; for while they recognized the presence of suffering in the world, their aim was to cultivate an inner detachment which made them immune to it. They have a modern counterpart in Schopenhauer, who saw the world "subjected to futility" through the operation of a blind, purposeless will, and who sought salvation, after the Buddhist pattern, through the extirpation of the will in the individual.

The problem of theodicy in modern theology has been predicated on the assumption that the occurrence of evil in the world is incompatible with the goodness of God and therefore in need of justification.[4] This assumption is almost universal. A notable exception is to be found, once more, in Nietzsche, who, despite his early enthusiasm for Schopenhauer, rejected Schopenhauer's Buddhist doctrine of the renunciation of the will and recognized the part of suffering in the promotion of the purpose of nature. He saw the distinctive contribution of the saint, as we noted above, in the fact that the suffering of his life is "felt as the spring of the deepest sympathy and intimacy with all living creatures."[5]

Sympathy with the sufferings of living creatures, whether they be human beings or such animals as human beings are capable of forming some kind of relationship with, is accepted as something incumbent upon Christians, who owe their being as Christians to the suffering of Christ *for* them. But extension of this sympathy to the inanimate creation is a different matter; it seems to be an invitation to the "pathetic fallacy," which is charged against poets who impute their human feelings to natural objects. Whether the practice of the poets is to be laid to fallacy or to inspiration is a question we may leave aside. For Christians it is an element in the perception of nature to which they are opened through the Spirit, so as to see in it reflections of the light that shines in their crucified Lord.[6]

2. The second element is the perception of nature in the light of the gospel. The groanings of creation, which are joined in by those who have the Spirit, are heard as the travail

pangs of the new creation. Christians, therefore, perceive the world around them under the sign of hope. Here again we may recall the figure of the two concentric circles: as Christians are "born anew to a living hope through the resurrection of Jesus Christ from the dead" (1 Pet. 1:3), they compose the first circle around the center from which hope radiates; but the radiation cannot stop with them, it radiates beyond them to the created world and suffuses it with the light of hope.

This is undoubtedly the most extravagant, the most audacious, the most ecstatic aspect of the Christian hope. It is impossible to describe it in sober detail. The Bible speaks of it in the fantastic imagery of apocalyptic. But the validity of the hope does not depend on the plausibility of any description that may be offered of it. It has its ground in the resurrection of Christ from the dead, on which we base our hope for the (implausible enough) "redemption of our bodies" (Rom. 8:23), which are indissolubly linked to the elements of the world and would be useless without them. The resurrection of Christ is thus the link that binds the consummation of the world to its creation, and the decisive proof of the faithfulness of God. Christians who believe in the resurrection cannot restrict their hope to a future life for themselves; they extend it to the whole created world, which, as it proceeded from God in its entirety in the beginning, will, through his faithfulness, attested in the resurrection, proceed toward him in its entirety at the end. The word that was in the beginning, and through whom all things were made, will receive its appropriate response from all things—"and earth repeat the long Amen."

3. The third element in the Christian perception of nature is the recognition of the responsibility that rests upon us for the fulfillment of God's purpose with nature. Paul concentrates this responsibility in prayer, but I think we may legitimately expand the concept of prayer to embrace the whole of worship, of which prayer is the central and definitive ingredient. What Paul says of prayer may be said of worship

as a whole: (*a*) Worship is an activity to which we are moved by the presence of the Spirit; (*b*) worship is an extravagant, or ecstatic, activity in which we exceed the bounds of the comprehensible;[7] (*c*) worship is an activity in which we become engaged in the transcendent purpose of God.

Worship is an act in which we elevate ourselves to God ("Lift up your hearts"). It is not a blind venture into the beyond. It is the response to the condescension of God who in Jesus Christ has come down to us and taken upon him our flesh, which is "consubstantial" with the matter of the world. The response finds its most concentrated expression in the Lord's Supper, or Eucharist, in which representative elements of the world, by which our life is sustained, are brought in offering to God as a prayer that the consummation of our bodies through the incarnation, passion, and resurrection of Christ may be continued and extended to the whole material world.

The view that the Eucharist enshrines a sacramental view of nature as a whole received its most impressive statement from William Temple,[8] and it is widely received among Anglican theologians, who find it "congruent with the contemporary scientific perspective on the evolution of the cosmos from inorganic matter, through living organisms, to man."[9] What it entails for our perception of nature may be gathered from the evolutionary analogy. The process of evolution as it leads from the inorganic to the organic (if we may confine ourselves to its first stage) does not involve the transmutation of the former into the latter; in some strange way, which some call a "leap," the organic "emerges" from, or supervenes on, the inorganic; but the inorganic continues to be what it is. On the sacramental view, in like manner, water, bread, wine, and all the elements of the world of nature continue to be what they are and to possess the properties ascertained by the natural sciences; but above and beyond (or "in, with, and under") their natural properties the elements are elevated as bearers of higher properties, which, in turn, reflect back on their natural properties and color the perception of those who use them. All natural objects continue to be what they are, and they are to be used according to their natural properties, but to those who perceive them in the light of the incarnation they become charged with the promise of something more than what they are, and they will be treated accordingly.[10]

A single illustration may be sufficient to indicate the manner of the approach—and the difficulties surrounding it. The most natural feature of nature, especially human nature, is the process of generation by sexual intercourse. According to traditional Christian teaching, sexual intercourse is confined to marriage, and to Roman Catholics marriage is a sacrament. In this way sexual intercourse is elevated two degrees above the natural level: (*a*) it is tied to a relationship between persons which engages them at other levels of their being, and (*b*) this personal relationship in turn is seen as the sacramental material of a relationship that transcends it, viz., the relationship between Christ and the church, as presented in Eph. 5:22–33. Zinzendorf (who was not a Catholic) spelled out the implications in a very concrete manner: since the relationship between husband and wife is analogous to the relationship between Christ and the church, he taught his followers that they should treat marital intercourse as a sacrament, and in the performance of it fix their thoughts on the union between Christ and the church. A counsel of perfection? Bonhoeffer wrote, "To long for the transcendent when you are in your wife's arms is, to put it mildly, a lack of taste, and it is certainly not what God expects of us."[11] But is the alternative a total dissociation of sex from transcendence? The sexual revolution of our time may be described as an attempt to do just this, to assert the naturalness of sex as nothing but sex; and the proliferation of handbooks on sexual technique has ostensibly no purpose beyond this. Yet the joy of sex (to borrow the title of one of the most widely read of these books) is something more than the satisfaction or pleasure to be obtained through perfected technique in the performance of the act; for human beings, sexual intercourse, involving as it does a relationship with another human being, opens the door to a joy that transcends the experience itself.[12] It is, as the writer of Ephesians says, "a great mystery" (Eph. 5:32), something charged with a meaning beyond itself, to which it provides access. Sexuality, as was noted in a previous chapter, has often been regarded as the key to the mystery of nature. Biblical religion has consistently and vigorously opposed this view. But it has not opposed sex as such; only, it regards sex as a clue to the mystery which transcends nature, viz., the purpose of God with nature; and it regards sex as performing this function when it transcends itself into the love which has its model in Christ, who "loved the church and gave himself up for it." The theme of the passage in Ephesians is a call to husbands to love their wives, not to perform their conjugal rites, and thus to elevate their relationship, in common with that of children and parents and that of slaves and masters, into an instrument of the purpose of God, which is advancing through conflict to victory (Eph. 5:21 to 6:9).

Sexual experience has been cited as an example of the way in which all the processes of nature may be perceived by Christians as charged with promise of a transcendent consummation. The perception of nature in this light clearly resembles the transfiguration of nature so often celebrated by the poets, but it also differs from it in an important respect. The poetic celebration of nature, as we noted when considering it earlier, tends to be selective; it dwells on those aspects of nature which are suffused with light. But there are many dark things in nature in which it is difficult to discern any light at all. An unprejudiced and dispassionate view of nature must perceive both sides, both the light and the dark.[13]

The light of the gospel is the light that shines in the crucified and risen Lord, and it sheds over all things the promise of judgment and consummation. It is the promise of judgment shed over all things by the light of the gospel that guarantees the continuing identity of all things in the consummation. The created world shares in our need of redemption, and in that need it joins with us in a concert of groaning; but this groaning is not the expression of a desire of creatures to become other than they are, as philosophical eschatologies tend to imply, when they envisage such goals as the deliverance of the soul from the body, the return of the many to the one, the resolution of the particular into the universal, and the like.[14] The Christian hope looks to no such transformation of the structure of the world, neither by the return of all things to the source from which they took their origin, nor by the dissolution of all things in an infinite from which all characteristics of finitude have disappeared. Since everything that God has created, including the world of nature, is good, everything is destined to participate in the consummation. Only, every created thing must be judged, so that all that mars its goodness may be negated and it may be brought to the goodness in and for which it was created.

Thus a Christian perception of nature in the light of the gospel is one that involves discrimination. And it is obvious that it faces many difficult problems in practice. But there is one thing that sustains the hope and overshadows the difficulties: cross and resurrection are not equipollent. Both are integral to the gospel, which involves both judgment and redemption, both death and life. But in this dialectic (if the term be permitted) there is a preponderance of the second element over the first. This is the theme of Paul in Romans 5; as he surveys these two elements in their various aspects and effects, the second is always "much more" than the first: "If many died through one man's trespass, much more have the grace of God and the free gift in the grace of that one man Jesus Christ abounded for many. . . . If, because of one man's trespass, death reigned through that one man, much more will those who receive the abundance of grace and the free gift of righteousness reign in life through the one man Jesus Christ" (Rom. 5:15, 17). Therefore the experience of Christians under the cross and resurrection does not consist of an alternation between suffering and hope. The cross and the resurrection form an irreversible sequence; the risen Lord is "the living one," who is "alive for evermore" (Rev. 1:18); the death he died is behind him, once for all (Rom. 6:9f.). The Christian life follows the same sequence from death to life, or, as Paul elaborates it, from suffering through endurance and confirmation, to hope, and its dominant note is joy, because the hope is the glory of God (Rom. 5:2f.). The glory of God is the completion of his purpose with his children, in which they are brought to glory (Heb. 2:10), and it is this glory in which the creation is destined to share (Rom. 8:21).

Such a view of the consummation of nature may well seem an impossible dream, in the face of all in nature that is cruel, ugly, wasteful, and absurd. The answer is not to deny that nature shows all these characteristics, but to recall that the hope of glory for humanity is faced with the same contradiction. If we believe that God will complete his purpose in the creation of us human beings, in spite of what we are, we may surely believe that he will complete his purpose with the world of nature, of which we are a part. And so, when all things are made subject to him, God will be all in all (1 Cor. 15:28).

Notes

Chapter 1. The Problem of Nature in Theology

1. Speaking to a group of ministers on this theme some years ago, the writer asked when was the last time any of them had preached, or heard, a sermon on the text, "Consider the lilies of the field, how they grow," and he drew a complete blank.

2. The suggestion that the categorical imperative itself might be the product of a natural process had not been made in Kant's time, but it would not have troubled him; for, as he held, the command of duty implies freedom, and he saw no way in which freedom could be derived from anything other than itself. Nature tells us what *is,* the categorical imperative tells us what *ought to be;* and there is no way that leads from *is* to *ought.*

3. Augustine, *Soliloquies* I.ii.7.

4. Cited from John H. Leith, *Creeds of the Churches* (Doubleday & Co., Anchor Books, 1963), p. 115.

5. Gerhard von Rad, *The Problem of the Hexateuch, and Other Essays* (McGraw-Hill Book Co., 1966), p. 134.

6. The contrast between the faith of Israel and the Canaanite cults may be best seen in connection with human fertility. In the latter, fertility is sought through the performance of sexual rites at the sanctuaries; in Israel, it is accomplished by "annunciation," not only in the case of Mary (Lk. 1:30) but with Sarah (Gen. 18:10), with Hannah, who was clearly Mary's model (1 Sam. 1:17), and with Mary's kinswoman, Elizabeth (Lk. 1:13).

7. Origen, cited in Henry S. Bettenson, ed. and tr., *Early Christian Fathers* (Oxford University Press, 1956), p. 330.

8. The alienation of some Jews from the faith of the Old Testament takes the form of a shift from the political to the cosmological

parameter of belief in God. A good example is to be found in the Nobel Lecture delivered before the Swedish Academy by the distinguished Jewish writer Isaac Bashevis Singer on December 8, 1978. Singer said: "Although I came to doubt all revelation, I can never accept the idea that the universe is a physical or chemical accident, a result of blind evolution. . . . There must be a way for a man to attain all possible pleasures, all the powers and knowledge that nature can grant him, and still serve God—a God who speaks in deeds, not in words, and whose vocabulary is the cosmos" (*The New York Times*, Dec. 9, 1978).

9. Friedrich Schleiermacher, *The Christian Faith* (Harper Torchbooks, 1963), pp. 126f.

10. Ibid., p. 127.

11. Dietrich Bonhoeffer, *Letters and Papers from Prison* (Macmillan Co., 1953), Letter of July 8, 1944.

12. Ibid., Letter of May 5, 1944.

13. Dietrich Bonhoeffer, *Creation and Fall* (SCM Press, 1959), p. 14.

14. Ibid., p. 10.

Chapter 2. The Mystery of Nature

1. Aristotle, Fr. 45.

2. Friedrich Schleiermacher, *On Religion* (Harper Torchbooks, 1958), p. 43.

3. Keats, *Letters*, ed. by Maurice Forman (Oxford University Press, 1935), p. 64.

4. Wordsworth, "Lines Composed a Few Miles Above Tintern Abbey," lines 27f.

5. The title of Wordsworth's poem is an odd misnomer; for immortality, in the sense of life after death, is not mentioned at all. The intimations recollected from early childhood are of life before birth.

6. Beaudelaire, *Oeuvres Complètes* (Paris: Pleiade, 1951), p. 880.

7. Thomas Carlyle, *Sartor Resartus* (1870), p. 40.

8. John Stuart Mill, *Autobiography*, World's Classics (Oxford University Press, 1958), pp. 116–121.

9. Charles Darwin, quoted in Charles Coulston Gillispie, *The*

Edge of Objectivity: An Essay in the History of Scientific Ideas (Princeton University Press, 1960), pp. 305f.

10. Perry Miller, *The Transcendentalists: An Anthology,* p. 165, quoted in Tony Tanner, *The Reign of Wonder* (Cambridge University Press, 1965), p. 20. This book traces the persistence of the theme in American literature from the Transcendentalists to the present day.

11. Wordsworth, "The Prelude," Bk. II, lines 247–250, quoted in Tanner, *The Reign of Wonder,* p. 4.

12. Tennyson, "In Memoriam," Prologue.

13. Quoted in Charles Coulston Gillispie, *The Edge of Objectivity: An Essay in the History of Scientific Ideas* (copyright © by Princeton University Press), p. 196. Reprinted by permission of Princeton University Press.

14. Schiller, "The Gods of Greece," quoted in Charles Taylor, *Hegel* (Cambridge University Press, 1975), pp. 26f. Reprinted by permission of Cambridge University Press. Taylor gives the original:

> Unbewusst der Freuden, die sie schenket,
> Nie entzückt von ihrer Herrlichkeit,
> Nie gewahr des Geistes, der sie lenket,
> Sel'ger nie durch meine Seligkeit,
> Fühllos selbst für ihres Künstlers Ehre
> Gleich dem toten Schlag der Pendeluhr,
> Dient sie knechtisch dem Gesetz der Schwere,
> Die entgötterte Natur.

15. Goethe, in Gillispie, *The Edge of Objectivity.*

16. Ernst Cassirer, *Rousseau, Kant, Goethe* (Princeton University Press, 1970), p. 62.

17. *Encyclopaedia Britannica* (1964), Vol. 13, p. 671.

18. Alfred North Whitehead, *Science and the Modern World* (Macmillan Co., 1925), p. 103.

19. Morton White, *Science and Sentiment in America* (Oxford University Press, 1973), pp. 74f.

20. Letter of Nietzsche, quoted in A. S. Pringle-Pattison, "The Life and Opinions of Friedrich Nietzsche," in *Man's Place in the Cosmos* (1897), pp. 161f. It may be added that Nietzsche's death took place to the accompaniment of a thunderstorm of unusual violence.

21. See, e.g., "Song of Myself," Sec. 15.

Chapter 3. The Religion of Nature

1. Basil Willey, *The Seventeenth Century Background* (Doubleday & Co., Anchor Books, 1953), Ch. II.

2. Sir Thomas Browne, *Religio Medici,* Pt. I, §16.

3. *Calvin: Institutes of the Christian Religion,* ed. John T. McNeill, Vol. 20 of The Library of Christian Classics (Westminster Press, 1960), *Institutes* I.v.

4. Thomas Burnet, *The Sacred Theory of the Earth,* quoted in Basil Willey, *The Eighteenth Century Background* (Beacon Paperback, 1961), pp. 17ff.

5. Bishop Joseph Butler, cited in Willey, *The Eighteenth Century Background,* p. 84.

6. Charles C. Gillispie, *Genesis and Geology* (Harper Torchbooks, 1959), p. 9.

7. Calvin, *Institutes* I.xvi.

8. Jonathan Edwards, *Images or Shadows of Divine Things,* ed. Perry Miller (Yale University Press, 1948), Introduction, p. 1.

9. C. H. Dodd, *The Parables of the Kingdom* (London: James Nisbet & Co., 1935), pp. 21f.

10. Edwards, *Images or Shadows of Divine Things,* p. 79.

11. Ibid., p. 71.

12. Schleiermacher, *On Religion*, p. 70.

13. From Emerson's original essay on "Nature."

14. Ibid.

15. Emerson, "Divinity School Address."

16. Ibid.

17. Ibid.

18. Perry Miller, ed., *The American Transcendentalists* (Doubleday & Co, Anchor Books, 1957), p. ix.

19. Emerson, "Nature."

20. Ibid.

21. Ibid.

22. Emerson, "Divinity School Address."

23. Lord Byron, "Childe Harold," C.IV.clxxviii.

24. The writer's copy of Henry Drummond's *Natural Law in the Spiritual World* belonged to his grandfather, whose name is inscribed on the flyleaf, with the date, September 1888—it is the twenty-first edition.

25. Drummond, *Natural Law in the Spiritual World,* p. vi.

26. Ibid., pp. 110f. Edwards also observed the mole, but he noted something else: "The mole opens not his eyes till he be dead" (*Images or Shadows of Divine Things,* p. 123). Edwards does not elaborate on this, but apparently he saw in it a type of our advancement from darkness to light in the resurrection.

Chapter 4. The Philosophy of Nature

1. W. K. C. Guthrie, *A History of Greek Philosophy* (Cambridge University Press, 1962), Vol. I, p. 29.

2. Werner Jaeger, *The Theology of the Early Greek Philosophers* (Oxford University Press, 1947).

3. If it were not known that the word "metaphysics" had a fortuitous origin in the fact that Aristotle's work on this topic (which he called "first philosophy") was placed "after the Physics" in the corpus of his writings, the word itself might suggest something that goes "beyond physics." But since it has come to mean an inquiry of a different order, metascience is less ambiguous.

4. According to Jaeger, Empedocles' powers of Love and Strife stand for something quite different from the forces of attraction and repulsion in modern mechanical physics, since they are derived from experience of life (Jaeger, *The Theology of the Early Greek Philosophers,* p. 138). But is the same not true of the forces of attraction and repulsion?

5. Plato, *Phaedo* 95ff.

6. Plato, *Timaeus* 92C. There is a contradiction between the ascription of supreme perfection to the created world, with which the dialogue ends, and the doctrine presented earlier (48ff.) that the forms can only be imperfectly reproduced in the refractory material available for the creation of the world.

7. Plato, *Timaeus* 29E. Of the innumerable echoes of the thought in Christian theology it may be sufficient to cite one from the early church and one from modern times: Athanasius, *On the Incarnation* 3; Karl Barth, *Church Dogmatics* II/2, p. 168.

8. It is perhaps with reference to its theology that Plato spoke of "a likely story" *(mythos),* and not to the dialogue as a whole, which attempts to offer a sober, scientific account of the world, though his feeling, expressed twice (*Timaeus* 27C, 48D), that it should be begun and continued with prayer, tends to put it in the realm of theology.

9. Alfred North Whitehead, *Process and Reality* (Macmillan Co., 1960), p. 8.

10. Aristotle, *Nicomachean Ethics* VI.7.1141lab.

11. Thus the postulate of God appears in Aristotle, not as in Kant, in the area of the practical reason, where he functions as underwriter of the moral will, but in the area of the theoretical reason, where he functions as the cause of motion (*Metaphysics* XII. 7.1072b).

12. An analogy from the realm of law, with which people are more familiar, may make the distinction clearer. Only laws that are specific can be enforced by the courts. But it is considered important that all specific laws should be in accord with general principles of justice and equity; and a list of such principles is contained in the Bill of Rights. These are not directly enforceable as they stand; they are statements of principles intended to guide the legislatures in the enactment of specific laws and the courts in the determination of specific cases that come before them, and if a question arises whether a law passed by a legislature, or a judgment of a court, is in accordance with the principles, it has to be answered by the Supreme Court. If we attempt to treat these principles as enforceable laws, we are led to contradictory conclusions ("antinomies" Kant called them), as is shown by the endless disputes about the application of some of them, such as freedom of speech, the right to bear arms.

13. Kant, *Critique of Pure Reason* B359.

14. Walter J. Bate, *Coleridge* (Macmillan Co., 1968), p. 182.

15. Coleridge was probably one of the first to bring the knowledge of Kant to England.

16. The peripeteia in Coleridge's poem should not sound strange to readers of the Bible who recall that when the people of Israel in the wilderness "became impatient on the way," and the Lord sent fiery serpents upon them to bite them, "Moses made a bronze serpent, . . . and if a serpent bit any man, he would look at the bronze serpent and live" (Num. 21:4, 9). Clearly there is a smell of ophiolatry here, and it is not surprising to read that Hezekiah in his puritanical zeal for reform "broke in pieces the bronze serpent that Moses had made, for until those days the people of Israel had burned incense to it; it was called Nehushtan" (2 Kings 18:4). The Fourth Evangelist, however, was not so iconoclastic, and he recaptured the unifying

vision of Coleridge: "As Moses lifted up the serpent in the wilderness, so must the Son of man be lifted up, that whoever believes in him may have eternal life" (Jn. 3:14f.).

Analogies of this kind, which abound in the Wisdom writings of Israel, are not intended as casual resemblances, but as "visible connections which point to an all-embracing order in which both phenomena are linked with each other" (Gerhard von Rad, *Wisdom in Israel,* p. 120; Abingdon Press, 1972).

17. Milton, *Paradise Lost* V, lines 469–479. If the archangel's indebtedness to Neoplatonism is not sufficiently clear in these lines, he says later in the speech (lines 493–497):

> Time may come when men
> With angels may participate and . . .
> perhaps
> Your bodies may at last turn all to spirit.

18. Samuel Taylor Coleridge, *Aids to Reflection* (1825; London: Bell, 1913), p. 181.

19. A similar suggestion that the process of reality resembles a legal proceeding is contained in the sole surviving and much discussed saying of Anaximander (Jaeger, *The Theology of the Early Greek Philosophers,* p. 34).

20. It may be noted that neither Coleridge nor Simone Weil finds a place for the third person of the Trinity in this connection, though in other places Coleridge developed a doctrine of the Trinity in terms resembling Hegel's.

21. "Gothische Himmelsstürmerei" (*Werke* XIII, 89).

22. Walter Kaufmann, *Hegel* (Doubleday & Co., 1965), p. 195. The outstanding exception to this judgment is J. N. Findlay (*Hegel,* pp. 269ff.; Macmillan Co., Collier Books, 1962), who in addition sponsored the first translation of Hegel's *Philosophy of Nature* into English (Oxford University Press, 1970).

23. The critics have been mostly theologians, but not exclusively; one is the philosopher (and no friend to Christianity) Karl Löwith, who uses Hegel's own words to describe what Hegel did to Christianity, in "Hegels Aufhebung der christlichen Religion" (*Vorträge und Abhandlungen,* pp. 54–96; Stuttgart, 1966)—the point could not be carried over into the English translation, "Hegel and the Christian Religion," in *Nature, History, and Existentialism* (Northwestern University Press, 1966), pp. 162–203.

Chapter 5. The Science of Nature

1. "The Invasion of the Pseudoscientists" by Boyce Rensberger, *The New York Times,* Nov. 20, 1977.

2. There is a curious kind of postscript to the story of the loss of the self that may be added here. Alfred J. Ayer, whose book *Language, Truth and Logic* (Oxford University Press, 1936) was the original manifesto of logical positivism, and who appears to be regarded as the most eminent living philosopher in England since the death of Bertrand Russell, has lately written his autobiography. A reviewer in *The New York Times Book Review* of Jan. 22, 1978, complains that it is an autobiography without the *auto* (self). Twice in a relatively short review he makes the complaint: "It [the book] is all about Ayer, yet quite unrevealing of Ayer. His life from 1910, when he was born, . . . is here in creditable, at times engrossing detail; but there is strangely little self to go with it." The final sentence of the review was: "Ayer remembers what he did, where he went, who he met, what he read, what, intellectually, he at one time or another accepted; but he cannot, or will not, tell us who he was."

3. Stuart Hampshire, quoted in Michael B. Foster, *Mystery and Philosophy* (London: SCM Press, 1957), p. 94.

4. *Time,* Aug. 1, 1977.

5. Hugh T. Kerr, "Ecosystems and Systematics," *Theology Today,* Vol. XXIX (April 1972), pp. 113f.

6. Stephan Körner, *Kant* (Penguin Books, 1955), p. 13.

7. Alfred North Whitehead, *Religion in the Making* (Cambridge University Press, 1927), p. 21.

8. Whitehead, *Process and Reality,* p. 8.

9. William H. Walsh, *Metaphysics* (Harcourt, Brace and World, 1963), p. 81.

10. "Profile of I. I. Rabi," by Jeremy Bernstein, *The New Yorker,* Oct. 3, 1975, p. 50.

11. Eric L. Mascall, *Christian Theology and Natural Science* (Ronald Press, 1956), p. 132.

Chapter 6. The Creation of Nature

1. The sentiment was expressed by the Athenian stranger in Plato's *Laws:* "Men say that we ought not to enquire into the

supreme God and the nature of the universe, nor busy ourselves in searching out the causes of things, and that such enquiries are impious" (*Laws* VII. 821). Plato himself was not deterred from inquiry into the creation of the world, but he considered it fitting to begin it with prayer (*Timaeus* 27C).

2. Plato, *Timaeus* 29E.

3. Barth, *CD* II/2, p. 168.

4. "Gott, das Nichts und die Kreatur," Peter Brunner, *Kerygma und Dogma* (1960), p. 177. The final words clearly echo the last line of the passage from Schiller which is quoted in the following note, and the sequel to which is quoted by Hegel at the end of his *Phenomenology.*

5. Last lines of Schiller's poem "To Friendship":

> Freundlos war der grosse Weltenmeister,
> Fühlte Mangel, darum schuf er Geister,
> Sel'ge Spiegel seiner Seligkeit.

6. Whitehead, *Process and Reality,* pp. 521–524.

7. Cf. Isaak A. Dorner, *A System of Christian Doctrine,* 4 vols. (Edinburgh, 1880–1882), Vol. II, pp. 9f.

8. Gerhard von Rad, *Genesis, A Commentary,* rev. ed. (Westminster Press, 1973), p. 52.

9. Cf. Milton's version of the divine freedom, which he puts into the mouth of God himself:

> Though I, uncircumscribed, myself retire
> And put not forth my goodness, which is free
> To act or not. Necessity and chance
> Approach not me, and what I will is Fate.
> (*Paradise Lost* VII, lines 170–173)

10. The most notable exponent of this doctrine of the divine freedom in recent theology is Karl Barth. For a fuller discussion, see the article by the present writer on "The Freedom of God in the Theology of Karl Barth," *Scottish Journal of Theology,* Vol. 31 (1978), pp. 229–244.

11. "The Way Towards the Blessed Life" *(Anweisung zum seligen Leben),* in *Fichte's Popular Works* (London, 1873), pp. 467ff.

12. Whitehead, *Process and Reality,* p. 519. Cf. Alfred North Whitehead, *Adventures of Ideas* (Pelican Books, 1942), p. 154.

13. J. N. Findlay, *Ascent to the Absolute* (London: George Allen & Unwin, 1970), p. 225.

14. Ibid., p. 30.

15. Ibid., p. 141.

16. Ibid., p. 206.

17. A. E. Taylor, "The Philosophy of Proclus," in his book *Philosophical Studies* (Macmillan Co., 1934), p. 166. Taylor, who was a devout Catholic Christian, may be presumed to have shared the view he ascribes to Christian theologians.

18. Findlay, *Ascent to the Absolute,* p. 30.

19. M. Heidegger, *An Introduction to Metaphysics* (Doubleday & Co. Anchor Books, 1961), p. 6.

20. Hugh Montefiore, ed., *Man and Nature* (London: Collins, 1975), p. 27. The reference is to Feuerbach's *Essence of Christianity,* Ch XI.

21. Paul Tillich, *Systematic Theology* (hereafter cited as *ST*), 3 vols. (University of Chicago Press, 1951–1963), Vol. I, pp. 249–252. Tillich's treatment of the Trinitarian dogma follows in *ST,* Vol. III, pp. 286–291, but that too, it may be added, is largely in terms of principles.

22. Theosophy has become an especially opprobrious term in Protestantism. Yet it is only by an accident of history that theology came to be called *theo-logia* (talk of God) rather than *theo-sophia* (wisdom of God). Both *sophia* and *logos* are respectable Biblical words, and it was environment rather than heredity that led the latter to be preferred to the former. Sophiology, a term coined by some modern Russian theologians, is a curious hybrid.

23. *Theogony* is the title that Hesiod gave to the poem in which he offered a mythical account of the generation, or genealogy, of the Olympian gods.

24. Jacob Boehme, *Aurora,* xxiii.15ff., cited in John J. Stoudt, *Sunrise to Eternity: A Study in Jacob Boehme's Life and Thought* (University of Pennsylvania Press, 1957), pp. 195f.

25. Schelling, *Werke,* 2te Abt., Vol. III, p. 123.

26. Friedrich Schelling, *Of Human Freedom* (Open Court Publishing Co., 1936), p. 34 (*Werke* VII, 359).

27. Ibid., p. 32 (*Werke* VII, 357).

28. Ibid., p. 33 (*Werke* VII, 359).

29. Ibid., p. 30 (*Werke* VII, 356).

30. Ibid., p. 51 (*Werke* VII, 375).

31. Preface to Stoudt, *Sunrise to Eternity,* pp. 7f.

32. Barth, *Church Dogmatics* (hereafter cited as *CD*), II/1, §28, pp. 257ff.

33. Barth, *CD* II/1, pp. 320f.

34. The choice of the term is doubtless significant.

35. Tillich, *ST* I, pp. 250f.

36. Tillich, *ST* I, p. 178.

37. Jacob Boehme, *Von der Gnadenwahl,* i.3, cited in Stoudt, *Sunrise to Eternity,* p. 203.

38. Schelling, *Of Human Freedom,* p. 87 (*Werke* VII, 406).

39. Tillich, *ST* I, p. 179.

40. The distinctive and most critical aspect of voluntarism is presented in its ethics: the good is what God has willed; he does not will it because it is good; and he might have willed otherwise. Thus if God had published the Seventh Commandment without the negative, which was omitted (accidentally, or, I suspect, mischievously) in one historic printing of the English Bible, adultery would have been well-pleasing to God.

41. It is the soteriological aspect of voluntarism that interested Luther, not the cosmological, the freedom of God's grace, not that of his power. When he said that there is no Why to the will of God *(Gottes Wille hat kein Warumbe),* it was not his intention to ascribe irrationality to God, but to assert God's freedom to forgive sinners by his grace despite their condemnation under his law. It was not so much an abstract primacy of will over intellect, as rather a concrete primacy of grace over merit, or of gospel over law.

42. Karl Barth, *Romans* (Oxford University Press, 1933), p. 386. Barth was careful to avoid this kind of language in his later work, e.g., *CD* II/1, p. 298.

43. Jacob Boehme, *De Signatura Rerum* ii.6, quoted in Stoudt, *Sunrise to Eternity,* p. 202.

44. Jacob Boehme, *Mysterium Magnum* iii.5, quoted in Stoudt, *Sunrise to Eternity,* p. 200.

45. Schelling, *Of Human Freedom,* pp. 74f. (*Werke* VII, 395).

46. If Nietzsche's doctrine has often been misunderstood in ways that can be shown to be contrary to his intention, the persistence of these misunderstandings points to the circularity of any attempt to derive form from a formless dynamic.

47. Sigmund Freud, *New Introductory Lectures on Psychoanalysis* (W. W. Norton & Co., 1965), pp. 73, 77.

48. Max Scheler, *Man's Place in Nature* (ET of *Die Stellung des Menschen im Kosmos,* 1928).

49. Aristotle, *Metaphysics* XII.1074b.

50. Hilary Armstrong, "Platonism," in *Prospect for Metaphysics,* ed. Ian Ramsey (London: George Allen & Unwin, 1961), p. 99.

51. Findlay, "Towards a Neo-neo-Platonism," *Ascent to the Absolute,* pp. 254, 262.

52. Findlay, *Ascent to the Absolute,* p. 263. This contention, I think, overlooks the intermediary role of the Craftsman in effecting the transition from the perfect forms in the realm of pure intelligence to their embodiment in a world in which their perfection cannot be fully reproduced.

53. Philo, *De opif.* 16–19, cited in C. H. Dodd, *The Interpretation of the Fourth Gospel* (Cambridge University Press, 1953), p. 67.

54. Findlay, *Ascent to the Absolute,* p. 262.

55. Hegel referred contemptuously to Schelling's identification of the depth of God with indifference as "the night in which all cows are black" (*The Phenomenology of Mind,* p. 79; Harper Torchbooks, 1967).

56. On Hegel's use of the concept of spirit in the achievement of his synthesis, see below p. 93.

57. J. N. Findlay, *Hegel: A Re-examination* (Macmillan Co., Collier Books, 1962), p. 271. It is doubtful if Hegel would have taken "intellectual sobriety" as a compliment, in view of his famous statement in the Preface to the *Phenomenology:* "The truth is . . . the Bacchanalian revel, where not a member is sober" (p. 105).

58. Schelling, *Werke* I, pp. 212ff., quoted by Karl Löwith, *From Hegel to Nietzsche* (Doubleday & Co., Anchor Books, 1967), p. 115.

59. Karl Barth, *Protestant Theology in the Nineteenth Century* (Judson Press, 1973), p. 420. It is not clear what the implied concept of freedom is that Barth opposes to the alleged Hegelian necessity. If necessity is understood as necessity on the part of God to act according to his own nature, the alternative would seem to be sheer arbitrariness; but Barth himself recognizes in another place that this is an intolerable concept of freedom, and, indeed, he applied to it the same expression as he applied to Hegel's God: "God Himself, if conceived of as unconditioned power, would be a demon and as such his own prisoner" ("The Gift of Freedom," in Karl Barth *The Humanity of God,* p. 71; John Knox Press, 1960).

60. Tillich, *ST* I, p. 252. It is a question whether the exclusion of God from action in the temporal order is compatible with what Tillich says, with acknowledgment to Hegel, regarding the inclusion of "temporality within the Absolute" (p. 275). He asserts, on the one hand, that there is "an absolute break, an infinite jump" between "the finite and the infinite" (p. 237)—here he is speaking, with Kierkegaard, of what he calls "distorted temporality" (p. 275). When he states, on the other hand, that "everything finite participates in being-itself and its infinity," and by the same token, derives from the infinite the power of being, it is hard to see why the infinite should be excluded from the temporal sphere. For Barth's attempt to bridge the gulf between Hegel and Kierkegaard, see his *CD* I/2, and 14.

61. Cf. Schubert M. Ogden, "What Sense Does It Make to Say 'God Acts in History'?" in his book *The Reality of God* (Harper & Row, 1966), pp. 164–187; Gordon D. Kaufman, "On the Meaning of 'Act of God,' " in his book *God the Problem* (Harvard University Press, 1972), pp. 119–147. If it is not a caricature of these studies to say that their conclusion is that God does everything in general but nothing in particular, one is tempted to wonder if there is an organizational model at work here, with God as the chairman of the board, who concerns himself only with broad questions of policy but takes nothing to do with the day-to-day operations of the company.

62. Tillich, *ST* I, p. 243.

63. Tillich, *ST* I, p. 185.

64. Tillich, *ST* I, p. 243. Tillich appears to be referring to the transcendental self.

65. Tillich, *ST* I, pp. 157f.

66. Barth, *CD* II/1, p. 343.

67. Barth, *CD* II/1, p. 298; II/2, p. 25: Barth is alluding to 1 Cor. 2:10 and Rev. 2:24.

Chapter 7. The Role of the Spirit

1. The reader of *CD* II/1 should not be misled by the fact that reference to the Trinity usually includes mention of the Spirit. In Barth's trinitarianism the role of the Spirit is an extension or duplication of that of the Son. There is a revealing passage on p. 317, which makes no mention of the Spirit, and which lends credence to Cyril Richardson's thesis that if the attempt is made to extract the

Trinity from revelation, the extract is a binity (Cyril Richardson, *The Doctrine of the Trinity;* Abingdon Press, 1958).

2. There can be little doubt that Boehme's doctrine of the seven spirits of God, though ostensibly derived from the book of Revelation, owes a good deal to the doctrine of the *Sefirot* in the Jewish Kabbalah, with which he was acquainted. The ten *Sefirot* (the precise meaning of the term is hard to determine) are used to account for the derivation (some would say emanation) of the world from God; and, like Boehme's spirits, some of them (the first four) have to do with processes within God himself and the rest with the continuation of the process outside the Godhead. Boehme and Kabbalists alike came under the suspicion of pantheism (cf. Gershom Scholem, *Kabbalah,* pp. 96–116; Quadrangle/The New York Times Book Co., 1974).

3. Schelling, *Of Human Freedom,* p. 32 (*Werke* VII, 358).

4. Ibid., p. 87 (*Werke* VII, 406).

5. Ibid., pp. 51ff. (*Werke* VII, 375).

6. Ibid., p. 34 (*Werke* VII, 359).

7. Ibid., pp. 74f. (*Werke* VII, 395).

8. Ibid., pp. 51f. (*Werke* VII, 375).

9. Ibid., pp. 35f. (*Werke* VII, 360f.).

10. Tillich, *ST* I, p. 249.

11. Tillich, *ST* I, p. 251.

12. Augustine, *On the Trinity* XIII.24.

13. Leonard Hodgson so described Augustine's method in his book *The Doctrine of the Trinity* (London: James Nisbet & Co., 1943), p. 145.

14. Augustine, *On the Trinity* V.12–17. In the words of Burnaby, "The third 'Person' is related to the other two as gift to giver; and this relation denotes an external possibility in the Godhead of 'giveableness' even before the existence of creatures to whom the Spirit might be given" (John Burnaby, *Augustine: Later Works,* Vol. 8 of The Library of Christian Classics, p. 21; Westminster Press, 1955).

15. Augustine, *On the Trinity* V.16. Cf. Burnaby, *Augustine: Later Works,* p. 34.

16. The "procession" of the Spirit is parallel to that of Jesus, who himself "proceeded and came forth from God" (Jn. 8:42; the Greek word is different, *exēlthon,* but it is so rendered in both KJV and RSV).

17. Aquinas, *Summa Theologica* Ia.37.1 and 3.

18. The earliest reference is in the Preface to Hegel's *The Phenomenology of Mind,* p. 181. Jacob Boehme also spoke of an eternal love-play in God, in which the Abyss *(Ungrund)* wrestles, sports, and plays with itself (Boehme, *Mysterium Magnum* v.3, quoted in Stoudt, *Sunrise to Eternity,* p. 201).
19. Barth, *CD* I/1, §8.
20. Barth, *CD* IV/1, p. 194.
21. Barth, *CD* IV/1, p. 52.
22. Barth, *CD* III/1, p. 54.
23. Barth, *CD* IV/1, p. 177.
24. Barth, *CD* IV/1, pp. 192ff.
25. Barth, *CD* IV/1, p. 202.
26. Barth, *CD* IV/1, pp. 186ff.
27. Barth, *CD* IV/1, p. 201.
28. Barth, *CD* IV/1, p. 203.

Chapter 8. Models of Creation

1. See above, Chapter 6, pp. 122f. Fichte went on to praise the evangelist John because he rejected the unthinkable statement of Genesis, "In the beginning God *created* . . ." and substituted, "In the beginning *was* the Word"—as if to say, "Away with that phantasm of a creation from God of something that is not in himself and has not been eternally and necessarily in himself."
2. Barth, *CD* II/1, p. 76.
3. In the P narrative of Gen. 1:1 to 2:4a the verb "create" is used in the introductory statement of the whole and thereafter only of marine and bird life (v. 21)—which, however, are also "made," as are all the other contents of the world, including the land animals (vs. 7, 16, 25, 26)—and finally of man (v. 27). Did the Priestly writer have that sense of the uniqueness of *barah* which the commentators attribute to him? Cf. von Rad, *Genesis,* p. 66.
4. The very name "nature" (in Greek *physis,* from *phyō,* "to bring forth," and in Latin *natura,* from *nascor,* "to be born") enshrines its generative power.
5. "Make" has such a broad range in English that it can be applied to the generative function in the phrase "make love."
6. It has been repeatedly pointed out that the *creatio ex nihilo,* "creation out of nothing," is not found explicitly in canonical Scrip-

ture, though Paul certainly comes close to it in Rom. 4:17. It occurs first in 2 Macc. 7:28.

7. Appropriately enough the Greek version of the Hebrew Scriptures (the LXX) rendered the coda which concludes the hexaemeron: "Thus the heavens and the earth were finished, and all the *cosmos* of them." There is a marked contrast between the Biblical and the Hindu views of the world in this respect: in the Hindu world "This is that; this also is that"; the Biblical world is one in which "Everything is what it is and is no other thing."

8. The psalmist's words recall Samuel Butler's lines on Aristotle:

> He had First Matter seen undressed;
> He took her naked all alone,
> Before one rag of Form was on.
> (*Hudibras*, Pt. 1, Canto 1, line 560)

9. The reference is to canonical Scripture. The cosmological argument is stated in the apocryphal Wisdom of Solomon, ch. 13, a book that shows the effect of contact with Greek culture, in which the argument had long been current.

10. It is one of the curiosities of language that English, which took so much of its vocabulary from Latin, did not take over *formosus,* a standard word for "beautiful." English took "form" from the Latin *forma,* but *formosus* survives only in Formosa, the old name of the beautiful island of Taiwan.

11. Heraclitus, Frag. B67.

12. Heraclitus, Frag. B53.

13. Heraclitus, Frag. A22.

14. Aristotle, *Eth. Eud.* VIII.1.

15. This is also true of the Chinese philosophy, perhaps even more true; for the relationship of the two chief gods of the ancient religion is hierarchical rather than hostile. It has been said that harmony is the dominant feature in the traditional Chinese view of reality, and that the adoption of the Marxist view that class struggle is the mainspring of social progress meant a radical break with the tradition.

16. *Zōon logon echon,* usually translated "a rational animal."

17. Isaiah Berlin, *Vico and Herder* (Viking Press, 1976), p. 153.

18. "Freedom of speech" in the Constitution of the United States has been interpreted by the courts to cover activities such as demon-

strations, marches, and rallies, which are described as "symbolic speech."

19. Cf. Aquinas, *Summa Theol.* I.44.3. The notion of nature as the art of God still flourished in the seventeenth century. Cf. Willey, *The Seventeenth Century Background,* pp. 57f.

20. Cited in Josiah Royce, *The Spirit of Modern Philosophy* (1892), p. 457. The authenticity of the letter has been questioned.

21. Plato, *Republic* VI.508.

22. Plotinus used it frequently.

23. Schelling, *Of Human Freedom,* p. 19.

24. See above, Chapter 6, p. 124.

25. Plato, *Timaeus* 29E.

26. Aquinas, *Summa Theol.* I.1.44, Intro.

27. *Summa Theol.* I.45.6.

28. F. C. Copleston, *Aquinas* (Penguin Books, 1955), pp. 138f.

29. See Chapter 6, p. 123.

30. The last phrase is from one of the anathemas attached to the original creed of Nicaea. Plato also noted in the basic passage that "the offspring of the good, which the good begat, is analogous to itself" (*analogon heautōi, Republic* VI.508).

31. Aquinas says that the internal procession of the divine persons results in perfect likeness, that of the creatures from the Creator in imperfect likeness (*Summa Theol.* I.45.6).

32. Cf. Bonhoeffer, *Creation and Fall,* pp. 24f.

33. This thought is perhaps present in the divine speech to Job (38:12, 19, 24).

34. Barth recognizes that "light is the symbol (and the prototype) of grace." But his insistence on the createdness of light as something "dependent, threatened and corruptible" forces him to argue that the "light from light" of the Nicene Creed is "quite unlike the Son of God," and thus makes of it a veritable *lucus a non lucendo* (*CD* III/1, pp. 118f.).

35. Claus Westermann argues that since it is the light that was pronounced good, and not the darkness (which God is not expressly said to have created), light has a preferred place; and, though the alternation of light and darkness is a "necessary part of the order of creation," the precedence of light indicates that there is something more to the history of creation than the rhythm of day and night, and of coming to be and passing away (*Creation,* pp. 43f.; Fortress Press, 1974).

36. Sir James Jeans, *The Mysterious Universe* (Cambridge University Press, 1930), pp. 77f.

Chapter 9. Creator Spirit

1. From the hymn "Gelobet seist du, Jesu Christ." The original is:

> Den aller Welt Kreis nie beschloss,
> der liegt in Marien Schoss;
> er ist ein Kindlein worden klein,
> der alle King erhält allein.

Luther celebrated the marvel again in his hymn "Vom Himmel hoch":

> Ach Herr, du Schöpfer aller Ding,
> wie hist du worden so gering,
> dass du da liegt auf dürrem Gras,
> davon ein Rind und Esel ass.
>
> Ah, Lord, who hast created all,
> How hast Thou made Thee weak and small,
> That Thou must choose Thy infant bed
> Where ass and ox but lately fed.
> (Tr. Catherine Winkworth)

Cf. also John Donne, Nativitie, *Holy Sonnets* 3:

> But oh, for thee, for him, hath th'Inne no room? . . .
> Sees't thou, my Soule, with thy faith's eyes,
> How he which fils all place, yet none holds him, doth lye?

2. Calvin, *Institutes* II.xiii.4.
3. That this declaration is intended as definitive is shown by the response of the disciples: "Ah, now you are speaking plainly, not in any figure! . . . By this we believe that you came from God" (Jn. 16:29–30).
4. Hendrikus Berkof, *The Doctrine of the Holy Spirit* (John Knox Press, 1964), p. 21.
5. This was the root of Luther's devotion to Mary, which continued after the break with Rome; by her profession of faith in the word of promise Mary showed herself the perfect model of an evangelical Christian.

6. This sense survives in modern English, oddly enough, only with reference to counterfeit money and libel.

7. Emil Fackenheim, looking at Hegel from a Jewish standpoint, correctly identifies the center of Hegel's religious thought in what he calls the two Trinities, "the pre-worldly trinitarian play eternally complete apart from the world, and the real trinitarian incursion into the world" (*The Religious Dimension in Hegel's Thought,* pp. 153, 202ff.; Beacon Press, 1970). Christian faith asserts that the bond between them is Love, and philosophy accepts this. But when it comes to what Fackenheim aptly describes as "the transfiguration of faith into philosophy" (title of Ch. 6, p. 160), the "mystery," or "paradoxical fact," of the transition from the ontological Trinity to the economic (as they are called in Christian theology) is referred to a divine self-othering, or "overreaching," which is best grasped in the comprehension of God as Spirit (p. 219).

8. I find unconvincing the arguments for replacing the traditional "Spirit of God" in Gen. 1:2 with "a mighty wind" (NEB; cf. von Rad, *Genesis,* p. 49). In the Old Testament the function of a mighty wind (lit., "a wind of God") is either to stir up a storm (Dan. 7:2) or to dry up flood waters (Gen. 8:1). But there is no suggestion of a storm here, and the waters still abound after the moving of the Spirit (Gen. 1:6). I am inclined to think that the significance of the moving of the Spirit is to be found in the fact that it is introduced at the point of transition from darkness to light.

9. Hegel, *Philosophy of Religion,* Vol. I, p. 200.

10. Barth, *CD* IV/1, p. 157; IV/2, p. 20.

11. "The Historical Roots of Our Ecological Crisis," *Science,* Vol. 155 (1967), p. 1203.

12. There is another difference between the two accounts which may be mentioned in this connection. In the first account, water, which abounds in the opening scene, represents the element of chaos and disorder which must be brought under control before the creation of an orderly world may proceed; in the second, it represents the vehicle of life and blessing which flows from God to all his creatures. Both beneficent and maleficent aspects reappear frequently in the Bible, and they remind us of the ambiguity of all things in the world.

13. The thought of God as one who is created at the end rather than one who created in the beginning was first advanced by Samuel Alexander in his book *Space, Time and Deity* (1920).

14. Langdon Gilkey, *Religion and the Scientific Future* (Harper & Row, 1970), p. 69.

15. Cf. Pascal: "It is impossible that God should ever be the end if he is not the beginning" (Fr. 488, Brunschvig).

Chapter 10. The Whole Realm of Nature

1. Apperception, meaning a mode of perception that is conscious of itself, would be a more appropriate term, but it is unfamiliar to most people, and perception will do.

2. According to von Rad, the thought is basic to wisdom in Israel "that effective knowledge about God is the only thing that puts a man into a right relationship with the objects of his perception" (*Wisdom in Israel,* pp. 67f.).

3. Stanley L. Jaki, *Science and Creation* (1975), pp. 126, 356. The thesis is elaborated in the same author's Gifford Lectures, *The Road of Science and the Ways to God* (University of Chicago Press, 1978).

4. The question is as old as Augustine, who tells us that it was the subject of what must be the oldest theological joke: someone answered the question, "He was preparing hell for those who pry too deep" (*Confessions* XI.12).

5. It is doubtful if Aquinas was consistent with himself on this point when he argued in his proof of God from the contingency of the world that, "if everything can not be, then at one time there was nothing in existence" (*Summa Theol.* I.2.3).

6. Kant, *Critique of Practical Reason,* 125; *Critique of Pure Reason,* B454f.

7. Schleiermacher, *The Christian Faith,* §39.1, pp. 148f.

8. Ibid., pp. 151f.

9. Ibid., p. 143. A puzzling question arises here: if creation is an implicate of absolute dependence, but it is not itself a matter of feeling, how can there be a feeling of absolute dependence?

10. Barth, *CD* III/1, §40, pp. 3, 31ff.

11. Kant, *Critique of Practical Reason,* 161. The other thing which aroused this sentiment in Kant is "the moral law within me."

12. Examples are Psalms 8, 19A, 104, 148. The author of the Wisdom of Solomon goes so far as to say that, while the sublime qualities of the created world ought to elevate the minds of those

who behold them to the Creator, these qualities are so impressive that, if some people do not see beyond them, this is understandable, if not excusable (Wis., ch. 13).

13. Aristotle, *Metaphysics* I.982b.

14. The writer recalls a sermon he heard more than half a century ago. The preacher was Professor James Moffatt, the place a church in Edinburgh, Scotland, and the occasion the introduction of the *Revised Church Hymnary* (1927), in the preparation of which Moffatt had taken an active part. The text was a line that appears in identical form in two different hymns: "Lost in wonder, love, and praise." The line occurs first in the hymn by Joseph Addison (1672–1719), the essayist and critic, which begins:

> When all Thy mercies, O my God,
> My rising soul surveys,
> Transported with the view, I'm lost
> In wonder, love, and praise.

It appears again in the last stanza of one of the best-known hymns of Charles Wesley (1707–1788), who gave wings of song to the revival initiated by his brother, John, "Love Divine, All Loves Excelling":

> Finish, then, Thy new creation;
> Pure and spotless let us be;
> Let us see Thy great salvation
> Perfectly restored in Thee;
> Changed from glory into glory,
> Till in heaven we take our place,
> Till we cast our crowns before Thee,
> Lost in wonder, love, and praise.

It is, of course, possible that Wesley knew Addison's hymn and reproduced the line from memory, consciously or unconsciously. I do not remember whether Moffatt discussed this question. His main emphasis was on the striking fact that two men of such different dispositions—Addison, the declared foe of "enthusiasm," and Wesley deep in something that looked very like it—should have lighted upon the same three components of adoration, and especially that both should have given the first place to wonder.

15. The advent of space travel, which has enabled a man to land on the moon and has given us the prospect of journeys to more distant regions, has doubtless dimmed our sense of wonder at "the

starry heaven above." But it takes only a moment's reflection to recognize that we have merely dabbled at the fringe, and that there is little likelihood of ranging farther afield unless the span of human life can be extended dramatically. The nearest fixed star in our galaxy, Proxima Centauri, is over twenty-five million million miles distant from the earth, so that even if it were possible to devise a vehicle to travel at the speed of light, it would take four years and four months to reach it—and, if we set our sights on a more distant target, say, the Great Nebula in Andromeda, we should have to travel for two million years.

16. Cf. R. Otto, *The Idea of the Holy* (1925), pp. 12–41.

17. In two hymnic passages in Jeremiah reference is made to "the fixed order," or "ordinances," of creation (Jer. 31:35f.; 33:25); in the latter passage the order is traced to a divine "covenant with day and night," presumably the Noahic covenant of Gen. 9:8–17. On the whole theme, see von Rad, *Wisdom in Israel,* II.

18. Kant, *Critique of Pure Reason,* B652.

19. It is a question whether the problem of evil can be treated dispassionately by one who has not suffered under it. Barth remarked of Leibniz that "at bottom he hardly had any serious interest (and from the practical standpoint none at all) in the problem of evil" (*CD* III/1, p. 392). But it is not apparent that Barth himself was any more deeply or passionately concerned with it. Not all who have written on the problem of suffering were acquainted with suffering in their own lives. It would seem that the problem has impressed itself more on people who were observers rather than victims of it.

20. Leibniz, *Principles of Nature and Grace,* 7.

21. Heidegger, *Introduction to Metaphysics,* p. 6.

22. From the Memoir by Norman Malcolm, quoted in Milton K. Munitz, *The Mystery of Existence* (New York University Press, 1974), p. 79.

23. Barth interprets creation as an act of free choice on the part of God (*CD* III/1, pp. 94ff.): God did not need to create (*CD* IV/1, p. 201); however, the alternative he rejected when he chose to create was not to not create at all, but "the world fashioned otherwise than according to the divine purpose, and therefore formless and intrinsically impossible" (*CD* III/1, p. 102).

24. Examples are Henri Bergson, C. Lloyd Morgan, and Pierre

Teilhard de Chardin. The last was a working scientist, but his science is viewed with suspicion by some scientists just because of the theological reflections he combined with it.

25. Robert South (1634–1716), *Sermons* I.ii.

26. Irenaeus, *Against Heresies* IV.39.1.

27. Ibid., IV.37.5. Although the parallelism between Christ and Adam was widely recognized, the particular aspect of it that relates to the infancy seems to have been peculiar to Irenaeus, and it has, of course, no Biblical foundation. There is also no trace of it in Christian art: the infant Jesus (with his mother) is probably the most frequent subject of Christian painting, but Adam and Eve are regularly portrayed as mature adults.

28. Testimonies to the devastating effects of sin on human nature could be quoted in abundance from Augustine and all the heirs of the Augustinian tradition. It may suffice to quote the eloquent answer that is given in the Westminster Shorter Catechism to the question, "What is the misery of that estate whereinto man fell?" (Q.19): "A. All mankind, by their fall, lost communion with God, are under his wrath and curse, and so made liable to all miseries of this life, to death itself, and to the pains of hell forever." The answer is "existential" in that it focuses on the effects of the Fall on human existence, and says nothing to suggest that the world, in which human existence is continued, is other than intact.

29. It has often been remarked that in the two best-known statements of the purpose of the mission of Christ in the New Testament, it is "the world" that is named as the object (Jn. 3:16; 2 Cor. 5:19), but the use of personal language in both passages makes it probable that it is the world of human life that is intended, and not the cosmos of Col. 1:20.

30. Two of the disasters that befell Job at the beginning arose from "natural causes."

31. Barth, *CD* IV/3, pp. 425ff.

32. Wisdom of Solomon 13.

33. Peter Brunner, "Gott, das Nichts und die Kreatur," in *Kerygma und Dogma,* Jg. 6 (1960), pp. 188f. Cf. the very similar treatment of the text by Karl Barth in *CD* III/1, pp. 100ff. The instability (defectibility) of created being is a theme that Augustine took over from Neoplatonism, and it reappears in Leibniz' concept of metaphysical evil.

Chapter 11. Nature Lost and Nature Found

1. Cf. Basil Willey, *The Eighteenth Century Background,* pp. 42f.

2. Cf. F. Ferre, *Shaping the Future* (Harper & Row, 1976), pp. 88f.

3. Hannah Arendt, *The Human Condition* (Doubleday & Co., Anchor Books, 1959), p. 228.

4. Ibid., VI, sec. 36. Pascal's position on this matter deserves special comment. His dismay at the "disproportion" between man and the "infinite spaces" disclosed by the Copernican revolution is well known. When he sought consolation in the fact that, though man is only a puny and feeble creature in comparison with the rest of the universe, he is superior to the universe, inasmuch as he knows it, while it knows nothing of him, he was seeking what Arendt calls an Archimedean point in self-certainty, and thus paying tribute to Descartes, of whom he was so critical.

5. Sir James Jeans, *The Mysterious Universe,* p. 134.

6. Joseph M. Kitagawa, "Experience, Knowledge and Understanding," *Religious Studies,* Vol. 11 (1975), pp. 205f.

7. Saint Francis, as is well known, went so far as to preach to the birds (as Saint Anthony had earlier preached to the fish); but he got away with this only because he was a saint.

8. Charles Sherrington, *Man on His Nature* (Cambridge University Press, 1951), p. 265. The account he gives of the life cycle of the liver fluke is a veritable horror story.

9. From Albert Schweitzer, *Kultur und Ethik,* cited in Barth, *CD* III/4, p. 349.

10. In the rural communities of earlier times (such as the one familiar to this writer in his youth) the domestic animals were not regarded as objects radically distinct from the farmer and his family, but rather as extensions of the family, and they were given names, to which they sometimes learned to respond. The coming of the industrial era and the mechanization of agriculture has weakened this tie, but the growth in the number of animal pets that are kept by city dwellers and others may be an index of a felt need to express the sense of oneness between human and other forms of life.

11. Contrast the absence of scenery from many modern novels, which concentrate on the personal relationships between the human characters. For example, Iris Murdoch, one of the most sophis-

ticated novelists in England today, tends to shut off her characters from the external world, like a sequestered jury. But in fairness, it may be added that Jane Austen, who was a contemporary of Sir Walter Scott, did much the same.

12. Martin Buber, *I and Thou,* tr. by R. G. Smith (1937), p. 11. *Between Man and Man* is the title of a collection of essays by Buber published in 1947 (London: Kegan Paul).

13. Cf. Wordsworth, "I have felt a presence . . . ," in his poem "Lines Composed a Few Miles Above Tintern Abbey".

14. The passage (*I and Thou,* pp. 7f.) is brief and oracular, and Buber nowhere, to my knowledge, returns to the theme in his later writings.

15. Wordsworth's "Intimations of Immortality" were such recollections of preexistence.

16. James Brown, *Subject and Object in Modern Theology* (London: SCM Press, 1955), p. 117.

17. Leslie Paul, *The Meaning of Human Existence,* 1949, cited in Brown, *Subject and Object in Modern Theology,* p. 113.

18. Francis Thompson was a devout Catholic. He is noted for the excessive Latinity of his diction.

19. Buber, *I and Thou,* pp. 23f. Cf. Brown, *Subject and Object in Modern Theology,* p. 118. Brown suggests an affinity with the thought of Spinoza (p. 138), but this seems hardly justified in the light of Buber's sensitivity to the dialectic of Hegel, as he described it on the following page.

20. Buber, *I and Thou,* p. 25.

21. According to Tillich, the existentialism of Sartre has some Manichean traits (*ST* II, p. 39).

22. *Luther: Lectures on Romans,* tr. and ed. by Wilhelm Pauck, Vol. 15 of The Library of Christian Classics (Westminster Press, 1961), pp. 235ff.

23. Cf. Heinrich Schlier, "Das, worauf alles wartet," in *Interpretation der Welt,* Festschrift für R. Guardini (Würzburg, 1926), p. 605.

24. "Existence (of all creation) seen from the goal to which the apostle looks, is always, so to speak, an intentional existence" (*Schlier,* "Das, worauf alles wartet," p. 602). Schlier describes openness and motion toward the future eschaton as a "uniform and basic characteristic of all creatures" (p. 606).

25. Ibid., p. 600.

26. How impossible it is to take the words of the prophet in a literal sense becomes apparent if we translate them into terms that are more familiar today: Does he mean that bacteria will cease to damage cells and pneumococci will live happily with lung tissue?

27. The difficulty in regard to human nature and destiny may be seen by comparing two words of Jesus: (1) "From the beginning of creation, 'God made them male and female' " (Mk. 10:6); (2) "When they rise from the dead, they neither marry nor are given in marriage, but are like angels in heaven" (Mk. 12:25).

28. The interpretation of Rom. 8:26 is notoriously difficult. The traditional interpretation ascribes the *stenagmoi alalētoi* to the Spirit; but if this is all that the Spirit can do, it is difficult to see how the Spirit can come to our assistance. It is preferable to follow the NEB, which ascribes them to us, as expressions of the work of the Spirit in us: "Through our inarticulate groanings the Spirit himself is pleading for us." The distinctive function of the Spirit, however, is to articulate our inarticulate groanings and so present them to God. Paul seems to think of the presence of the Spirit in Christians in a manner analogous to the incarnation, in which the Son of God accomplished his divine mission in the medium of our human nature, with all its weaknesses, and, like us, agonized in prayer. Cf. G. W. H. Lampe, *God as Spirit* (Oxford University Press, 1977), p. 89.

29. Pope John Paul II makes impressive use of this passage in his encyclical *Redemptor Hominis* of March 15, 1979, p. 89, but he focuses on the redemption of "man," as the title indicates, and he interprets the language of the apostle about the plight of the world in terms of its effects on human life. Nowhere does the redemption of *the world,* which is the theme of the passage, appear in the document: "Does not the previously unknown immense progress—which has taken place especially in the course of this century—in the field of man's dominion over the world itself reveal—to a previously unknown degree—that manifold subjection to 'futility'? It is enough to recall certain phenomena, such as the threat of the pollution of the natural environment in areas of rapid industrialization, or the armed conflicts continually breaking out over and over again, or the prospectives *(sic)* of self-destruction through the use of atomic, hydrogen, neutron, and similar weapons, or the lack of respect for the life of the unborn. The world of the new age, the world of space flights, the world of the previously unattained con-

quests of science and technology—is it not also the world 'groaning in travail' that 'waits with eager longing for the revealing of the sons of God'?" (quoted in *The New York Times,* Mar. 16, 1979).

30. Walter Kaufmann, *Nietzsche* (Meridian Books, 1956), p. 142.

31. Nietzsche, *Thus Spoke Zarathustra,* Pt. I, Prologue, 3, tr. Walter Kaufmann, in *The Portable Nietzsche* (Viking Press, 1954), p. 124.

32. Nietzsche, "Schopenhauer as Educator," in *Thoughts out of Season, Collected Works,* V, pp. 149–152. This essay was written in 1874, well after Nietzsche's break with Christianity, but before he had developed the ideas of the overman, the will to power, and the eternal recurrence.

33. Nietzsche's coinage in *Zarathustra,* Pt. I, Speech 3 (tr. Kaufmann, p. 142).

34. Nietzsche, *Zarathustra,* Pt. I, Prologue, 3 (tr. Kaufmann, p. 125).

35. Kaufmann's suggestion that "redemption" is "a word that must have come readily to the mind of Wagner's young friend" (*Nietzsche,* p. 148) may be correct; but it may be assumed that Nietzsche had heard the word before.

36. *Zarathustra,* Pt. I, Speech 22, sec. 2 (tr. Kaufmann, p. 189).

37. Schlier, "Das, worauf alles wartet," p. 615.

38. A favorite formula of Nietzsche's; he derived it from Pindar.

39. Nietzsche, "Schopenhauer as Educator," p. 154.

40. Cf. Kaufmann, *Nietzsche,* p. 129.

41. Nietzsche, "Schopenhauer as Educator, p. 154."

42. See especially Schleiermacher, *On Religion,* pp. 35ff.

43. Nietzsche formed a high regard for Emerson at an early age and retained it throughout his life. There are similarities as well as affinities between the two men, notably the absence of a systematically reasoned philosophy, and reliance, instead, on insights and intuitions. Nietzsche may have been alluding to this when he wrote, "dass ich Emerson als eine Bruder-Seele empfinde (aber sein Geist is schlecht gebildet)" (from a letter to Overbeck, December, 1883, *Briefwechsel,* p. 239). He held a low opinion of Schleiermacher, whom he once described as "der weibische, geistreichelnde Schleiermacher, den man überall bis zum Ekel lobt oder tadelt" (from a letter to Erwin Rohde, December 9, 1868, *Briefe,* 2,279).

Chapter 12. The Destiny of Nature

1. Cf. Barth, *CD* IV/3, pp. 375ff.
2. Ibid., pp. 140f.
3. The verb *sympatheō* occurs only twice in the New Testament (Heb. 4:15; 10:34); the noun *sympatheia,* never.
4. The problem of theodicy in modern theology is generally dated from the *Theodicy* of Leibniz (1710). In the orthodoxy which preceded it the sufferings, to which Christians are exposed, were treated as elements in the discipline by which God is advancing his purpose with them. The treatment of the trials and tribulations of the saints in Ch. XVIII of the Westminster Confession of Faith (1646), for example, may strike the modern reader as heartless; but the point is that they are interpreted in the context of God's purpose of salvation, however narrowly that purpose may have been conceived.
5. Nietzsche's emphasis on suffering has been a source of puzzlement to some of his interpreters (cf. Kaufmann, *Nietzsche,* pp. 121f.). No doubt it was influenced in part by the poor health from which he suffered throughout most of his life, and which was accompanied by a peculiar sensitivity to his natural surroundings. He was by disposition a lover of nature (though he spent long hours writing in solitary rooms), and he believed that his best thoughts came to him on his long walks: he said that the idea of "the eternal recurrence" came to him by a rock on the shore of Lake Silvaplana in the Upper Engadine, where he spent several summers. As regards the saints' sympathy with living creatures, it may not be entirely accidental that when Nietzsche collapsed on a street in Turin on January 3, 1889, he had thrown his arms around the neck of a horse that was being flogged by a coachman.
6. Peter Brunner, commenting on the words of Isaiah,

> Sing, O heavens, for the Lord has done it;
> shout, O depths of the earth;
> Break forth into singing, O mountains,
> O forest, and every tree in it!
> (Is. 44:23)

writes: "The language of a text like this, which is by no means an isolated case, cannot be understood as a mere prophetic figure or an anthropomorphic animation of nature, but must be understood in the light of the fact that creation as a whole, which is from the beginning determined by the word (of the Creator), is from the first beginning embraced in God's saving will and at the end of all things actually attains to this primordially determined grace. . . . (Then) the sighing of the creature will be changed to resounding praise" (*Kerygma und Dogma,* Jg. 6, 1960, p. 192).

7. Most people would probably find it hard to answer if they were asked to say what they are doing when they worship; and to people who do not worship, the practice must appear incomprehensible, if not silly (cf. 1 Cor. 14:23).

8. William Temple, *Nature, Man and God* (London: Macmillan Co., 1935), especially Ch. XIX.

9. Hugh Montefiore, ed., *Man and Nature,* Report of a group appointed by the Archbishop of Canterbury (London: Collins, 1975), p. 60. The theme is further developed in an essay entitled "A Sacramental View of Nature" by A. R. Peacocke, pp. 132–142 in the same volume.

10. Teilhard de Chardin's view of evolution was also sacramental, but with a significant difference: he found his model in the mass, and the mass is held to effect a substantial change of the bread and wine into the body and blood of Christ. Evolution was conceived by Teilhard, accordingly, as a substantial transmutation of the world, through successive "spheres," into the body of Christ (cf. Ernst Benz, *Evolution and Christian Hope,* pp. 224ff.; Doubleday & Co., Anchor Books, 1968).

11. Bonhoeffer, *Letters and Papers from Prison,* Letter of Dec. 18, 1943.

12. An analogy from music may be pertinent: a player may perform a piece with technical perfection, but fail to express the "soul" of the music.

13. It is rare to encounter such a view among those who write on the subject. Most lay a disproportionate weight on one side or the other, and so they are distinguished as optimists or pessimists. The best attempt at a balanced view known to this writer is that given by W. Macneile Dixon in his Gifford Lectures, *The Human Situation* (London: Arnold, 1937), pp. 73–90.

14. Philosophical eschatologies are rare at the present time. One is to be found in Findlay, *Ascent to the Absolute,* pp. 58–77.

Index